An Abrahamic Theology for Science

An Abrahamic Theology for Science

KENNETH L. VAUX

Wipf & Stock
PUBLISHERS
Eugene, Oregon

AN ABRAHAMIC THEOLOGY FOR SCIENCE

Copyright © 2007 Kenneth L. Vaux. All rights reserved. Except for brief quotations in critical publications or reviews, no part of this book may be reproduced in any manner without prior written permission from the publisher. Write: Permissions, Wipf & Stock, 199 W. 8th Ave., Eugene, OR 97401.

ISBN 10: 1-55635-098-8
ISBN 13: 978-1-55635-098-6

Manufactured in the U.S.A.

Thanks to Joey Lenti and Adam Ericksen for their assistance in editing and proofreading this manuscript.

Contents

Introduction 1

1. Avicenna/Maimonides 15
   the alethic vector

2. Robert Boyle 39
   the aesthetic vector

3. Pierre Teilhard de Chardin 67
   the etiologic vector

4. Albert Schweitzer 87
   the eschatologic vector

5. Amartya Sen 121
   the axiologic vector

6. Leon Kass 155
   the agapic vector

Conclusion 183

Introduction

THOUGH A THEOLOGIAN BY training (my teacher, Helmut Thielicke, wrote the essay on "Theology" in the *Encyclopedia Britannica Macropedia*), I have worked in the world of science and medicine all of my professional life. A few texts call me "the first bioethicist."[1] I coined the term "biomedical ethics" nearly forty years ago—about the time when another of my teacher/mentors, Joseph Fletcher, popularized "situation ethics." My third principal mentor, Paul Ramsey, called me a philosopher of theology. Ramsey was actually one of an amazing circle of theologians beginning in the 1950s who sought to give theology and theological ethics an acceptable face for the secular university by calling their work "religious studies." I have written books on these three teachers: Thielicke, Fletcher and Ramsey. They all sought to interpret science and medicine to theology, and bring these beliefs and values to bear on science. The careful reader will also see the tracings of other teachers in this work—John Hick at Princeton, Tom Torrance at Edinburgh, Carl Friedrich von Weizsäcker at Hamburg and Wolfhart Pannenberg at Munich.

Actually, I began university studies as a biology major and have spent most of my professional life teaching in medical schools—first in Houston, then Chicago. My theology follows Kierkegaard, Barth, and the Niebuhrs, and I am deeply fascinated by Judaism and Islam. I have written or edited nearly two dozen books that would best be called "homilies." I am at heart, a preacher in the Reformed-Presbyterian religious tradition.

Late in my career teaching theology, and after refocusing my work on interfaith issues and war, I was awarded a sabbatical leave and was encouraged to go back to science by my two sons (a physician and a linguist), two daughters (the theologians of our family), and my wife (our best scholar). I had left the discipline of bioethics a decade ago when one had to declare a specialty in genetic or thanatological ethics, and I was unwilling to microspecialize. I had just written the first of two books on war among Jews, Christians, and Muslims. This study began with Avicenna, the Muslim

---

[1] S.B. Rae and Paul M. Cox, *Bioethics* (Grand Rapids: Eerdmans, 1999) 1. See also Albert Jonsen, *The Birth of Bioethics* (New York: Oxford, 1998).

physician sage who inspired the golden age of science and theology and ethics in medieval Andalusia. As I composed my thoughts in the hometown of Maimonides and Averroës—Cordoba, Spain—war was brewing again with Iraq. I opposed it and have made my case in *Ethics and the War on Terrorism* (Wipf & Stock, 2002), *Ethics and the Gulf War* (Westview, 1992; Wipf & Stock, 2003) and *Jew, Christian, Muslim* (Wipf & Stock, 2003). I have been reading for years on the connection between monotheism and war and science and culture and religion. I see the destiny of Israel in world history to promote truth and justice, and of America to further the worldly agenda of Puritanism, to advance science and empirical truth. War is not the *raison d'être* of either people in today's world.

So, my research on monotheism and war brought me back to theology and science. I have always found this subject a correlate to the issues of "war and peace" and "rich and poor." These subjects, along with "life and death" are among the courses I teach at Garrett-Evangelical Theological Seminary, in Evanston, Illinois.

The particular location from which I write this essay is the hospital and clinical setting where persons experience the ravages of disease and refreshments of health in their bodies and minds. The biomedical world, not physics or chemistry, is my milieu, though biomedicine is rapidly converging with the realms of natural science, mathematics and technology. My early work was more in natural science and technology. The dissertation on cybernetics and a human future was an attempt to relate the biblical mandate "subdue the earth" (Gen. 1: 28) with the bioelectronic age. Published as *Subduing the Cosmos: Cybernetics and Man's Future* (John Knox Press, 1970), this was followed by a project undertaken while on a Danforth fellowship in Munich on the theological history of science in the Judeo-Christian tradition entitled *Being Well* (Abingdon, 1997). This work was fashioned in consultation with Wolfhart Pannenberg, Karl Rahner and Johannes Metz in the university's theological faculties.

All during these years working on biomedical theology and functioning as a clinical bioethicist, I saw human needs and pathos and the profession of care as parts of the impulse behind science and theology. I continue to write as a clinical/pastoral thinker driven by that vocation to the rigors of science and theology. I write as a Christian for the church—her pastors and laity—scientists, philosophers and common folk who think hard about life in this world. I hope that searchers into science and theology from other faiths, especially our sister Abrahamic faiths, will also take a look.

My suspicion or hypothesis is that the monotheistic Abrahamic theology that gave rise to science in the first place (e.g., Judaism in the classical world, early medieval Islam, and Puritan Christianity) can best sustain the rigorous truth quest, ethical incandescence and hopeful horizon that science will most certainly require in the challenging decades ahead.

I construct this edifice on the foundation of six building blocks. I have, in fact, used a phrase to describe them: *six mariners across the membrane of science and theology*. The six persons studied here penetrate and permeate in their work this membrane between science and theology. They intrigue me with their theoretical and practical wisdom. They represent four faith traditions and various branches of science. Though half are physicians, all are healers in the broadest sense. Here they are in historical order:

- Avicenna—Muslim—physician, philosopher, theologian, eleventh century (adding Maimonides, Averroës, Hildegard)
- Robert Boyle—Anglican Christian—scientist, theologian, seventeenth century (adding Torrance)
- Albert Schweitzer—Reformed Christian—physician, theologian, twentieth century
- Pierre Teilhard de Chardin—Catholic Christian—paleontologist, twentieth century (adding Torrance, Weizsäcker)
- Amartya Sen—Hindu (secularist)—economist, twentieth century (adding Moltmann)
- Leon Kass—Jew—Physician, philosopher, theologian, twentieth century (adding Polkinghorne)

Others were considered, and a woman was desperately needed. I therefore added a section on Hildegard of Bingen, who in addition to being an astute philosopher, was a practitioner in stones, herbs and healing to match Avicenna. Maimonides and Averroës are companions to our path under the robes of Avicenna. Pythagoras, Aristotle and several Indian and Asian sages could be here. Isaac Newton, John Wesley, Marie Curie, and Stephen Jay Gould were also considered. The contemporary parade of scientist-theologians, who are now writing searching studies: Arthur Peacock, John Polkinghorne, Ian Barbour, Tris Engelhardt, to mention only some of those writing in English, are subliminally and sublineally present in this work.

I know that this project is controversial. I have worked among scientists and among skeptics in the university all of my life. I know their profound skepticism of religion, if not theology. This cynicism is all the more heightened in the aftermath of 9/11 and the religiopolitical undercurrents of that crisis. What good could come out of Sinai or Nazareth or Mecca, it might be asked. I have also known many persons of science who are also persons of faith. I am not concerned here to condemn the one group or commend the other. My thesis is quite simple. Theology has grounded and founded, prompted and promoted science in the past. Can it continue to do so today? Secondly, theology has had a profound impact on ethics. Of all cultural "factors," religion is perhaps the most profound vector of morality. Indeed I am dubious of any ethic derived from within science itself or one based solely on secular reason. Theology can and must sustain a shepherding function for science and technology. I make no triumphalist claim. I find the moments of religious hegemony over science just as appalling and stifling as the contemporary hegemony of a scientific and secular ideology over the same realm. I simply hope in this book to characterize a kind of theology which can ground and guide science and technology into the twenty-first century and beyond.

Science and Theology

The interplay of science and theology is inescapable. Kepler's laws, Newton's absolute space and Einstein's enlargement on quantum mechanics are all theological not scientific assumptions. In the meanings of Plato and Augustine these are *theoria* and *theologia*. Beliefs and values riddle every aspect of scientific knowledge and technological appropriation. At the same time we see in cultural terms a great wall of imposed secularization in science and thoughtless sacrality in religion. Today, cooperation and reciprocal edification is needed as never before. Science is always partial, provisional and, by definition, evolving within cultural change. Theology is the same. Theology is the activity of relating our ever-deepening knowledge of God with science, which is our ever-changing and ever-growing knowledge of the world. Theology, in other words, requires reflection on creation by the very nature of its concern. Science, of necessity, brings forth theological reflection about nature as soon as it moves from descriptive tasks to explanatory: What is it? Where did it come from? Where is it going? What makes it work? What avenues is it meant to pursue? These are the questions science puts to theology. It can, of course, bracket and set these questions aside as imponderable or unanswerable. If this occurs the enterprise called science is totally truncated, devoid of conceptual and practical power.

The dialogue between science and theology (religion) has in recent years gone deep and broad. It has been instructive and constructive to both endeavors. Major currents of theology—neo-orthodox, liberation, process, and the like—have had their premises and methodologies sharpened and enriched by dealing with scientific questions. Science has been shaken from its dogmatic and amoral delusions. The value of the work of pioneers Ian Barbour, Tom Torrance, Arthur Peacock and John Polkinghorne has been inestimable, literally, in creating a field enlisting a wide circle of theological and scientific participants preparing a literature, securing sponsors and grants, developing curricula, establishing institutes and engendering broad public discourse. The modern consideration, of course, stands at the end of a long history.

If we survey the history of science we see it as an admirable discipline seeking knowledge about nature—operational knowledge. It seeks regularities, patterns and the constitution of nature from the shadowy beginning of celestial study at Stonehenge or Pythagoras' articulation of what had been known for two millennia in China—that numbers, calendar and counting somehow configure reality. From the dawn of conscience (science), the human mind has sought to avert danger and understand natural process. That natural reality is numerical and nominal—inviting our construal and designation—is the first step of a theology for science. Science, by its nature, is ameliorative investigation. It seeks to help and heal humanity and creation. It is *Tikkun Olam*—mending of the world.

With the collapse of Mycenaean theology and the waning of the remarkable age of Hesiod and Homer, the natural theologians, as they were called by Plato—the first physicists and physicians—Thales, Heraclitus, Anaximenes, Anaximander, Democritus and others—seek to define the stuff and the processes of the world. Pythagoras makes a simple discovery that the length of a string determines the pitch (note). Mathematical physics is born. In the middle ages, these skills of conceiving, measuring, counting, and testing—brilliantly furthered the classical and ancient arts of trial and error, correction and experimentation—are activated by supplying scientific hypotheses. The clock and countless machines to facilitate work emerge from rigorous conceptualization and construction.

Theology often discouraged science in the early Renaissance although we see in Francis Bacon the impetus to constrain nature towards human goods as a divine imperative. In 1543, Copernicus confronts Catholic cosmology with his *De Revolutionibus Orbrium Coelestrum,* conveying an ill-conceived threat to theology by displacing the earth's centrality in the universe by brother sun. Actually humans are as glorious and tragic after

Copernicus as they were before. Newton's *Principia* flows from a worldview where profound faith and scientific formulation are totally compatible. The present holder of the Isaac Newton chair at Cambridge, Stephen Hawking, still exudes that spirit. Our case study of Robert Boyle will document this theological reappraisal. The laws of gravitation and motion stubbornly claim that the regularities of nature are God's handiwork. Haydn's *Creation* captures the theological-scientific exuberance of the age. The Lisbon earthquake did not reverberate as far as Cambridge.

The two subsequent centuries are hard going for a viable theology for science. The age of nineteenth century biology—Lamarck, Darwin, Pasteur and Koch pursue science with a disdain for theological censorship even though closer retrospection shows great impulses of faith and hope in these thinkers. It was rear-guard ecclesiastics who fulminated resistance, not only on the basis of bad science, but also bad theology.

The age of contemporary physics, though initially skeptical, seems friendlier to theology and more encouraging of dialogue. Maxwell, Planck, Einstein, Weizsäcker and others have redefined time, energy, matter, velocity, indeed the depth composition and dimension of the vast universe. Theories are no longer laws of nature. Even Kant's critical assertions are conceived less positivistically, allowing for more profound, even mystical and moral speculation.

Theology meanwhile has moved, in the Kierkegaardian-Barthian revolution and in process thought, to explicate the faith with biblical and historical rigor, affirming the classical call of theology to relate revelatory convictions to the worldly dimension of nature and history. Ultimately faith is about human destiny before God. In liberation theology—closely akin to neo-orthodoxy and to process thought—a moral and political focus is maintained. Human fulfillment and resistance to degradation is sought with the aid of scientific and technical endeavors as these help sustain and enrich the lives of all people in the world.

In the play *Copenhagen* (Kierkegaard's home city), playwright Michael Frayn has us see the interaction of another great Dane, Niels Bohr, with the physicist Wernher Heisenberg about the Germans' attempt to use the nascent nuclear knowledge and technology to build a bomb in the early 1940s. With an eerie contemporary relevance, the Nazis would fill the warheads of the already-in-use Werner Von Braun rockets. A lesser figure in this drama was my teacher, Carl Friedrich Von Weizsäcker, a German physicist and son of Hitler's ambassador first to Denmark, then to the Vatican. Weizsäcker, as a young physicist at Göttigen, struggled with the theological meaning of the new age of nuclear physics that was unfolding.

He went to Karl Barth and asked if he could continue. In his enigmatic way Barth said, "If you believe as Christians always have that Christ alone holds the power to end the world—you may continue."[2] A subtle affirmation. Much like that of the young student—Weizsäcker—when he asked the senior Heisenberg what he should do to study philosophy, Heisenberg answered, "first, study physics."[3] The enigmatic retorts of these two giants—of theology and science—show that a new age of searching dialogue would become imperative and crucial to human survival on earth.

The "art that is long" (Hippocrates) recedes to a horizon where theology and science, beliefs and manipulative magic converge. In the Vedas, where we have perhaps the oldest theological ethics, reality and goodness—*Gott und Gut*—intertwine. *Ritain*—in Sanskrit—can be translated as truth and right. When the privileged Gautama, who would become Siddhartha Buddha, ventured out into the unprotected world he was devastated by the spectra of

- An old withered man
- A leper
- A funeral
- A venerable monk contemplating compassion

The call to science and theology! In the three millennia before the Christian era and before this ethos would create Indo-Europe through its migrations the four ideals of the Vedas and Upanishads were

- to satisfy human desires
- to seek prosperity not woe
- to execute duty
- to seek spiritual perfection

Just as the Shāman, in all traditions, is a scientist-pastor, so these primordial impulses suggest a common path for science and theology, ethics and technology.

---

[2] Personal conversation with Weizsäcker in 1972, when I was a fellow at the Max Planck Institute in Munich, which Weizsäcker directed at the time.
[3] Conversation with Weizsäcker (Munich, 1972).

Ethics/Technology

Though the rapprochement of theology and science is problematic, we must formulate a working association of the two realms in order to provide an ethic for the technology derived from that theology. The connections between ethics and applied science (technology) are compelling and evident. While human reason is necessary for the processes of moral reasoning—starting principles, modes of analysis, coherent and consistent argumentation, marshalling of evidence, avoidance of inappropriate arguments (e.g., *Ad Hominem*, etc.), rational ethics tends to be formalistic (that's to say, it starts with the values and principles of a given perspective—utilitarian, Machiavellian, naturalistic, etc., and reasons through to courses of action). Rational ethics is not able to identify higher goods, the *summum bonum*, norms beyond relativity, because it cannot posit an ultimate good or God. Indeed *Gott* and *Gut* are codependent concepts that provide normativity and ultimacy for humanity. Moral philosophy therefore can help us work out positions for action given the underlying principles of a given system, nothing more. Theology is needed for comprehensive science.

The history of ethics from Protagoras and Thrasymachus' first principles of "man as the measure of all things" and "might makes right," down through contemporary philosophical ethics working out the principles of Kant, Hegel, and Mill is an effort to ground morality in natural reason and to establish an acceptable moral stance for public order reaching beyond parochial options—identifying values worthy of pluralistic loyalty and adherence. The more contemporary decisions become conflicted, however, the more metaethics or normative ethics derived from metaphysics (which in the thought of this essay is theology) is sought beyond the limitations of the ethics of natural reason. Examples of such conflicts are the conflict between values of freedom and coercion on abortion; Deciding whether potential threat from another nation is a reason to preemptively make war or demand a regime change; or choosing between helping the poor to basic human needs—food, education, health care—or concentrating wealth in national security or international hegemony. If we go with Kant or Marx and start to define the content of an ethical position, or the substance of love or justice, we enter the realm of theological ethics, of prophetic esteem for human persons (souls) and religious values.

My argument in this study is that we can distill the essence of theological ethics for science by doing a fine-grained analysis of a handful of scientists' work, all of whom labor generally out of the Abrahamic heritage (with Hinduism, Buddhism and Chinese ethics seen as historically cognate or resonant religious movements— and/or godless, per Rodney Stark). It is my thesis that from this distillation (not dilution) of representations a clear and compelling theology commends itself to humanity because of its particular relevance to the scientific project.

A Critical Moment

A word seems necessary about the critical importance and urgency of the case I am about to set before you. Two compelling reasons present themselves, one from science and technology, and the other from theology and ethics. From the science/technology side there is widespread consensus that the immediate future portends awesome, perhaps ominous issues.

We may be approaching what have been perceived in the past as zones of natural quarantine. From the perspective of theological ethics, the imperative has never been so strong to draw scientific activity into the sphere of its understanding and counsel lest we deteriorate further into the "two cultures" of totally dissociated discourse. It is the nature of theology to form a comprehensive and instructive body of knowledge concomitant to science. If this vital conversation is missing, both realms—science and theology—lose their integrity and purpose. Even in the words of an anticlerical Carl Sagan, science requires skepticism, awe and hope—prophetic and proleptic theology.

Take three representative activities of recent science: The human genome and the research and therapeutics which that endeavor is generating; contemporary neuroscience; and nanotechnology. The thresholds of the beginning, ending and meaning of life touch the realm of mystery.

A. The cluster of issues of genetic research and therapy centering on the Human Genome Project, including stem-cell research and cloning, have elicited a frightful pause, several actual and proposed moratoria, and, as we will note in the chapter on Leon Kass, endeavors of national deliberative bodies around the world to ponder and provide guidelines for these newfound reaches of knowledge. Genomics and the related science of proteonomics serve as an example of the ambivalent wonder and horror found in this realm.

Now that the human genome has been described a myriad of techniques is being researched and marketed to bring that knowledge into human service. We can alter particular sequencing processes, splice or move genes on the matrix of their structure, splice in transgenic material (from other species), modify or modulate germ cells and turn on or turn off salutary or deleterious processes. In the hematological disorders, for example, we can enter corrections for hemophilias or anemias, though we are not quite sure what anomalies will be introduced with the corrections.

The classical theological themes of forbidden knowledge (Genesis: "You shall surely die if you eat the forbidden fruit"); of requisite consent based on foreknowledge of outcomes and of an acceptable balance of goods achieved over costs and risks, becomes very elusive. Since these matters go to the core mysteries of life and death, of hope and suffering, they are more amenable to theological analysis and scrutiny than say, legal, economic or philosophical consideration. Here we deal rather with issues of transgression and redemption—theological matters. Only such wisdom is commensurate to the issues.[4]

B. Issues in neuroscience may go even closer to the quick of soul, the *humanum,* to the moral issues of life and death, of possibility and limitation. Here, at this sacred threshold, we confront the dialectics of obligation and prohibition. That our minds are analogues of computers, amenable to mathematical and technical modeling and manipulation; that chemical (drugs), surgical, even behavioral interventions and improvements are prescribed or proscribed, constitutes another provocative innovation within science that calls out for theological comprehension and active ethical guidance. This need arises both for individuals and families who must choose courses of action and for society in its science policy and law. When we deal with the continuum of entities: brain, mind and soul, we find that science and therapeutics itself remains cautious and wary even though significant promise for human good may lie near at hand.

When Francis Crick reductionistically contends that we are " nothing more than a bundle of neurons" in his *Astonishing Hypothesis: The Scientific Search for the Soul* (London: Simon and Schuster, 1994), he points more to the problem than the solution of our crisis. Yes, brain, mind and even soul arise as epiphenomena of and devolve onto cells and genes, just as genes devolve onto chemicals, atoms and quarks (high and low). Yet while such reductionism has answered some questions and provided some significant knowledge data (e.g., neuropeptides, chemico-electrical dynamics of neurological vitality and morbidity), the more important issues, especially at the clinical level of living, dying, thinking and feeling, concern the whole

---

[4] See Celia E. Deane-Drummond, "Wisdom," in *Biology and Theology Today* (London: SCM Press, 2001).

brain, the soul, the person in one's history, environment and relation to normativity and ultimacy. In this reality we are drawn to Avicenna and Sen's "one and the many" or Torrance's "divisibility which discloses totality." "Heal the sick and cast out demons" was the subject of Paul Tillich's sermon upon my graduation from Princeton Seminary. The command still pertains even within this most "tender tissue" of our humanity.[5]

C. Mechanical technology presents another enormous challenge, again at the sacred modules and moments where life and death is concerned. A compelling constellation of issues arises when nanotechnologies are applied to the human organism. The issue is not so much the miniaturization but the ends these microtools will serve. A recent report from a team of Sheffield University scholars speaks of the utopian and catastrophic possibilities:

> The utopian vision predicts the technology will clean up the environment free humanity from disease, ageing and death, and will provide material abundance that will eradicate poverty. The dystopian vision is the "grey goo" scenario, predicting that nanotechnology would signal the end of the world, as the biosphere is destroyed by out-of-control self-replicating robots.[6]

Nanorobotics, the first wave of the technology, is on the verge of amazing human applications. Dismantling toxic chemicals circulating in the body, even inflicting intracellular damage; cruising the bloodstream monitoring signals of cardiovascular disease (hyperlipidemias, precursors of carcinogenesis, etc.); forming optical images on the retina, bringing sight to the blind; rebuilding or recircuiting injury to neural cords allowing the lame to rise up and walk; even "external computers uploading our minds enabling immortality and survival" (p. 5.) The ethical eschaton has arrived.

These developments rehearse the challenges we will explore in the age of Descartes, Newton and Robert Boyle when the machine/soul interface was also at stake. The micromachines may self-replicate and take over everything but the more real theological danger is that we will transfer our existence, more and more, to the plane of machine and computer, accelerating the present justice discrepancy of use among the rich and the poor, becoming less free, more robotic and less fully alive, bereft to face life's

---

[5] See Fraser Watts, ed., *Science Meets Faith* (London: SPCK Press, 1998), especially sections on brain and neuropsychology, 50ff.
[6] *The Guardian* (July 28, 2003) 5.

suffering and dying, its joy and renewal, which is the akedic clue to its nature and meaning. In sum, the preceding three developments in scientific thought and action—genomics, neuroscience, and nanoscience—call for transcendent reference, ultimate grounding and bearing and normative direction—the bequest of theology to human perception.

Premises and Presuppositions

A provisional word is required at this point about my understanding of some very weighty matters of philosophy of science assumed in this essay. The notions of *reality, nature,* and *truth* are either objective and ontological or subjective and nominal entities —human constructions. I hold the position of tentative realism, postulated on the basis of the first three commandments, that reality, for example, really is, but it is not exactly as we perceive it, know it and describe it. The same goes for *nature* and *truth.* These ultimacies belong only to God, yet God has us take them as real and to think and act on that basis. The statement "Jimmy's mole is malignant melanoma" is jam-packed with dubious assumptions about *reality, truth* and *nature*, yet we think and act with all the humility of provisionality. We act with courage and plea for forgiveness when we are wrong. I contend that the scientific method is our finest approximation of earthly *truth* just as methodical faith is our finest approximation of that even more elusive, divine *truth*. Arthur Peacock states the realist assumption regarding science:

> Geology, cell-biology and chemistry—in the last two centuries these sciences have progressively and continuously discovered hidden structures in the entities of the natural world that account causally for observed phenomenon" (*Theology in a Scientific Age*, p. 12).

Thesis

Theologically I hope to expand the aforementioned hypothesis and offer an analysis of theology for science that is one of cautious realism, much the same as the philosophy of science offered earlier. While the reader must wait until the argument unfolds to unpack this statement, the theology I propose in this study is the realism of Torrance without the lingerings of his protestant scholastic objectivism and positivism and the dynamism of Moltmann without the lingerings of his Blochian and Marxian historicism. These two, along with Pannenberg—whose mentoring influence will be evident throughout this study—are preeminent systematic theologians who have put their minds to late twentieth-century science. They appropriate profoundly the biblical and Judeo-Christian heritage into the scientific realm. Their work joined to the pioneering insights of cleric scientists such as Peacock and Polkinghorne, and those dually competent synthetists like Ian Barbour and Alister McGrath coalesce a theocentric analysis, carrying a torch into the twenty-first century.

I will add a small additional element, an Abrahamic-Akedic theology for science. As I have pondered our six pioneering bridge-builders I have drawn what seems to be a salient normative theme from each of their work and woven these together to constitute a template of characteristics for a contemporary theology for science. As I thread together six intrinsically lovely and harmonious patches the interstitial needlework and border blending will become the theology I offer for science—a comely quilt, I trust and hope. A sound science—desirous of authenticity—is truthful, beautiful, reflective of beginnings, endings and good; moral, just and loving. The constituent ingredients, which will be elucidated as each chapter unfolds, are:

- *alethic* : Avicenna/Maimonides
- *aesthetic* : Boyle
- *aetiologic* : Teilhard de Chardin
- *aeschatologic* : Schweitzer
- *axiologic* : Sen
- *agapic* : Kass

The theology I envision as celebrative of and conducive to science relates the reality of God in correlation to the world of dynamic panoply and field of space/time. In this context/continuum God is manifest (though remaining totally distinct) as truth, good and beauty on the spatial axis and as the One who was, is, and will be on the temporal axis. Just as the infinity of deity touches tangentially on space, the eternity of deity touches tangentially on time as God, in and through creation, is the giver, sustainer and consummator of each dimension. If science is true to this incipient theology it will exhibit alethic, aesthetic, aetiologic, aeschatologic, axiologic and agapic dimensions. As Irenaeus of Lyon taught, the divine agapic/akedic act (event) subsuming self-giving, self-limitation, incarnation, temptation, death, resurrection and the fulfillment of life enters, assumes and transfigures the cosmos. Unassumed it is unredeemed or vacant and impotent, assumed it is redeemed and pulses proleptically in this world with eternal and infinite life.

As all of our exemplars of theology for science exhibit (especially our keystone figures at the apex of this study—Teilhard and Schweitzer), space/time and the entire *entourage* of creation is in a state of emerging and fading—an irrational paradox. That which is—is not, and that which is not, is, as the One impulse, propulse and tropulse of Creation in topsy-turvy wonder "gives and takes life" (Job 1:21) "bringing from nothing all that is" (1 Cor 1:28). "Eternity," says Pannenberg, "has to do with the totality and fullness of life." It is a datum or quantum of cosmic, physical, historical reality—the resurrection of the God become man—Jesus—by which eternity and infinity—the realm of God seizes space/time. In grasping this time and all time by end-time, creation is rendered whole and full.

The journey commences. The history is indubitably replete with examples of the conjunction of theology and science. A period of amnesia and forthright animosity seems to have waned. We know that humans are irresistibly *Homo Religiosis* as well as *Homo faber*. Intriguing voyagers appear on the horizon. They embark on a new journey on turbulent seas. Like Othello, the Moor, looking out from the Cyprus fortress onto the horizon, we tremble at the terrors without and within. Yet with courage we sail forth. The mariners we have chosen have compassed, gyroscoped and transacted this Perfect Storm. As this world endeavor now ascends that sheer vertical wave crest, they invite us to join their portentous voyage.

1
Avicenna/Maimonides
the alethic vector

AL ANDALUS. THE FAINT lure of an *halvalero* over the Granada evening turned into a commanding staccato of flamenco after 9/11. Fratricidal animosity among Abraham's children—Americo-Israel vs. Arab—had the world on the brink of calamity in Palestine and Iraq. Where to look for peace and wisdom? What was ancient Andalusia? A pulsing center of the Roman Empire? An Iberian Peninsula jutting out like the Rock of Gibraltar toward the new world? The yearning if not the sunsetting where the Apostle Paul concluded his ministry? Here beginning in the seventh century CE the Muslim world would gain a European stronghold as its poised mission, initially thwarted, toward the fragile dawnings of tribal peoples who would begin to become consolidated Europe under Charlemagne. Here in Granada, Cordoba and Seville, Jews, Christians and Muslims would interact with magnanimity and mutual edification until the Inquisition. Here Maimonides, Averroës and Aquinas—all protégés of Avicenna of Isfahan—would find common insight in medicine, mathematics, philosophy and theology. Here Greek wisdom would synergistically intertwine with Judaic and Islamic monotheism to evoke the dawn of Western science. From the Crusades onward a fateful trifurcation had set in.[1] Recently, phenomena like global warming, weapons of mass destruction and religious war have increased the breach of irenic truth and justice—the atmosphere of science.

So on New Years of 2003, after forty years absence from Spain, I returned. Not only Pan-Abrahamic peace but also theology for science took its strong beginnings here in early medieval Andalusia. Here devout theologians who laid the foundations not only for the modern age of science, but for the concord and rapprochement among monotheistic theology, philosophy and knowledge, more generally, are first found. In Avicenna of Isfahan, Iran and Maimonides and Averroës of Cordoba, Spain, the age reaches its zenith.

---

[1] See Kenneth L. Vaux, *Ethics and the War on Terrorism* (Eugene, OR: Wipf & Stock, 2002).

It was these clinician sages—offering Boethius' *consolatio philosophia* and strong comfort (Isaiah 40) to Abraham's terrorized seed—who preserved and transmitted Greek science and philosophy to medieval and renaissance Europe. Aristotle's *De Anima* and *Metaphysic*—the science of antiquity when theologized through Platonic Augustinianism, into Jewish mysticism then into the soaring visions of reality of Thomism and of Islamic Sufism—would constitute faith and science for half a millennium. Even the Renaissance and Reformation, which would convey Christendom's greatest scientific and political force into Puritanism, were marked by the sacred biblical and empirical heritage derived from this Andalusian awakening.

The more I read in preparation for this pilgrimage the stronger a more Western-Asian profile arose for the founder of this movement. The sure foundation for an ongoing theology for science in the west was provided by Avicenna (980–1037 CE), the Persian physician-philosopher who is the inspiration of Maimonides of Cordoba and the "Great Philosopher" of Thomas Aquinas. Our construction of an extant theology for science, a useful knowledge and helpful technology, begins therefore near Isfahan, Iran and Baghdad, Iraq where today a crisis of war, causing science and faith to tremble, finds its epicenter.[2] Like Maimonides, physician and guide to Prince Saladin in Palestine, and Thomas, the wise doctor to priest and physician in Upper Europe, Avicenna is physician and counsel to the Amir Ibn Mansúr al Sāmani at Bukhārā. His lasting contribution to a theology for science is alethic (Greek *aletheia* = truth)—an absolute insistence on honesty and veracity with a stern repudiation of falsehood. Assurance of truth was best insured as subjectivity verged toward objectivity, relativity toward transcendence. Let us unfold this dimension of theology so crucial to true science.

Avicenna: Biography

The crèche is found throughout Spain at *Navidad*. In the great cathedral of Seville (tragically built atop the Almohad Mosque, though the magnificent Giralda minaret built in 1196 still stands) the visitor finds a vast desert oasis looking all like Andalusia with wise men, shepherds, and all the *Sagra familia* in what looks like a cave on the Campo de la Mancha. If ever a wise man came from the East it was Avicenna.

At ten years of age he knew the Qur'an by heart along with much of the corpus of Arabic poetry. The theologian must become the physician

---

[2] Vaux, *War on Terrorism*, 106ff.

and by sixteen he had mastered Greek and Latin medicine and had already innovated medical treatments for the sick. In my 25 years in the medical school I often observed an impressive theological and ethical commitment in my Muslim medical colleagues. Though I somewhat agreed with my colleague—hematologist Stanley Schade—that the "only theists were the Muslim doctors," I also found devout Jews, Catholics and Protestant Christians, like himself. The intensity and through-going synthesis of medicine and theology was indeed impressive among Muslim doctors as it was with Seventh Day Adventists and Hutterites.

Likewise Avicenna. When he became intellectually confused or morally bewildered as he pondered the Greeks, he would resort to the Mosque to receive ablutions (at Minarets like Giralda). Often he would stay to pray until dawn. After illumination he thanked God and bestowed alms on the poor. He read Aristotle's *Metaphysics* forty times. Its meaning only became clear when he found Al Farabi's commentary. These brilliant ninth and tenth century Muslim translators and commentators would convey that wisdom into the Latin and European world.

In 997 CE he performed a miraculous cure on the Amir, which Avicenna saw as an empirical miracle. The honors following this cure gave him access to the library of the Samanids (which subsequently burned—a tragedy like the Alexandria library fire) and set his life course in a scholarly direction. At Hyercania, he wrote his *Canon* of medicine which guided Western medicine—at Louvain, Montpellier and elsewhere— until the seventeenth century. Imprisoned during the war between Isfahan and Hamadan, he spent the last twelve years of his life in service to Abu Addaula of Isfahan.

Though Averroës found his work pantheistic, especially the now lost text *Philosophia Orientalis* (this text is mentioned by Roger Bacon), Avicenna's influence was pervasive and surprisingly lasting. Radically empirical, irrepressibly faithful, he established a foundation for a theology of medicine of our time. Of course, his insights do not come *de novo*. Mention must be made of several threads he wove together, like an Andalusian fabric, to prepare the early modern mind for a theology for science. Hellenic and Hebraic sources have set the stage.

Hellenic and Hebraic Sources

Avicenna sought initially to reconcile Greek philosophy with the traditional Semitic (Hebraic) wisdom called *hikmah*. This ancient sagacity chronicled in wisdom literature of Ancient Near Eastern lore and Hebrew

Scripture trails back into the perennial *Logos* or understanding found in all cultures—Asian, African, and aboriginal. This wisdom sees a synthetic portrayal of divine power and expression apprehended and reiterated in human thought, faith and act (craft).

This apperception, though more full of fear, trembling and awe than the more critical and rational Greek intellect, shared with it the same confidence in human insight and instinct and the same sense of responsibility before the divine life-giver and law-giver. Titling a major work *Oriental Philosophy,* Avicenna intended not only to claim a kind of Asiatic illumination but the conviction found in Greece and Egypt that all human perception and technique were given in *Tao. Scientia Inductiva* (Aristotle) and *Scientia Deductiva* (Plato, monotheism) were now complementary.

The old Greeks like Thales, the poets like Homer, the pre-Socratics and the Golden Age philosophers, Plato and Aristotle, lived and worked in this confidence and piety. Pythagoras, from across the Mediterranean, two millennia before the Andalusian masters, sensed a mystic form and format behind all human ingenuity. For him mathematics, theology, and music touched and mimicked this divinity.

Epistemology

In much the Pythagorean manner, Avicenna held the priority of modes of knowledge to be grounded in metaphysics, followed by mathematics and then natural (physical) science. Put another way in his book on the "Divisions of the Rational Science," Avicenna sees all knowledge (science) involving two parts: theoretical and practical. Theoretical knowledge, for example, the science of God's unity or astronomy, seeks certainty beyond any human effect.[3] Practical science (ethics, for example) combines a theoretical theme—truth—with the good in human behavior. In practical knowledge something is sought which is far greater than certainty. Moral habits and happiness (Aristotle's *Nicomachean Ethics*) are sought here and now and in the hereafter. A third mode of knowledge pertains to society and politics. As with Pythagoras, political action, human ethics and science itself were in constant interaction. Forced from Samos by Polycrates' tyranny in the sixth century BCE, the Pythagorean brothers, like the early Muslims, sought knowledge in order to effect human liberation. Truth was in order to goodness.

---

[3] Avicenna, "On the Division of the Rational Sciences," trans. by Mushin Mahda, in Ralph Lerner, *Medieval Political Philosophy* (New York: Free Press, 1963).

As one begins to probe science and conscience, knowledge and technology, as a Western person, one quickly becomes aware of a profound alteration of the human mind and its confidence in knowledge that has occurred since Avicenna, Aristotle and Pythagoras, to say nothing of Aquinas and Calvin. The revolution of epistemology brought about by Descartes, Hume, Kant and the "makers of the modern mind" has left us with a haunting sense of agnosticism. Now the age of post-modernity, post-positivism and deconstructionism allows a new sense of truth and goodness. Though it certainly rests on different grounds than on those of premodern metaphysics or Newtonian physics, confidence in particular perceptions and convictions is again possible. The reader cannot miss my appreciation of Avicenna. From my view, the retrieval of ancient wisdom is even more complex than a Derridian allowance. With Whitehead, I believe that good science and worthy application of that science and exertion of *technē* requires both knowledge and belief, both Greek rationalism and Semitic monotheism.[4] All of this Kant quite rightly saw as a human disposition—informed by a *Weltanschauung*—a view of reality—which Avicenna saw as wisdom. His was an interwoven truth as monotheistic unity and ethics found concord with moral law. My purpose in this project, as the reader will rightly discern, is in concord with Seyyed Hossein Nasr in his 1981 Gifford Lectures on natural theology: "To resuscitate the sacred quality of knowledge."[5]

The descriptive thesis of this work is invoked to support a normative thesis. I seek to show that not only have the science and technology, which have now spread throughout the world and become universal been derived from a certain theology and ethic (Abrahamic), but that the usefulness and helpfulness of that science still depends on that tradition. When science probes realms of danger (for example, nuclear science), stem cell genetic research or mechanistic modeling of the human brain, the normative tradition provokes critique on its own child. Is this true and how will it be used is the critical gift of this intellectual posture. But beyond this descriptive argument I present a normative contention that a vital theology and ethic growing out of this heritage exemplified by these six religious scientists can best guide us into the future.

---

[4] A. N. Whitehead affirmed that without Greek *Logos* and Hebraic "time" there would be no modern science. See Whitehead, *Science and the Modern World* (New York: Mentor, 1925) 13.
[5] Seyyed Hossein Nasr, *Knowledge and the Sacred* (New York: Crossroad, 1981) viii.

Which leads us to return to Avicenna. For the "prince of physicians" and for Islamic science generally, the first verses of the Qur'an refer to knowledge and science:

> Recite (*iqra'*): In the name of the Lord who createth, createth man from a clot. Recite: And thy Lord is the Most Bounteous, who teacheth (*'allama*) by the pen, Teacheth man that which he knew not.[6]

Mohammed said, and Avicenna believed, that the first thing that God created was reason. Whether drawing on his esoteric "oriental" philosophy, a kind of mathematical, Gnostic mysticism—on his Semitic monotheism and *creatio Imago dei*—or on his intellectual propensity toward Aristotle— Avicenna placed epistemology central in his philosophy and theology. For him as for his masters, Al-Kindi (b. 801 CE) and Al-Farabi (b. 870 CE), there were two forms of knowledge: divine knowledge (*al-'ilm al-ilāhī*) and human knowledge (*al-'ilm al-insāvī*). Knowledge of God, divine revelations, mysteries like the creation *ex nihilo*, or resurrection, were conveyed through prophets to the receptive soul. Philosophy or science is the process of human knowledge. Because of the three roots of his consciousness (and conscientiousness)—Esoteric, Hebraic, and Hellenic—the important feature of his epistemology was not so much the demarcation of divine and human knowing but the synthetic and integral quality of all knowledge, per se. Theology, said Karl Rahner, is the science of faith. Science it could be said is the faith of knowledge—the search for veracity and certainty. Weaving together the monotheistic and noetic reason into one concept, Avicenna provides foundation for the theology for science we propose and will exemplify from our six scientists.

For this reason, the interweaving of Hebraic (Abrahamic, Mosaic, Prophetic) knowledge with Greek (Aristotelian) *scientia*—Thomas Aquinas found Avicenna and Maimonides partners in the intellectual quest. To reconcile the knowledge receipt of Ancient Israel with Aristotle's probing of the mind seemed to be the task of his times as universities began to form around Europe.[7]

There is also an integration of the theoretical and practical, the scientific and moral in Avicenna's *Episteme*. Nasr, in his Gifford lecture of 1981 sees a broad heritage forming from ancient China, through the Hebrews to

---

[6] Qur'an 96:1–5 (Pickthall translation).
[7] See David B. Burrell, "Aquinas and Islamic and Jewish Thinkers," in Norman Kretzmann (ed.), *Companion to Aquinas* (Cambridge: Cambridge University, 1993) 60.

Christian sages, now manifest in the medieval Muslim scientists. Scientific enlightenment is the concomitant of personal virtue:

> The man of virtue . . . can see where all is dark. He can hear . . . where all is still the darkness, he alone can see light. In the stillness he alone can detect harmony.[8]

Though this epistemological premise is controversial, it has a long heritage. Kepler claimed that the one who would fathom nature must contemplate it with a certain reverence (*Betrachten*).

In a recent interview with two leading astronomers, commentator John McLaughlin noted a sense of profound "awe" as both contemplated the vast universe, its origin and prospects. But in their responses they made clear that awe—and certainly not faith—was necessitated by the phenomena or the data. My claim in this chapter is intermediate to that view in that I see responsible utilization called for by the knowledge that is forthcoming from the glory of creation. I believe with Einstein that knowledge is cumulatively reliable and ethically imperative when he affirmed: "God doesn't throw dice;" and, beyond this mountain just ascended, rises another, but we need never climb this one again, and we move on.[9]

An Abrahamic Epistemology

Mention of Albert Einstein moves us to another feature of Avicenna's epistemology. Referring to what he finds as a sympathetic kind of epistemology in the Christian tradition, particularly the innovations of Luther, Nasr finds in scientists like Paracelsus, shaped by that critical tradition, an "Abrahamic quality in which the wedding between faith and knowledge was a definite possibility" (Nasr, *Knowledge and the Sacred*). I contend that this radical Abrahamic consciousness first makes it way into Western science through Avicenna. This mode of epistemology stimulates scientific and technological breakthroughs, not only in the Andalusian Renaissance but also in the work of the Benedictine monks as they fashion all sorts of scientific and technological improvements in their *orare et laborare* spirit and by the Puritan scientists in England in the seventeenth century. Critical alethic science grounded in monotheistic ultimacy and monolatry will abide no falsehood or fabrication and demand excellence, elegance and ethics—the rudiments of pure *theoria* and *praxis*.

---

[8] H.A. Giles, Chuang-Tzū: *Taoist Philosopher and Chinese Mystic* (London, 1961) 119, quoted in Seyyed Hossein Nasr, *Knowledge and the Sacred* (Albany, NY: SUNY, 1989) 8.

[9] Author's paraphrase of Einstein.

What are the impulses and characteristics of an "Abrahamic epistemology?" The significant break in human history marked by Abraham's call to pick up and move out to this unprecedented summons fashions in the three Abrahamic faiths (Judaism, Christianity, and Islam) a mode of science and technology, which has striking features to the faith itself. Some of the characteristics are, as follows:

- The imperative to wrest the knowable by *venturing* into the unknown.
- Since divine grace and faithfulness mark our adventures into space and time we can *expect* insights and results from our inquiring and experimentation.
- It is our responsibility to seek knowledge and technology that is *ameliorative*, that improves the human plight and diminishes its tragic enigma.
- Our epistemological endeavors should be marked by drawing *hope* in resistance to that which harms people and claims a new world into the present from salutary future prospects.[10]

Case Study: Forbidden Knowledge

A new form of an old question in the age of stem cell research and reported human cloning concerns whether there are certain things we are forbidden to know and do. This anxiety is actually very old, recurring across the centuries, as vivid in the ages of the Exile Priests' writing Genesis to Paul the Apostle, Avicenna or Paracelsus, as it is today. The question itself begs an Avicennian universe. Who is there to forbid anything, especially pure knowledge, which is ethically neutral—Society, God, some nemesis inherent in the very process of probing and manipulating nature? The very mention of a prohibition or sanction smacks of censorship to those schooled in the Cartesian, Kantian and Enlightenment ethos. Yet, the foreboding persists today even among the most liberated and autonomous scientists. The dread seems to cut to the very center of our sense of responsibility.

One of the most widely read books in the town of Granada is *Tales of the Alhambra* by Washington Irving (Paris: A&W Galignani, 1832).[11] An American diplomat in Spain in 1829, he wrote, as in his *Legend of Sleepy*

---

[10] Seyyed Hossein Nasr, *Three Muslim Sages* (Cambridge: Harvard University Press, 1964) 25.

[11] Incidentally, this 1832 edition of *Alhambra* is one of the classics being released for free electronic download as a PDF file at http://books.google.com/—with all the attendant controversy that surrounds the "digital age."

Hollow, a mixture of history and legend to convey the deepest dreams and fears of the common people. He tells the tale of the Moorish King Aben Habuz who reigned over the Kingdom of Granada. An old and gullible man, he took into the company of Alhambra palace an ancient companion of Mahomet. After studying the dark sciences of the Egyptian priests he discovered in a pyramid whose sacrosanctity he has violated by exposing an ancient book of the wisdom of Solomon. This book bestowed on him superhuman knowledge and longevity—proven by his 200 years (though deprived of youthfulness). The ever-besieged king was lured into the promise of complacency when Ibrahim assured him that he need not physically fight the encroaching Christian powers if he would only play-act each assault on a chessboard set up in the Tower over the Albicin. Every time he dashed the toy soldiers on the big game board, the approaching enemies were put to rout. Finally, the king succumbed to the wiles of a beautiful Christian maiden. The spell was lost, the power was gone, and the damsel and old Ibrahim were lost in the deep subterranean recesses of Alhambra. Forbidden knowledge, itself procured, turned ruinous when prideful arrogance ruined potency and efficacy. Forbidden knowledge involves breaching divine quarantines: disobeying divine deontology, reverential detailing of sense data and intellectual interpretation and creating life, causing death. The gift of divine disclosure about the world requires inordinate speculation and concoction. Knowledge in *Mishnah* requires detailed and careful study of *Torah*. *Madrassas* insist on careful repetition. Puritan knowledge is fine-grained experiential perception.

Dimensions of Avicenna's Epistemology

In order to create a milieu where the pursuit of knowledge and its application was creative and encouraging rather than cautious and dreadful as if knowledge were forbidden, Avicenna fashioned an epistemology having three dimensions: (I) Mathematical, (II) Theological, and (III) Eschatological. At age twenty-one *Ibn Sinā* wrote his first three books: *Kitāb al-Majmü* on Mathematics, *Kitāb al hāsil*, on the sciences and *Kitāb al bira wa'l-ithm* on ethics. The beginning of knowledge in all wisdom tradition is empirical and moral insight.

I. In the mathematical realm he affirmed the ancient Pythagorean conviction that truth, because of its divine source, began with quantitative and formalistically logical qualities. The great Alhambra in Granada, or the Cordoba Mosque Cathedral convey the genius of *Pre-reconquista* Islamic art focused in geometric, organic and logographic modes of expression. Kepler believed that "quantity was the mode of Job's expression" (see *Cosmographicum*). The foundational quality of human perception and reason deals with numbers, symbols, forms and patterns. Symbolic logic, logical positivism and scientific epistemology witness to the power of this window into reality. Leibniz, Spinoza, and their followers fashioned knowledge based on the sciences, mathematics and philosophy. Even the newcomers, human and social sciences, have fashioned an enterprise of knowing grounded in statistics. The era of quantifiable knowledge extends into our own century. The mind makes a great leap into truth and justice—into the realm of the divine—with its probe of this formal universal order.

II. We have mentioned the sacred dimension of knowledge. Not only is God the ground of all truth and knowing, there is a knowledgeable God accessible to the human mind and there is a divine permeation of the world and human thought, which illumines many other realms of knowledge. Avicenna affirms the connection between God and objective knowledge, which is

> proof that He has knowledge of all objects of knowledge. Since it is established that He is a Necessary Being, that He is One, and that the universe is brought into being from HIM and has resulted out of His Being; since it is established further that He has knowledge of His Own Essence, His Knowledge of His Essence being what it is, namely that He is the Origin of all realities and of all things that have being; it follows that nothing in heaven or earth is remote from His knowledge—on the contrary, all that comes into being does so by reason of Him: He is the cause of all reason, and He knows that of which He is the Reason, the Giver of being and the Originator.[12]

Here the ingredients of classical Greek ontotheological epistemology are joined to Semitic monotheism. The one necessary Being, by definition, is prior to and cognizant of all other contingent beings. The unity and sufficiency of this Being constitutes the etiology, which becomes the circumference and teleological purpose of all other beings. Nothing in all reality therefore, is remote to this Being. Rather He is the rationale and salience of all beings and objects.

---

[12] Avicenna, *On Theology* (London: John Murray Ltd., 1951), A.J. Arberry, trans., quoted in Anne Fremantle, *The Age of Belief* (New York: Mentor, 1954) 136.

III. Finally, there is a proleptic (impending, coming) aspect to Avicenna's epistemology. This again is an Abrahamic and prophetic dimension in that it construes reality historically and eschatologically. The One not only perceives, observes, analyzes and contemplates but also anticipates and waits. Avicenna believed that comprehensive or full knowledge was not confined to form or matter, the yield of the mind and senses. Knowledge involved grace (*barakah*), what we would today call serendipity or surprise; along with the more generic mental substance we would call revelation. Knowledge involved unity (*Tawhid*), which entailed coherence, or what we would name unified theory. Edward Wilson's *Consilience*[13] is one of the latest scientific attempts to gather all knowledge into a comprehensive framework. Finally, there is an eschatological aspect to epistemology. Here we subsume Greek *telos*, inherent into another Semitic, Abrahamic meaning, which is hope. Knowledge, which has dimensions of veracity and morality, allows the dimension of prediction, foretelling (prophesy) cybernetic consequentiality and expectation based not on illusion, but on desirability, goodness and justice. Far from being mere wishes or values, outcomes can be trusted in Avicenna's mathematical theology and eschatological epistemology, then proved to be solid ground for useful science and helpful technology.

A Crisis in Knowledge

By way of summarizing this section on Avicenna's epistemology, we need to mention a special aspect of eschatological intelligence, which is a sense of alarm and of warning. We will see this aspect of theologico-scientific wisdom later portrayed by another Semitic thinker—Leon Kass. Seyyed Nasr begins his Gifford Lectures (1981) with a sense of urgency and crisis more profound than even those delivered by Stanley Hauerwas (2001), Karl Barth (1950), Reinhold Niebuhr (1939), or Albert Schweitzer (1934)—other Gifford laureates who wove eschatological/apocalyptic dimension into their lectures on "natural theology." Nasr titles his first lecture "Knowledge and its Desacralization."

Theologically speaking humans are given the grace of knowledge (*gnosis*) as the gift for industry (work) and responsibility. They are given *agnosis*—silence and the inscrutable—in divine response to faithlessness and injustice. The known and living God, evoking and empowering the human knowledge project in His work, is also *deus absconditas, deus anonymous*. Using words like *secularization, scientism, positivism*, and *cosmolatry*,

---

[13] Edward Wilson, *Consilience: The Unity of Knowledge* (New York: Vintage Books, 1999).

Nasr wants to decry an irreverence and violence that has become set in Western epistemology and technology in wake of the project of Descartes, Hume, Kant and Comte.

The Enlightenment of Western Europe, one of whose fruits is an ascending accumulation of knowledge, has not witnessed to a concomitant wisdom. She has therefore unleashed much destruction and degradation along with much nobility, freedom and progress. This ambivalence also gives us reason to revisit ancient humanistic and sacred traditions, which define scientific endeavors in spiritual and ethical terms.

Traditions

The tragic has seriously confined, as well as defined the intellectual project. Copernicus, Galileo and many other pioneers of knowledge have been censured and worse. Avicenna himself was labeled a heretic, though his work finally prevailed. In general, faith has stimulated the research and implementation of knowledge. We think of the Benedictine Monks, Albertus Magnus and Thomas Aquinas, Paracelsus and his experimental colleagues or the Puritan geniuses—Thomas Sydenham, Robert Boyle, and others who investigated, categorized and described reality with great imagination and rigor.

The characteristics of creative science and conducive religiosocial science policy and ethics include, among others, what Nicholas of Cusa called "learned ignorance" (*Docta Ignorantia*) and what the apostle Paul called "knowledge added to virtue" (2 Corinthians 8:7). Learned ignorance is the posture of humility, creative doubt and holy perception, formulated by Nicholas of Cusa, a brother of the Deventer community in the Netherlands—a mathematician, physicist as well as metaphysician and theologian. "The highest wisdom," he wrote, "consists in this, to know . . . how that which is unattainable may be reached or attained unattainably."[14] Paradox, contradiction, negation may be the threshold, where knowledge becomes wisdom.

Having worked most of my career in the faculties of science and medicine, I have often seen the great learning that is implicit in acknowledged ignorance and the profound error, even danger, seen in presumed knowledge or compulsive task. Knowledge acquisition is often like the biblical truth—a process of negation. Negative theology affirms that the main project of belief is to dispel penultimate or idolatrous truths. In sci-

---

[14] Jasper Hopkins, *Nicholas of Cusa on Learned Ignorance: A Translation and an Appraisal of De docta ignorantia* (Minneapolis: A. J. Banning Press, 1981).

ence, truth often comes in a long, successive project of dispelling, discarding, disproving and ruling out of the false. The Human Genome Project is such an example. As anomalies are cast out, the norm appears. When error is cast out truth is self-illuminating and self-verifying. When idols are iconoclastically removed—God appears, self-evidently and not of our making. This is Abrahamic science.

Here are all the elements of Hebraic-Islamic theology passed through the Hellenistic lens. That the creation came into being by the power of One who conceived and planned it, that this unfolding plan does not mechanically proceed (thus obviating freedom and creativity) but unfolds reflectively (as lunar light) through the vice-regency (*cooporatio dei*) of human beings, all through a pattern of avoiding evil and achieving goodness in moral (technical) freedom— this is the essence of a theology for science. A theological background, in other words, safeguards and scrutinizes the process of knowledge and technology, guiding it toward its appropriate redeeming expansion in the world. Not to be confused with spiritual salvation (soteriology), redemption, in Abrahamic-Akedic terms has to do with the ongoing development (Teilhard) and apocalyptic renewal (Schweitzer) occurring within the world of human endeavor. We can believe what we see and know because our senses are endowed in divine goodness. Our faith and the derivative helping impulses to help, further stimulate divine disclosure, which is the surprise and synergy of science.

Ethics

The direction of Avicennan and medieval Andalusian thought follows the logic and movement of Hellenic and Hebraic science and wisdom. Truth is in order to goodness in order to beauty. In such a conducive theology and ethics that we present for science and technology we find six dimensions:

Dimensions	*Exemplars*
Alethic . . . Truth	AVICENNA
Aesthetic . . . Beauty	ROBERT BOYLE
Aetiologic . . . Creation	TEILHARD DE CHARDIN
Aeschatologic . . . Finality	ALBERT SCHWEITZER
Axiologic . . . Ethical	AMARTYA SEN
Agapic . . . Love	LEON KASS

In learning science and craft, this human display follows the Platonic pattern and sequence. In Hebraic terms, divine energy and presence in creation offers a way of being with others in the world, which often in freedom is expressed as either honor or rejection. In the drama of failure, sin and injustice, a disorder is set in motion, which promotes the divine response of love, sacrifice, forgiveness and moral renewal so that the original, eternal and ultimate possibility might be regenerated.

Ethics, thus, is positioned at the very heart of the theological realm as it is in the scientific and technical realm. In Judaism and Islam ethical imperatives find a much higher place in the way of life than they find in Christianity. The Pauline-Augustinian worldview accents so strongly the fall, rescue and salvation that even the finest human endeavors are fraught with suspicion. Ironically, or paradoxically, Christianity follows Judaism with its accent on freedom and responsibility and generates enormous scientific and technical endeavor especially in the three eras of Andalusian, Medieval, and Mediterranean culture, Renaissance and Puritan England and Holland, and Enlightenment Europe and America.

Eschatology

After Christianity becomes "this worldly" in Constantinian secularism it remains to Islam to reintroduce the eschatological into Abrahamic theology and science. It is eschatology that sways the future. God, the author of the beginning is, as well, the arbiter of the end. Whether, in Aristotle's *Telos* as the inherent purpose or in the Abrahamic last Judgment and derivative hope, eschatology is a fruitful theological theme by which to critique, enrich and animate science. When Templeton Prize winner John Polkinghorne writes of *The End of the World and the Ends of God*,[15] he comes to this tangent of our theme. When Leonardo da Vinci turns to his turbulent series of sketches on apocalypse depicting ocean waves and deep chaotic flooding or when Andalusian writers and artists: Velázquez, Murillo and Picasso ponder physical catastrophes in the perennial aftershock of the Lisbon earthquake, we feel the tremor of this awareness.

Science is born in response to apocalypse and eschatology. We hold back the chaos in building dikes or contriving antibiotics. We respond to paradise hopes in food production and distribution. We yearn for a divine kingdom where wars will cease (economics), swords will be forged into plowshares (technology), light will illumine the night (electricity), and the pure, clean water of Abrahamic and Islamic eschatology will flow free (water purification technology). In medicine, we hope to realize the dream where injury and death is averted and we live long and well.

---

[15] John Polkinghorne, *The End of the World and the Ends of God* (Trinity, 2000).

Avicenna contends that we are obliged to constantly hold to mind our dying, the resurrection and the afterlife. His curious phrase, we must "remember" the afterlife, captures the Islamic mystical paradox. Standing still at attention (*achten*)—or kneeling or lying prostrate in obeisance—are matters of concentration on what is real, lasting and eternal. The ministries of good deeds drive away evil. Attending human need enlarges the rule of Allah in this world. The divine future is proleptically advanced as divine righteousness is manifest in our human world (Calvin).

For Avicenna revelations or prophesies concord with universal intellect where the mind of the Deity is conveyed across to the human mind and creative spirit establishing all things true, good and beautiful. Eschatology is the transmission of knowledge and hope across the dimension of time. This emanation, often called light, removes darkness, illumines the unknown, shows the way. These emanations (Plotinus) or messengers (angels) proceed from eternity into time, future into present, fulfillment into our refracted incompleteness. [16]

Avicenna, here, is expositing the ancient doctrine of the immortality of the soul. This substance in person- infusing mind, spirit, and body is divine investiture. Since it belongs to God, it cannot be harmed or perish. The earthly process of its maturation and refinement is involved as the Spirit elicits thought and inspires works within the human person and community. It is the immortality of the soul that is the constitutive doctrine of Islamic eschatology. Here we are linked with the hereafter, the beyond. Here we are rendered accountable for how we use this life. Semitic and even generic universal values, find expression here. We are given endowments and experiences. We make good use or abuse of these moments or opportunities. Though the doctrine pertains to personal souls, our collective activities of thought and action are part of the freedom, destiny and judgment of God. In Abrahamic or Semitic religion, as in its precursor Indo-European faith, there is no radical separation of the "One and the many." In Islamic thought, as in Judaism and Christianity, we sense that professions, for example, medicine, law, economics (business), ministry, education, even science and engineering, are recipients of divine calling and the bearers, therefore, of special culpability and responsibility.

Conclusion

We too have journeyed in and out of the reality spirit and of the physical world. We have oscillated, with the help of a sublime genius, Avicenna,

---

[16] Avicenna, "On the Proof of the Prophesies," in Lerner, *Medieval Political Philosophy*, 101.

between God and creation, theology and science, ethics and technology. In the segments of this opening chapter, we have traveled from metaphysics to epistemology from theology to science, from eschatology to ethics. It has been a journey within and beyond. It has been a trafficking of the author (hopefully, along with you, esteemed reader) up and down the ladder of heaven.

I have sought to lay a foundation for a larger exploration of theology for science and a correlative ethics for technology. As I look out my balcony window here in Seville, Spain, I see the grand cathedral, 500 feet away. Here the Inquisition began in 1481, continued through Dostoevsky's day when the old Grand Inquisitor walked by this very cathedral and that unwelcome visitor raised the dead little girl from her funeral carriage. Those horses still clip-clop down the stone alley beneath my window. The Inquisitors constructed this massive cathedral, with its 70 domes, *solo dei gloria*, so that "all the world would think we were mad."

I hope that my reader will not reach such a conclusion regarding the construction of this work. As I shared in the introduction, it is a building that culminates a life-long work in science and theology. The complex history and present challenges of these themes invite such expansive formulation. I hope that you will journey along. I will lead you like the restless guide who hounded me in the casbah in Tangier, hoping that you will help me decipher the labyrinth and find a way through.

Excursus: Maimonides

A resplendent edifice (deeply moving to this writer, whose scholarly world has sought to show the profound interdependence of the Abrahamic faiths) mounts the small university city. *La Mesquita*, now the Catholic Cathedral of Cordoba, is at heart a Muslim Mosque, one of the leading three or four in the world. Built on top of the Visigoth Christian Church (dating to the fifth or sixth century) which topped the Greco-Roman temple, adjacent to the Jewish quarter and Maimonides' home, the structure symbolizes that day of rapprochement if these faiths ever enjoyed such a day. My *hostala*, the Baghdad, is just two hundred meters from the great tower of the Mesquita, which houses the remnants of the eighth century minaret. My *hotelier*, Ahmed, is from Jordan. As we nervously wait to hear if America will begin bombing Iraq again, Ahmed laments that it is a difficult day for Muslim Arabs to be alive. Life, I assure him, is equally terrifying to Christians and Jews. If only we could walk these streets again with Averroës,

Maimonides, and perhaps Thomas Aquinas, who also lived in a Muslim domain, until the Inquisition and *Reconquista*.

As a footnote to my opening chapter of this book on Avicenna, I wish to add some reflections on Maimonides and Averroës. During all my years in the medical school the name of Maimonides fascinated me. We studied the Code (Oath) of Maimonides and some medical schools even recited it on commencement to medical practice. Actually, our twelfth century *Qadi* from Cordoba had nothing to do with the Oath. It is a nineteenth century document. The esteem owed this wise physician, philosopher, and theologian is obviously great. He is the codifier of the Rabbinic tradition (*Mishnah*, *Talmud*) and discoverer/interpreter of many processes and diseases, such as the menstrual cycle and certain mental illnesses. He is the philosopher, par excellence. His corpus of material is so rich and varied that he deserves more than scant mention in this volume, for at least this reason.

As medieval Catholic Europe begins to form and as the morally ambiguous events of crusades, inquisition and *Reconquista* give shape to the present age of European and of American cultural dominance in the world, Thomas Aquinas—the greatest mind the Christian Church has produced—looked to two colleagues for primary inspiration: Avicenna and Maimonides. He knew that Christian philosophy, science, theology and ethics must be true to the Greeks (Aristotle) and to Hebrew scripture. Maimonides was his "wise man." For David Burrell, one of his foremost interpreters, Western science and philosophy begins, ironically, in Baghdad.

Being true to the Greeks and Hebrews means being true to natural reason and real-world empirical knowledge and to the God humans come to know as The God of Abraham and Israel—the God of history. While Thomas rejected the heterodoxy of Avicenna, Averroës and Maimonides, perhaps even sharing what in general society and the church was a vitriolic hatred and fear of Jews and Muslims, he sought Truth wherever it was to be found. The doctrine of the eternity of the world—the cosmology of Aristotle, Avicenna and Averroës, was problematic—though the *Logos* Theology of John and Paul (Colossians and Ephesians) spoke of something coeternal between God and the world. Maimonides hovered near Christian truth in Thomas' view. He started with the Abraham and Mosaic discovery, revelation and deliverance in freedom and law.

Romantic views of the twelfth and thirteenth centuries at this outer edge of *Dar al Islam* will not hold. Fanatic right wing Muslim movements and resentful Christian leaders made life difficult for Jews. Hounded and harassed, Maimonides' family wandered through Southern Spain when he was thirteen years old. They finally settled in Fez, Morocco, where he spent the next ten years. The family eventually moved to Palestine, then Cairo. While Richard the Lionhearted was fighting the crusades (reportedly he asked Maimonides to be his personal physician), he served as Muslim Court Physician in Cairo. Like Jesus and Schweitzer, he also attended the sick masses every day . . . Jews and gentiles, nobles and common people, judges and policemen, friends and enemies . . ."[17] The spiritual leader of the Jews in Egypt, he completed his magnum opus, *The Mishneh Torah*, in 1178. This compilation of ten volumes of Talmudic law remains a standard classic to this day. In 1190, he finished his philosophical masterpiece, *The Guide for the Perplexed*. He also wrote medical treatises on drugs, asthma, regimes of health and sexual intercourse.

Fred Rosner summarized the legacy of Maimonides:

> Maimonides died on December 13, 1204 and was buried in Tiberius, Palestine. The Christian, Moslem and Jewish worlds mourned him. His literary ability was incredible and his knowledge encyclopedic. He mastered nearly everything known in the fields of theology, mathematics, law, philosophy, astronomy, ethics, and of course, medicine. As a physician, he treated diseases by the scientific method, not by guess work, superstition or rule of thumb. His attitude towards the practice of medicines came from a deep religious background, which made the preservation of health and life a divine commandment. His inspiration lives on through the years and his position as one of the medical giants of history is indelibly recorded. He was physician to Sultans and Princes, and as Sir William Osler said, He was "Prince of Physicians." The heritage of his great medical writings is being more and more appreciated. To the Jewish people, he symbolized the highest spiritual and intellectual achievement of man on this earth; as so aptly stated, "from Moses to Moses there never arose a man like Moses" and none has since.[18]

Maimonides' contribution indeed moves into the center of science and theology not only as it shapes Judaism, but also as it becomes a part of general Abrahamic culture. That Thomas Aquinas would single him out (with Avicenna) as architects of a new vision of God and the world is not surprising. Let us mention three central concepts that he contributes to our unfolding vision of a theology for science and an ethic for technology.

Maimonides' intellectual diary with the perplexed student, Joseph, is much like Thomas' ongoing doctrinal dialogue. Like Socrates, both medieval writers seek to probe deeper and deeper after the truth of God and the world. Maimonides instructed Thomas to seek the delicate reconciliation of reason and revelation. Both accents were intense in Rabbinic Judaism since the founding of the Talmud schools in Palestine and Babylonia. Hebrew conviction was always caught on the horns of a dilemma between purity to the Torah and the particular emphasis of

---

[17] see *The Art of Luke: Maimonides Medical Writings*, forward by Fred Rosner, M.D. (Haifa: Maimonides Research Institute, 1992).

[18] Fred Rosner, "Moses Maimonides (1135–1204)," *Annals of Internal Medicine* 62 (1965) 373–75.

faith seeking purity and continuity in embattling circumstances always lured, as is all Abrahamic religion, by assimilation and cosmopolitans interests. The purist and eclectic tendencies have always been pronounced in Jewish history.

David Burrell, in *The Cambridge Companion to Aquinas*, singles out three key areas in which to trace Maimonides' influence:

- The "eternity" or temporal limitedness of the cosmos
- The meaning structure of divine names
- The issues of providence

Ex nihilo theology was a crucial imperative of Judaic and Islamic theology of creation. Without this biblical doctrine both the nature of God and that of the world was compromised. Avicenna and the Talmudic heritage were able to reconcile this radical theocentric notion of creation, with emerging scientific insight through the incorporation of Logos ideas from Neoplatonic philosophy. For Rabbi Maimonides, there are not intermediary divinities like causation and essence. God alone is the direct creator and Lord of all creatures. Eternity belongs to God alone and to those on whom He bestows *creator spiritus* (derivative being).

Maimonides' doctrine of the law, will and truth of God revealed through Moses, maintains that initiation being and the ultimate grounding and guiding of the world is in God alone. That He "shares His glory with none other"[19] means to cut away from all demiurgic, demonic, fecund and autonomous cosmogonic faiths. There is not another "alongside" or "over-against" reality. This insistence solidly grounds creation and derivatively, science in a divine sustenance and purpose Concomitantly it anchors human technology and its ethical guidance in the commandments (words) of God.

Nasr, in his Gifford Lectures, links this intellectual appropriation and ethical action. Knowledge is virtue, he claims, in the broad wisdom tradition represented by Islamic Sufism, Christian mysticism and Jewish *Halakah*. To assert, to know truly, is to act rightly. Today the divorce threatens. "Exteriorized action" is a term evoked when science, seen as objective and "value neutral," is torn from its "value-laden" technology. Those who pioneered the genetic knowledge of disease, Dr. Lejeune of Paris, for example, the first to describe Down Syndrome (Trisomy 21), sensed the ominous power entailed in naming, in this case, a syndrome. He pleaded to the National Institutes of Health not to use this knowledge obtained via amniocentesis, to abort the "designated" fetus. For Nasr, naming was the highest form of invoking the divine name in prayer—an act that concentrates mind and will to do the possible under God—a profound responsibility.

Maimonides, the first Rabbi to comprehensively link Greek world knowledge with the Hebrew God knowledge, sees a critical connection between semantics and ontology. In the intriguing panoply of Hebrew "names of God" getting it right is contingent upon "doing it right." "Merciful and gracious ... long suffering

---

[19] Isa. 42:8.

(*hesed*)"[20] is a name and knowledge of God posited on the basis of character and action. Thomas pushes Maimonides by contending that the things (*Res significata*) must be distinguished from the mode (*modus significandi*) so that the actions of God—even those accomplished through human agency—are not independent virtues (power), but actions rooted in the Essence of Godself. Now science can never be severed from theology—nor theology from science.

Finally, Maimonides reflects on the nature of divine providence. This provides further inspiration for Thomas Aquinas. Surprisingly, Maimonides demands a wider realm of freedom and chance in things that happen in the world than does Thomas. He says, "It is not my own belief. . . . That this spider has devoured this fly because God has decreed and willed something concerning individuals."[21] In his *Guide to the Perplexed*, Maimonides affirms that ". . . a divine overflow . . . of providence watches over everyone endowed with intellect" drawing that entelechy toward its consummate purpose.[22] Again, we see the propensity towards freedom in Judaism and the obverse emphasis on causality, even fatality, in the Greeks and Muslims. The importance of the Maimonides, Averroës, Thomas Aquinas convergence in Western thought is that an exquisite balance of necessity and freedom comes to a characterize scientific and technological work. Chance and necessity, as Bergson and others have shown, intertwine in the theological worldview contributed by "the Prince of Physicians."

Excursus: Hildegard of Bingen (1098–1179)

Though a brilliant and incisive new science is incubating in Andalusia north in the heartland of Europe, a parallel movement of equal experimental wonder, scientific rigor and theological inspiration is taking place in the Benedictine cloister of Disibodenberg by one Hildegard of Bingen. Hildegard has long fascinated me because one of the eminent scholars of her life and work, Barbara Newman of Northwestern University, and dear family friends, the Willy Hahn family of Bingen, have called her genius to our attention. She again represents the serious and serene science that arises within consciousness steeped in the eschatological kingdom.

Dedicated as a "tithe" to God, Hildegard—the tenth child—was initiated into the Benedictine cloister at Disibodenberg on All Saints Day 1112. Even as a young child she realized that she had special insight and was a "prophet" or "Visio." An anchorite Nun, her residence was attached to the Abbey with a small

---

[20] Psalm 103:8ff.

[21] David Burrell, *Cambridge Companion to Aquinas*, 81.

[22] Burrell, *Cambridge Companion to Aquinas*, 81.

garden where she cultivated healing herbs. A special vision in 1141—perhaps related to an epileptic seizure—summoned her to "write what you see or hear." Etching with a slate pencil on small wax plates, she started her book *Scivias* ("know the ways"). From then on the Monk Volmar (1141–1173)—himself an intriguing figure—was her secretary until Gottfried, then Guibert of Gembloux—the brilliant Walloon monk assumed that role for the remainder of Hildegard's life work. Filled with doubts about her visions in 1146–47 she wrote Abbot Bernard of Clairvaux (1090–1153) for counsel and advice. He could not quell her doubt but encouraged her work. The European Synod held at nearby Trier (1147–48) received report of her "prophetic visions" with affirmation. Pope Eugenius III read *Liber Scivias* and encouraged her ministry.

Scivias is divided into three sections explaining in 26 visions the work of creation and redemption. Part I, "Under the curse of sin," deals with the work of creation, the fall of Lucifer and the creation and fall of man in six visions. Part II, "The Fiery work of redemption," deals with the work of redemption by Christ and the continuation of the mystery of salvation by the Church, in seven visions. The thirteen-vision Part III—"the ripening abundance of the times"—deals with the secret of salvation (a building raised by the *virtudes*—the powers of God). This imaginative theology seems to embrace the Judaic notion that God is erecting with humankind the antidote and answer to the fall wherein a construction of creation—beginning with the stones—is fashioned against evil and for fulfillment. After *Scivias* is completed in 1151 her work falls into six periods:

- 1158–1163 *Liber Vitae Meritorum* (Book of Life's merits)
- 1163–1174 *Liber Divinorum Operum* (Book of Divine works)
- 1151–1158 *Liber Simplicis Medicinae/Physica* (Natural science), *Compositae Medicinae* and *Causae et Curae* (medicine), *Subtilitatum diversarum Naturem Creaturum* (science)
- 1150–1160 *Lingua Ignota* and *Litterae Ignotae* (Languages)
- 1148–1179 *Ordo Virtutum* and 77 liturgical chants
- 1146–1178 Letters

Her major encyclopedia on science and medicine is a theological rendition of a divine therapeutic cosmos as well as a manual of practical compounding of medicaments along with an herbal, bestiary and lapidary.

Music

The polymath Hildegard's music, now recorded by excellent ensembles worldwide—including Sequentia and Anonymous Four—captures the blissful order of the Gregorian idiom with serene new accents from nature and her own mystical soul. She composed and wrote texts for 77 songs and a mystical play, the *Ordo Virtutum* (Journey of the *anima*—the human soul—toward virtue). *Diabolus* was sung and played by Volmar while the sisters sung the human and angelic parts of the liturgy. Volmar spoke vociferously and sang raucously which caused great pandemonium in the congregation.

Linguistics

In a less known and explored part of her work but important to ours, Hildegard invents a new language—*lingua ignota*—and her own secret writing—*litterae ignotae*. 300 of the 900 words are drawn from the extant texts on medicine and botany.

Stones and Metals

Book Four of the *Physica* is devoted to precious stones—lodestone, alabaster, burnt-lime and pearls. She also sees the therapeutic efficacy of the eight metals, including steel. In the book *Die Heilsteine der Hildegard von Bingen* (Tübingen, 1997) Michael Gienger shows the exquisite geological fascination and knowledge (purely worldly/not revelation) and the underlying theology that brought Hildegard to this interest. We find here an Hebraic attraction found in Wisdom (e.g., Sirach) that God is founding and building—with humankind as *mitarbeiter*—a mineral house in the earth to reconstruct a paradise for the flourishing of life after the transgression of Lucifer and the angels and subsequently Adam/Eve and the protohumans. The Hebrew notion (Akedah and Torah are fundamental to Hildegard) that humanity is created to rebuild the "good world" (*Shalom/Tikkun Olam*) is behind and under the "stone story." The specific beauties of the underworld: onyx, sapphire, *lapis lazuli*, topaz, diamond and the rest each have their own distinctive beauty and efficacy. Creation, Hildegard believed, was the garment or *grundstoff* of God—*specula*/reflecting glass. Stones impart color, light, dazzle, and, anticipating electromagnetic theory, energy and world-soul (Plato).

Science and Medicine

The medicinal works have long enjoyed the title *Hildegardmedizin* among the peoples of Europe, even the world. With a Wesleyan emphasis on healing remedies she focuses this work on the preventive and curative uses of plants, trees, animals, metals, precious stones and the elements (wind, air, fire, water), all those goods for life that Wisdom finds on and in the earth for the delight and utility of humans and for its own inherent good. A naturalist, she described the local fauna and flora and reviewed the knowledge sources extant in her day. The influence of Isadore of Seville, Galen, Pliny and Soranus is clearly felt. From a holistic vision her herbalism and bontanics fathom the constitution and efficacy of herbs, vegetables, flowers, honey, milk and sugar. In the *Physica* she lists thee remedies alongside the illnesses. Like Galen of old, and Avicenna, her contemporary, she describes the preparation, doses, application and form of administration (lotions, pills, poultices, irrigations, etc.) of all the substances. The remedy is generally a juice administered in pulverized form—a powder dissolved in wine or water.

Though natural science in the twelfth century was taught in the Cathedral and Convent schools, subjects bordering on crafts—botany, zoology (husbandry), gemology and medicine were taught in more popular settings, in the Encyclopedias of antiquity and in guilds. Hildegard bridged these bodies of scholastic and popular knowledge and functioned as a physician as did Avicenna, Maimonides and our medieval exemplars of theology for science. The *Macer Floridus* (eleventh century) was the most commonly used book on medicinal herbs as Northern Europe awaits the scientific revolution beginning in the thirteenth century, as Greek and Arabic works are translated in Andalusia, Italy and elsewhere where Abrahamic wisdom prevails.

Science and Wisdom

Hildegard's theological cosmology has been called one of the most significant world-conceptions of the middle ages: Earth and heaven, microcosm and macrocosm, seasons and ages of life—all gather in a synthetic cosmos. The book of Divine works (*Liber Divinorum*), a cosmologically conceived history of salvation, is representative of her wisdom. Barbara Newman writes: "For Hildegard, the moral interpretation of the east wind, the eyebrows, or the creation of fish was no decorative fancy, but mattered as much as the phenomenon themselves; for all creatures were fabricated for man (homo), the body for the soul, and the soul for the glory of God."[23] "Nature," wrote her near-contemporary Hugo von St. Victor, "is the book written by God's finger. God's constant creation (and recreation) is the ground of all healing and natural activity."[24] Hildegard attested to this, as did Robert Boyle 600 years later.

The Medieval Foundation of a Theology for Science

We have located the foundations of the building we are about to construct in the medieval period, so erroneously called the "dark ages." Here the theocentrality of the Hebrews and the rationality of the Hellenes converge. Here also *theoria* and *techne* join hands. Here, in a period condescendingly labeled that of the "Jews," "Muslims" or "Arabs," I find the monotheism, holism and ethical directionality which alone could supply foundation to the scientific edifice. Of the modern scientist-philosophers, Alfred North Whitehead best appreciates the crucial and constitutive role that the medieval world plays in the dawn of modern science. I summarize

---

[23] Barbara Newman, *Sister of Wisdom* (Berkeley, 1987) 21.
[24] Quoted in Newman, *Sister of Wisdom*, 72.

this opening section of our study referring to his masterpiece *Science and the Modern World*.[25]

He first acknowledges, as we will amplify in the next chapter on Robert Boyle, the enduring salience of the Stoic belief in order and the divine permeation of the world. It is divinity that has shaped the regulation and destination of the world and God has even obliged himself to adhere to that order and structure. "The Middle Ages (then) formed one long training of the intellect of Western Europe in (that) sense of order." (p. 12) Whitehead continues:

> The greatest contribution of medievalism to the formation of the scientific movement was the inexpugnable belief that every detailed occurrence can be correlated with its antecedents in a perfectly definite manner, exemplifying general principles. (p. 13)

> Faith in the possibility of science, generated antecedently to the development of modern scientific theory, is an unconscious derivative from medieval theology. (p. 14)

Whitehead then asserts that with the Benedictines and other monastic movements, prayer and work, thinking and making, science and technology, were so allied that they flourished along with "an interest in natural objects and natural occurrences" so that people experienced a "direct joy in the apprehension of the things which lie around us" (p. 16, 17). We will now see as we proceed that the Occident assumes a special burden as the sponsor of modern science specifically because of its spiritual and ethical heritage in the Orient. Beauty is now conjoined to truth, aesthetics to alethics.

---

[25] See A.N. Whitehead, *Science and the Modern World* (New York: Mentor, 1925).

Robert Boyle
the aesthetic vector

IT IS 1640. SIX centuries have passed since the sages of Spain brought their Jewish and Muslim Wisdom to ground and invigorate Christian philosophy and science. The Inquisition has driven the sibling sons of Abraham back into North Africa. Maimonides dies in Tiberius in Palestine. Christianity has held sway in Europe despite the threat of Suleiman the Magnificent at the eastern gates of Luther's fragile lands. Protestant and catholic cultures contest power on the continent while in England three complex Christian faiths intertwine traditions: The old Roman Catholic faith survives with its Irish and French roots but a century of religious struggle has left two other movements predominant—the Puritan and Scottish churches and the new coalescence of old and new traditions called The Church of England. It is the age of Robert Boyle.

The Age

And such an age! The first of a series of modern freedom revolutions that would transform human history swept England in the 1640s. These would continue through the American, French and German uprisings of the eighteenth and nineteenth centuries and then on to the Russian, Asian and African democracy revolutions in the twentieth. In that first fall of the line of dominoes, theology, science, even politics found new release from church, custom and then, colonialism. The thrills and terrors of an age of liberation would cause tremors in society. The seeds of Renaissance and Reformation had grown up in the cultural seedbeds of Europe made fertile, as we have shown, by the concepts and convictions of Judaism, Christianity and Islam in the continent's formative period. In England, an epicenter of this awakening, fashioned by this *zeitgeist*, we meet the likes of Isaac Newton, William Harvey, Christopher Wren and Robert Boyle. An inquiring newness and solid excellence characterizes their work. They create the age of modern science. In theology, the Puritan revolution, an aftershock of the Reformation, grounds religious expression in experience and questions Aristotelian hegemony, all in the spirit of scriptural rediscovery. It is an age of cultural exuberance and of paranoiac persecutions and witch-burnings. Even Boyle's mentor, Thomas Browne (1642, *Religiomedici*) consented to a prosecution at Bury St. Edmonds. Like the tumultuous twelfth to fifteenth centuries in Maimonides' Andalusia it was an age of pioneering rigor, synthesis and awakening, but also of fearful crusades and Inquisition.

It was an age of newfound practicality and particularity: think of Galileo's thermometers, Leibniz' calculus, or Boyle's air pumps. It was also an age of encyclopedic wisdom: think of Descartes' epistemology, John Ray's theology of nature or Isaac Newton's mathematical mechanics. Empirical specificity and Platonic/Aristotelian generality from the Greeks along with Semitic and Abrahamic *scientia*, wisdom, divine duty and worldly fervor had been transmitted to the age, as we have shown, by medieval Jews, Christians and Muslims. While delighting in classical insight, rigorous investigation would now cleanse theory and practice from all that would stifle and impede novelty. As Hippocrates and Galen had once brilliantly synthesized the rich phenomena of nature into a generalized whole, now Harvey dissected the cardiovasculature of 87 animal species, beautifully depicting, in the many, the overarching oneness. Milton's dream of an earthly paradise and Bacon's *Great Instauration* were at hand. Inspired by the symmetry that would become Newton's system, it was an aesthetic age, an age of beauty. But all too beautiful! The tragedy of Charles I would soon shatter the serenity. The music of the period, William Byrd's *The Battell* with the poignant "Marcher to the Fighte," "Retreat" and "The Burying of the Dead" or Captain Tobias Hume's "Death and Life" composed just a fortnight before Charles' decapitation, express the deep anxiety within the exuberance of the period. Like the death of Saddam Hussein's two sons Qusay and Uday, killed today as I write, some may be relieved to be rid of evil men, but we're not sure what will follow. Such was the age of Robert Boyle.

The Man

Robert Boyle, the physicist-philosopher (1627–1691) exemplifies the flourishing and the restlessness of the age. He epitomizes the ushering of a new empiric into the cosmic as the salience of Galen and Aristotle begins to wane. Behind this cultural change was an incipient theology, which would transform the science. This was an age that Thomas Carlyle described as one where persons of intuitive and inductive genius sought to see the earth's minutiae *sub species aeternitatis* and "... bring the law of the bible into actual practice in affairs on earth."[1]

Boyle was an extraordinary man of science. A father of modern chemistry, he pioneers the workings of pneumatics, hydrostatics and pyrotechnics. He is Hippocrates' airs, waters and fires come down to earth. He improved the air pump, studied the respiration of higher animals and discovered "the law"—Boyle's law that the volume of a gas is inversely proportional to the pressure. He elucidated the laws of motion—tides, oceans, solidity, plasticity and fluidity. He began to fathom color and heat, hot and cold. A passionate and compassionate intellectual, he anguished at the autopsies of young men who had drowned or suffocated while Oxford's Regius professor refused to stoop so low. This passion and compassion informed his scientific fervor and inventiveness. He studied chemistry, he claimed, to employ it in "the fight against stubborn diseases." His science arises from his theology and ethics.

His spirituality arises at a tender age. In his teens, while studying in Geneva (where he may have first heard of Calvin's *Institutes*), he was awakened one night in terror by the thunder and lightning that is common in the hills around the great lake. Fearing divine judgment at hand, he pledged, like St. Francis or Pascal, his life and work to divine pleasure and human good, should he be spared.[2]

His mind was drawn to the teachings of Jews, Christians and Muslims—casting out a net of inquiry for truth, wherever it might be found—to "ground his religion" (p. xxiii). In acute anxiety (we might infer, providential) he experienced something of a conversion while intensively studying Calvin's "catechism" (*Institutes of the Christian Religion*).[3]

This essay is rooted in that same "natural law" heritage generated into human history as Hebraic and Hellenic foundations provide the structure for Christian (including Puritan) and Muslim worldviews. Supplying the parameters and impulses for the origins of science, the elements of truth, now beauty are seen as indispensable qualities of discernment as the scientific endeavor proceeds.

---

[1] Thomas Carlyle, *Oliver Cromwell's Letters and Speeches.* Quoted in Mitchell Salem Fisher, *Robert Boyle: Devout Naturalist* (Philadelphia: Oshiver Studio Press, 1945) 15.

[2] Robert Boyle, *Works,* Life of Boyle vol 1, p. xxii, quoted in Fisher, *Robert Boyle,* 20.

[3] Flora Mason, *Robert Boyle* (London, 1914) 100. See also *Lismore Papers,* ed. Alexander Grosart, second series, five volumes, 1887–1888, quoted in John Harwood, *The Early Essays and Ethics of Robert Boyle* (Carbondale, Ill.: Southern Illinois Press, 1991).

Boyle's Ethics

From the moment of that Calvinist transformation Boyle was a person on the Way of transfiguring the world under the divine command. It is only recently that the connections between Boyle's science, theology and ethics have begun to become clear. John T. Harwood, one of his principal editors and interpreters, has brought out *The Early Essays and Ethics of Robert Boyle* in which he notes the words of Dr. Johnson in the preface to the *Dictionary* (1755), justifying the presentation of this work . . . "to the desire to communicate the works of great men of 'truth' and 'morality:' Hooker, Bacon, Milton and Boyle" (p. 15).

The connection between Boyle's natural philosophy (science) and moral philosophy (ethics) is an important link in the argument I seek to draw in this essay. Theology, I contend, is the natural link between science and ethics. For Boyle both science and ethics were aspects of communicative knowledge—offerings of service to the community. This ambition of godly disposition, biblical knowledge and human service is the locus of Boyle's ethics:

> An overriding Biblicism may be regarded . . . as a defining characteristic of Christian humanists. It was their regard for scripture which guided their extra-biblical pursuits (including science); their perception of a biblical concern for individual morality attracted them to the Roman stoics (e.g., Calvin); the need to understand the bible contextually drew them to the study of ancient history.[4]

Boyle's Theology

My study reverberates strongly with two recent sociology of science/theology studies by Rodney Stark. In *One True God* (Princeton, 2001) and *For the Glory of God* (Princeton, 2003) Stark develops the thesis that monotheism and Christianity are responsible for the historic and ongoing vitality of the scientific enterprise. "Christians developed science," Stark claims, "because they believed it could be done, and should be done."[5] Reason and viability joined with moral conviction of hope to offer a salience for the endeavor. He quotes my teacher, Charles Webster (now at All Souls, Oxford; previously director of the Wellcome Institute for the History of Science at Oxford): "No direction of energy toward science was undertak-

---

[4] Margo Todd, *Christian Humanism and the Puritan Social Order* (Cambridge: The University Press, 1987) 23. See also chapters 2–3.

[5] Rodney Stark, *One True God* (Princeton: Princeton University, 2001) 51.

en without the assurance of Christian conscience."⁶ The great historian of Puritan science knew the finer faith impulses behind scientific endeavors like those of Robert Boyle.

Stark rightly grounds science in medieval and Puritan theology. He wrongly caricatures Islam as possessing a capricious deity who could not be relied on to insure a knowable universe and a truthfully perceptive human mind. Early Islam is more grounded in Greco-Roman (Aristotelian) natural law than was Christianity. The deeper message of his two-volume study on monotheism is the broadly Abrahamic impulse and impetus at the basis of science. Our Puritan case study does prove Stark's point that the empirical mood resists Galenic and Aristotelian conceptualization and that that resistance exhilarates scientific work. The monotheistic impulse, however, including confidence in divine creativity, venturism and assurance of objective truth is the overriding element in all scientific advances including the Puritan.

For Boyle, theology undergirds science and science enlivens theology. Though deeply involved in scientific work with Puritan colleagues, in the Royal Society and Gresham College, for example, Boyle remained a reformer within the established church. He refused to support or frequent dissenter meetings. His prevailing passion seems to have been truth, order and efficacious work. He did however subscribe to many reformist beliefs and practices. At the behest of the now infamous Bishop Usher, Primate of Ireland, he studied not only Hebrew and Greek but Aramaic, Syriac and other Near-Eastern languages under Thomas Barlow, chief of the Bodleian Library and later Bishop of Lincoln. All this endeavor was undertaken to better receive the immediate address of the scriptures. One feels here both the humanist yearning for fresh and reliable texts and the more radical and countercultural impulse of Luther and Calvin for *Sola Scriptura*.

Like our son, a most pastoral sort, Boyle understood but did not discern a call to the Anglican ministry. He was, however, an astute theologian of the church and a strong benefactor of her mission in the world. He singly underwrote the Malay translation of scripture and contributed to the Welsh, Irish and Turkish bibles. He aided religious refugees in many lands. Founding the Society for Propagating the Gospel in New England, he foresaw promising evangelical and worldly endeavors on this new frontier.

In the closing lines of his Will and Testament he discloses his theology about science. Leaving his raw and unprepared minerals to the Royal

---

⁶ Charles Webster, *The Great Instauration* (New York: Holmes and Meier, 1975) 213.

Society he wishes them ". . . a most happy success in their laudable attempts to discover the true nature of the works of God and praying, that they and all other searchers into physical truths may cordially refer their attainments to the glory of the Author of Nature, and the benefit of mankind."[7]

The age of seventeenth century theology and science is a brilliant and creative age. It has all the vitalities and synergies of the age of Albertus Magnus and St. Thomas, and that of Luther, Paracelsus, Calvin and, dare we say, Servetus. But the theology of the period is also seriously distorted by the tendency toward pantheism and deism and the deification and absolutization of space and time implicit in the Newtonian revolution.

When a static and mechanistic space time apparatus is severed from the lineaments and impulses of the Living God of Abraham and the Akedah and the thought of the age is also colored by the Cartesian dissociation of subject and object so that a natural and trusting relation with the world is bewildered by a gnawing doubt and skepticism, hopeful science and helpful technology is hardly possible. Yet despite these drawbacks an underlying affirmation of a creating, sustaining and incarnating God and His good world is felt even though it regrettably seemed necessary to posit this temporary deistic, deterministic and dualistic interval. The continuity of the God of history and nature and the world of human construal and construction is strained though its energies are sustained.

Boyle, though, rises above the fray. He therefore leads us onward in a creative theology for science. For him the "book of science" (nature) and "book of God" (scripture) are complementary texts—free of contradiction. If the models of interaction between theology and science are (1) "interacting approaches to reality" (A. Peacock, R. Russell); (2) NOMA, or "non-overlapping magisterial areas" (e.g., S. J. Gould, *Rocks of Ages*); or (3) "two avenues to truth" (T. Torrance), Boyle represents the latter option. In affirming science as the penetrator and purveyor of efficient causes and theology of first and final causes, he affirms the dominion and glory of humanity under God:

> . . . that Divine providence had several Ends, in making the World, and the several creatures that compose it, some of which are hid to us and others known, is evident, some being made for the manifestation of the Glory of God, others for the usefulness of man, or the maintenance of the System of the world . . .[8]

---

[7] *Life of Boyle: Works*, p. clx, Quoted in Fisher, *Robert Boyle*, 23.

[8] *Theological Works of the Honorable Robert Boyle*, ed. Richard Boulton (London, 1715, III) 211.

With Hebraic and biblical resonance (Psalm 8) he claims that the material world is made as supply and substance for humanity in its destiny of *Tikkun Olam*, execution of justice and glorification of God. The world is not a manipulable ball of mud but a mysterious sacrament upon which plays out the divine-human drama. Some things are manifest, others cryptic, stimulating ordinary knowledge or revelation. Some acts are permitted, others forbidden. A proleptic and ethical drama is working its way out in this "interim time and space" where human experience, especially regarding mastery and control, is that best described by Matthew Arnold:

> . . . wandering between two worlds,
> one dead, the other powerless to be born

Or the Apostle Paul:

> . . . the whole world groans in travail seeking birth,
> gripped by futility by Him who subjected it in hope
> in order to set it free (*eleutherothesatai*).[9]

In this theology of nature we find paradox or paroxysm in creation itself within the lordship of God and the superintendence (stewardship) of humanity. Earth is not yet what it shall be. It is not what it could be or should be. Space and time, as Einstein showed, are provisional, fluid, contingent, relatively ordered phenomena. In very hard to grasp insight where the real world is distinct and discontinuous from this space and time it is true "that only the father who kills his son" (Arthur Miller, *All My Sons*) can "so love the world." A mystery of evil, of incompletion, yearning, of felt obligation and opportunity and of ultimate vindication and victory marks the plight and promise of humanity in God's created cosmos. As Benedictine physicist Stanley L. Jaki has shown in a fascinating series of books, the *Cosmopancrator Messiah*, vulnerable to the freedom of the world, becomes the "savior of science."[10] Sacrifice for the burden of loss and failure—the price of freedom—is the precondition for the sustenance and survival of the world. It is the indication and impulse of science.

Predictability and Spontaneity

If there is a God, ethicist Joseph Fletcher once told me, he would have to obey the laws of love. He could not do otherwise. Boyle, like Newton

---

[9] Rom 8:20–21 (author's translation)

[10] *Road of Science and the Ways of God* (1978), *Chance or Reality* (1986), *Absolute Beneath the Relative* (1988), *Savior of Science* (2000).

(and Fletcher), opts more for the predictability of "nature's laws" than for a radical creative freedom in God. This is in contrast to the more biblical Maimonides, who, when physician to the Caliph in Cairo, affirmed the radical, creative freedom of God present in the Abrahamic/Akedic heritage. In *Guide for the Perplexed* Maimonides contends that God can change His instantaneous governance of the universe in the same way that the Caliph could daily alter his riding habits through the streets of Cairo.[11] In his book *Faith*, G.K. Chesterton resonates that God says every morning to the sun "Get up!" and every night "Go down!" While this view affirms the sovereignty and power of God and certainly attests to the "surprise" and "serendipity," "deliverer of Israel" and the "miracle-working God and Father of the Lord Jesus Christ," it accents more the sheer will of God than the rationality of *Imago Dei* where God concedes to and works through the receptive structures of consciousness and conscience and the objective structures and processes of nature which He has placed in the world. While the "pure monotheism" of Judaism and Islam favors this metaphysical and metatemporal rendition the conversational/relational triune Godhead of Christianity affirms a more dynamic, multifaceted Creator—One who governs both in predictable decree and in spontaneous action.

Boyle's synthesis of Catholicism and Puritanism and of theology and science bridges this conflict. His theology—classically catholic and orthodox, gently irenic and eclectic in the Anglican spirit, yet inflamed and inspired by the reforming energies of Calvinism and Puritanism—exudes a Hebrew-Christian etiology and eschatology thereby exerting a confidence and guidance on the human activities of science. Just as the full beauty, goodness and truth of the One God must fill the world in all of its environs and epochs so the reality of the world—to whom God sent His beloved Son—ever abides in His mind and purpose. This is the meaning of the great *Shemah* and *Hashem* of Israel:

> Hear o Israel, The Lord our God is One . . . Therefore . . . you shall have no other gods

Boyle's Divine Chemistry

We have identified Robert Boyle with the aesthetic dimension of a theology conducive to truthful science and helpful technology. Just as theology and ethics are inseparably joined, so science and technology are conjoined. In this regard Boyle formulates a dynamic theology of the elements and

---

[11] Moses Maimonides, *Guide for the Perplexed* (New York: Dover, 1956) 128.

forces of the world—of the physics and chemistry of the cosmos. This theology of matter and form extends his philosophy into the realm of science. He offers this in his overarching philosophy of science as well as in his reflections on sight, light, heat, cold, fire, color and air. Like St. Francis he baptizes these elements with a divine aura. In their instrumentality and intrinsic worth and work they are God's creatures. These substances and processes of nature are given by the Creator, ordered purposively by His good Will for humanity and the creation, endowed with potencies for human affects and effects—worship and work—offered in order to His glory and liberating justice in the world. Boyle's reflections parallel those of his contemporary, John Milton:

> From the moment of creation God hath plac'd Metals and Minerals in the Mountains, Valleys and Veins of the earth and causeth them to grow there. . . . The spirit of man . . . will reach out far and wide as knowledge doth increase (Dn 12:4) . . . till it fills the whole world and the space beyond with "divine greatness."[12]

Boyle is a figure, much like Paracelsus (1493–1541) who, a century earlier, explored the "new theology" of Luther, incorporating that inquiring and reforming theology into the very fabric of his science and invention. Called "the Luther of science" his critique of Aristotle and Galen was bombastic, given the entrenchment of that medieval *weltanschauung*. As with Boyle, the matrix of his knowledge was chemistry, a science still mired in pre-empirical obfuscation. Starting as an alchemist, he turned the art away from magical concoction and gold-making into a thoughtful and deliberate science of matter. He still struggled with the naturalism and spiritism of antiquity and with iconoclastic genius refused to accept the caprice of the gods as the pervasive explanatory principle. He rather inquired after the empirical nature of water, air (wind), ether (space) and fire (light). He moved the world halfway toward Boyle. Behind it all was a view of God as vital, energetic—one who constitutes and animates world processes.

Boyle, with his sister Katherine ("the woman who made the greatest figure in all of these kingdomes above 50 years"—Burnet) patronized and participated in the "invisible college" focused in Worseley's labs in Oxford, investigating "physick, anatomy, navigation, staticks, magneticks, chymicks, mechanicks and Natural Experiments."[13] With his assistant, Robert Hooke, Boyle also became involved in Wilkens' labs in Oxford,

---

[12] Quoted in Webster, *Great Instauration*, ch. 3.
[13] Webster, *Great Instauration*, 56.

"the experimental philosophical clubbe," eventually superintending the entire scientific apparatus in Oxford subsuming the work of Harvey and his colleagues on circulation, respiration and aeration. Iatrochemists all, they surveyed and applied all physical elements toward the goods of human knowledge and health all under the purview of and offered to the Glory of God. This leads us across the aforementioned bridge of ethics to Boyle's science.

Boyle's Science

Seventeenth century science, as it would again be in the twentieth, was at heart a theological revolution. As then we are now witnessing a seismic change in our notions of ultimacy, truth and right. It is a crisis of the first commandments. There was the mathematical revolution: What constitutes infinity, contingency and the formalistic coherence of space-time reality? Leaders here are Descartes, Leibniz, Pascal and Newton. Then there was the experimental revolution: Why and how do things work as they do? Hooke, Harvey, Bacon and Boyle are prominent here. It was an age of scientific and Theistic martyrdom—dying for the truth and the right. In 1533 the Roman Church forced Galileo to recant his Copernican views, confirmed by telescope to the delight of his provocative anticlericalism. Boyle was there when he died at his estate near Florence. Giordano Bruno was burned at the stake for his atomic (and theological) theory in 1600. The religious (30 years) wars from 1618–1648 sacrificed many martyrs. Science, like theology is akedic. Truth and good are always disturbing, provoking vehement reaction among the vested interests and their minions who cling to the status quo. As truth displaces error (geocentrism) and right unseats wrong (witch-burning) the biblical wisdom is borne out:

> Blessed are the persecuted . . . They belong to the Kingdom of Heaven (Mt 5:10)

Boyle's religious conversion, a mystical and empirical event, became a paradigm for his scientific work. In a metaphoric way it involved air, fire, water and wind. With the full fury of da Vinci's Flood sketches he records:

> For at a time, which (being the very heat of summer) promised nothing less, about the dead of night that adds more terror to such accidents, Philaretus (the ideal of the truth seeker) was suddenly waked in a fright with such loud claps of thunder(which are oftentimes very terrible in those hot climes and seasons) that

> he thought the earth would owe an ague to the air, and every clap was preceded and attended with flashes of lightening so frequent and so dazzling, that Philaretus began to imagine them the Sallies of that fire that must consume the world. The long continuance of that dismal tempest where the winds were so loud, as almost drowned the noise of the very thunder, and the showers so hideous, as almost quenched the lightnines, ore it could reach his eyes, confirmed Philaretus in his apprehensions of the day of judgment's being at hand.[14]

There was a kind of apocalyptic mood in Boyle's science. Harold Nebelsick, an important theological historian of science, argues that what we find in Boyle is a revival of a Platonic mood in public philosophy, which would give rise to modern science.[15]

> In its neo-Platonic and Hermetic forms the concept of the divine as interpenetrating, rejuvenating and recreating all things served to help break the hold that the Peripatetics (Aristotelians) had . . . on the middle Renaissance mind.

This mentality contributes three elements, Nebelsick continues:

> . . . natural science depends on faith, imagination and a sense of order.

Beyond Platonism, Nebelsick finds

> . . . renewed interest in the ancient Scriptures of the Old and New Testaments which challenged . . . the Aristotelian deductive spirit (p. xiii, ff.).

Several streams, in other words, flowed together into Boyle's scientific thought:
- the Neoplatonism residual in the Augustinian tradition;
- fresh and critical study of the Scriptures;
- the revival of classical learning;
- apocalypticism (da Vinci and Newton);
- Hermetic and other "mystical ideas" about the soul and the world;

---

[14] Robert Boyle, *Works*, v. 1, p. xxii, (Quoted in Hunt, 19–20).

[15] Harold Nebelsick, *Circles of God: Theology and Science From the Greeks to Copernicus* (Edinburgh: Scottish Academic Press, 1985); *The Renaissance, the Reformation and the Rise of Science* (Edinburgh: T&T Clark, 1992).

- and the injection of Arabic wisdom and commitment to the transmission of the Abrahamic and Classical Tradition.

Together these streams become a mighty rushing river of cultural awakening, surging forward the ship of the new science. Elegance and enlargement became a "great instauration."

My own convictions follow Nebelsick because of the great emphasis he places on the "Arabic" appropriation of Greek science and philosophy including the emphasis on a unitary world, one eminently knowable and workable, all grounded in the God of Abraham as guarantor of order and purpose and the synergy of faith in that living God and worldly knowledge. My own research leads to the added affirmation of the importance of the monotheistic impulse: the strong (and derivative) iconoclastic (apocalyptic, revelatory) skepticism; the assurance that the mystery of divine love lies behind and beyond all the limitation and tragedy of life; and the obligation to do justice, impelled by the ground of our very being who calls us by Name. From Avicenna and Maimonides to Sen and Kass this is the message we are given for how theology and science are interrelated.

Boyle's science, in terms of its theological infusion, is intermediate to Paracelsus and, say, Lavoisier. His own apocalyptic experience informs his investigations into the natures and dynamics of airs and waters, ices and fires, heats and colds, even though these elements and forces are thoroughly disenchanted. Indeed, that is the point. Stripped of any divine or demonic necessity they are amenable to investigation. Like Leonardo, Boyle construes the physical universe in terms of the geography of his own soul and vice versa.

Again, the strange irony: Boyle is in Florence in 1642, just miles away when Galileo dies in his house arrest at Arcetri. Through his telescope Galileo saw new resplendent and dynamic heavens and, with Copernicus, set aside the stolid and fixed universe of Ptolemy and the medieval church. Boyle sees in nature not fixity but the same divine splendor and dynamism. He will become the muse of God's aesthetics.

An artist and optimist of this pre-modern era, Boyle saw intimations of the divine in nature. In the mind and heart of God he found love for and joy in the creation.' Why is the sky blue?' he asked. He anticipated Hegel's assertion, based on contemplation of sea and sky—"*Ewigkeit ist blau.*" He anticipated our present knowledge that among the wavelengths of light in the sun's spectrum blue oscillates at the highest frequency thereby refracting most readily through the air molecules in the atmosphere—*Voila!*—blue skies.

In the experiential or experimental imagination surprise and serendipity is expected. In Chesterton's words one hears a knock, opens the door and is surprised. The jaded and scientific mind hears the knock, opens the door and sees a lion. Only then is he surprised. Yuri Gagarin gazes from the Sputnik spaceship and sees no God. John Glenn from Apollo sees God in His handiwork. Darwin perhaps, but certainly Dawkins, eschews any "god of the gaps" and is agnostic about any design in nature. With Stephen Jay Gould or Carl Sagan he would be not only shocked but also offended by any divine involvement in nature or history. Steven Hawking, true to the honoree of his Cambridge chair, Isaac Newton, finds the beginning and end of human knowing in the mind of God. One sees what one is prepared to see.

Excursus: A Theology (and Science) of Radiance

It is Trinity Sunday in Oxford. The Lectionary in the Church of England leads the Priest at both Christ Church Cathedral and at Pusey Church to ponder the perplexities of the Holy Trinity. My thoughts, immersed in the work on Robert Boyle, focus on the themes of emanation, light, fire and radiance. As these topics were elucidated in sermon and the Mass, the shimmer shone, we can be sure, down the street of Corn Market and down along the High Street where Robert Boyle made residence nearly 400 years ago.

Ezekiel 36:23 promises:

> I will sanctify (brighten) among you my great Name which you have profaned (darkened).

And Revelation 2:1–4:

> The One who holds the seven stars in His hand
> The seven spirits of God are the seven stars
> The seven flaming torches are the seven Spirits of God

We have argued in this study that an aesthetical theology is the precondition for a vibrant science. In this Pentecost season we remember that this season of *Shavuot* (celebration of the law) was a time of ineffable light as tongues of fire accompanied the imparting of the Spirit as these gift-portions of Moses' Spirit were shared with the 70 elders (Numbers 11). This celebration of the "Way" is reenacted at Pentecost as the young church, an extension of *ecclesia,* the enlightened and "on-fire" community of God, is extended into the world. This theology of light, evanescence, flash and fire was referred to by the Chaplain of Christ Church as "quotidian beauty—the beauty of the common life of God's people in the world." The One who proclaimed "let there be light" is the very One who by His Will (Light, Spirit, Way, Word) created all things.

This theology of radiance is one of Boyle's great gifts to the world. It informs both theology and science. Air and moisture, color and fire all find review under his philosophy of perception, physics and divinity. The dean at Pusey and the retiring chaplain at Christ Church went one step further in their homilies, as scripture required. Both reminded all of us in the congregation that . . . "we beheld His glory shining in the Face of Christ" (2 Cor. 4:6). In the text of the transfiguration (Matt 17:2) the shining, transfigured one, we recall, is none other than the akedic/agapic figure:

> This is my beloved Son . . . listen to Him (Matt 17:5)

The "beloved son" of Abraham's Akedah (Gen. 22) is also the visage of "a man of sorrows," one acquainted with grief, "one in whom there is no beauty that we should desire him," "one from whom we averted our gaze" (Isa. 53). Yet, in sublime paradox, this disgrace is pure beauty. The refraction of sublime light through One in whom suffering becomes redemption and death becomes life, is pure radiance. This is also the aesthetic mystery of theology and science.

> Wake from sleep and rise from death and Christ shall give you light
> (Eph. 5:14)

The glory (radiance) of creation is both inherent and derived. God radiates glory (color) into his creature and in return receives glory. The rainbow, the refracted light spectrum, is the glory of God's greater love over the darkness the human world superimposes on creation. Humans-become-righteous are the renewed glory of the creation. In the words of Whitehead, speaking of the eternality of nature:

> A color is eternal. It haunts time like a new spirit. It comes and it goes, but where it comes, it is the same color. It neither survives nor does it live. It appears when it is wanted.[16]

Humans, wrote Calvin, are the "glory of God." John Philoponos, in sixth century Alexandria, not only refuted Aristotle's circular, uncreated and unending cosmos but asserted that the biblical Creator-God had made this world with an independent (free) though contingent reliance. Disputing Aristotle's assertion in *De Caelo* that stars were not fire balls, he followed the Apostle's ". . . one star differs from another in glory," asserting that in this world both implicit principles (composition, form, size, revolution) and divine implantations and destinations control the . . . color and brightness of stars.[17]

---

[16] Whitehead, *Science and the Modern World*, 88.
[17] Nebelsick, *Renaissance,* 13 (from *De Opificio Mundi*).

Boyle, with Philoponos and Calvin, saw the world as the theatre of God's glory. *(Deus hoc Fine Mundum Condidit ut Gloriae Suae Theatrum foret)*. It is too easy to equate science with deistic absenteeism or new age spiritism. These schemes do not deal with the God of nature and history, of time and space. Surer foundation, authorization and utilization of science are found in the God of Abraham. Though I ground this theocentric cosmology in the long wisdom of Confucius, the Vedas and Siddhartha, the Buddha, I stand particularly in the world-view of Judaic *Tanakh*, the Christian Gospel via the apostles and Paul, the Jamesian strand of Jewish Christianity and the Benedictine heritage. The Islam of Avicenna and rabbinic heritage of Maimonides, Aquinas, Calvin and the Puritans continue the pathway of heritage which I claim. Thielicke, Weizsäcker, Moltmann and Pannenberg, Torrance and the "ordained scientists" (e.g., Peacock and Polkinghorne) are my contemporary teachers. Within this lineage lies the work of Robert Boyle.

Robert Boyle: The Aesthetic Dimension of Theology for Science

This leads to the aesthetic dimension of reality in theology for science. In Isaiah 53 the cosmic Messiah "who had no beauty that we should look upon him" (v. 2) strangely becomes the One who will prosper. The One on whom "has been laid the Iniquity of us all" ironically "shall be fully satisfied," "who is rewarded with honor" (v. 12).

This is Messiah, the anointed Son of Man on a sapphire throne (Ezekiel 1:26), the divine, perfected human one within the realm of nature and history—the Infinite, Eternal, Holy One within the bounds and bonds of humanity within space and time. Theology struggles with the issue "who is God?" but also "who is man?" It probes the perfections of divinity and of the world. A full and complete science and correlated theology must deal with ambiguity, evil, the dark side, chaos and nothingness. Indeed in the all-embracing explanation (smoothing out irregularities) discord must transmute toward concord, disorder, order and chaos, cosmos. Purely deductive science, from Plato and Aristotle, has perfect ideals, ideas and forms. *Mens sana in corpore sano* is the human ideal. Puritan science, as we find in Bacon and Boyle, shows the more radical biblical sublimity—strength made perfect in weakness. Such is fitting for one working on air pumps, heat chambers and fire experiments.

That Boyle's theological science is so sublime may be a Newtonian anomaly. Actually he lives at the end of an age of harsh violence. The terror of the age is acute with threats of national and religious imperialism. Even his own time of Puritan Revolution, Commonwealth and Restoration is tumultuous. Yet his biblical seriousness and his careful observations of the properties and dynamics of matter, crafted with his assistant Hooker broadens and deepens his consciousness into a more serene and sublime comprehension of divine and natural process.

Philosophy of science claims that truer and better science is marked by symmetry, cohesion, cross-referential consistency, elegance and beauty. Thomas Kuhn's discussion of "Paradigm" shifts in the history of science finds breakdown and replacement of paradigms occurring when elegance wanes in one model and greater explanatory beauty is discovered in another. As he sought to construe and model the motion of the planets Kepler played with "oval curves" and found them "a cart-load of dung." Only when he tried "the elegance of the ellipse" did he hear the "music of the spheres."[18] At the heart of John Keble's theology, earthly beauty is the "glow of the divine," and Michael Polanyi notes the connection of beauty and truth.

The science of Harvey and Boyle, Newton and Ray, like the medicine of Browne and Sydenham and the architecture of Wren and the poetry of Herbert is a leap to a new expression of beauty. While it would be difficult to say in this age of post-modernism and deconstruction that explanations become more beautiful and that while, as Thomas Kuhn has shown, there is a certain sufficiency and deficiency with any model in any age, the seventeenth century seems to be an age of profound advance in science and in the correlated disciplines of theology and philosophy. Theological vitality, philosophical rigor and ethical earnestness make for useful science and helpful technology.

Indeed, in light of our thesis, the entire social organism of a given era possesses a certain beauty or grace which is fashioned, in part, by that culture's response to and amelioration of pain and its pursuit of justice and shalom. In light of our akedic thesis, for example, how does a given society show honor to its weakest and most vulnerable, say in providing education for all? Science, technology and especially medicine are near and long-range responses to these antipathies and ambitions. Since the Benedictines and da Vinci, the age of mechanics had been intrigued with muscles, joints, bones and limbs. The internal organs—heart and lungs—were after centuries of prohibition exposed to the experimental reach. The machinery of the common life—water, sanitation, transportation, farm-

---

[18] John Brooke, *Reconstructing Nature: The Engagement of Science and Religion* (Edinburgh: T&T Clark, 1998) 209.

ing and communication (printing) were allowing greater enrichments of life. While the age of plagues persisted their severity declined and a more congenial and hopeful age ensued . . . even for the poor. Science therefore was akedic work or worship. It was an offering, a sacrifice for justice and goodness (beauty) against the resistance of brute nature (Hobbes), the inevitabilities of fate, the injustices of inequity, and the brutality of disease and death. John Milton could perceive a yet unborn dream of hope streaming through the dark corridors of despair in this dawning age. This hope was channeled into the vehicles of science, technology, theology and ethics—all divine gifts.

In her excellent book *Theology in the Age of Scientific Reasoning* (Ithaca, New York: Cornell University Press, 1990), Nancy Murphy offers the Christian doctrine if the Trinity as the paradigm of elegance, coherence and beauty by which to comprehend, rationalize and evaluate science. This theoretical model (in the Hebraic and Hellenic sense) embracing both the form (substance) and action (process) of divine and material realms serves as a paradigm, in Kuhn's sense, to explain the conjunction of eternal and temporal under the sway of Grace. In this "overlapping realm" the "Totally Other" (Kierkegaard and Barth) plays and displays into the realm of nature and history as the divine dynamics of creation, incarnation and sanctification continue the process of redemption and restoration of the world.

In a subsequent work Murphy follows even more the lines of this essay by posing a kenotic model of the reality of God where absolute impassibility and other categories of Greek metaphysics are challenged by the more biblical God-picture of an out-going, self-giving, co-suffering, co-laboring being.[19] This model, though more elusive as a paradigm for science, does capture better a more Gruenwaldian notion of the glory of the divine condescension. This is the disarming notion of faith offered by Whitehead in *Science and the Modern World*:

> The faith in the order of nature which has made possible the growth of science is a particular example of a deeper faith. This faith cannot be justified by any inductive generalization. It springs from direct inspection of the nature of things as disclosed in our immediate present experience. There is no parting from your own shadow. To experience this faith is to know that in being ourselves we are more than ourselves: to know that our experience, dim and fragmentary as it is, yet sounds the utmost depths of reality: to

---

[19] Nancy Murphy and G.F.R. Ellis, *On the Moral Nature of the Universe: Theology, Cosmology and Ethics* (Minneapolis: Fortress Press, 1996).

know that detached details merely in order to be themselves demand that they should find themselves in a system of things: to know that this system includes the harmony of logical rationality, and the harmony of aesthetic achievement: to know that, while the harmony of logic lies upon the universe as an iron necessity, the aesthetic harmony stands before it as a living ideal moulding the general flux in its broken progress towards finer, subtler issues.[20]

Excursus: A Theologian for Science: Tom Torrance
Second Sunday in Trinity: June 22, 2003

A visit to St Michael's Inveresk Parish and her satellite congregation, Whitecraig, Scotland, brought unexpected pleasure, renewing friendship with parishioners I had served 42 years ago as student pastor. The text of the service was Paul's conversion experience in Acts where the foreboding words forecast:

"... I am Jesus whom you are persecuting (Acts 9:5)

"... I will show him (Saul) how much he will suffer for MY NAME (9:16)

"He is my chosen instrument to take MY NAME to the nations" (9:15)

In the afternoon at a Festival at St. Paul's Pilrig Street in Edinburgh, Ian Torrance, professor (and son of Tom Torrance), then Moderator of the Church of Scotland (now president of Princeton Seminary), preached on the "joy of Christ." This is something of an oxymoron in the Scots character, a theme, which I recalled in scripture, which is always associated with suffering (Isaiah 53, Heb. 12:2).

Science, in part is about delight and dissonance, symmetry and disfigurement. To what reality and inevitability shall we accede and what shall we challenge? The bible passages recalled the akedic focus of our inquiry. Science requires a theological ground not only to be anchored in truth and the right, but also to be positioned in a salutary way in the matrix of Utopia/Dystopia (the scenarios we seek to achieve and avoid) so that we sustain the theological heritage of seeking good and eschewing evil. Naming God and good, as well as wrong and evil, is part of the discerning and directing tasks embedded in the Abrahamic/Akedic thesis of this project.

Born into a missionary family in China, a Presbyterian minister in the Church of Scotland, Tom trained as a systematic theologian under Karl Barth at

---

[20] Whitehead, *Science and the Modern World*, 20.

Basel. He won the Templeton Prize for his work in science and theology in 1978. He devoted himself to these themes later in life after a distinguished career in theology including fundamental work on patristics, Calvin and Barth. *Theological Science* (1969), *Space, Time & Incarnation* (1969), *Space, Time & Resurrection* (1976), *Divine and Contingent Order* (1981) and *Reality and Scientific Theology* (1985) are some of the fruits of his labor in our field of inquiry.

Torrance was one of my first teachers in systematic theology at Edinburgh in the early 1960s when his interests in scientific theology and theology for science were already flourishing. In the 1940s and 1950s he worked carefully on Calvin's Institutes and Commentaries, which, as Boyle would discover, were masterworks of theological appeal to the scientific mind. Working on *Calvin's Doctrine of Man* (1949) and *The Eternal Ten Commandments* and *The Ten Words of the Lord's Model Prayer* (1957), he shows, against the backdrop of his study with Barth, an intrigue with epistemology and the Word of God as Truth, moral authority and the focal point of the conjunction of knowledge about God and man. If there is to be any theology for science it must come at this intersection where knowledge of the world unfolds within the knowledge of God (Calvin). The work on the *Dekalogishe Struktur,* which is essential to our exposition of an akedic perception of divine and human reality sees eternal verity in this cardinal expression of the Word (Logos/Wisdom) anchored in *Verbum Christi.*

Reformation studies, of necessity, led him into the issues of faith, grace and natural law as he explored the justification debate in Luther and Calvin. This inquiry continued in the debate of Barth and Brunner on natural theology. The struggle in the soul of the young theologian between the "wholly other" theology of Luther, Kierkegaard and Barth and the more "natural theology of the world" of Calvin and Schleiermacher would inevitably shape his interests in theology and science. Like Robert Boyle, Torrance seeks to assert the pure transcendence and non-adulteration of the God of Book One of Calvin's *Institutes* along with a providential theology where God is actually involved in governance and engagement with His world. A theology of science, much like the Puritan side of Robert Boyle, is emerging.

A set of books written in the late sixties and early seventies is crucial to this unfolding theology. *Space, Time & Incarnation* (1969) and *Space, Time & Resurrection* (1976) frame what I see as his crucial theological assertion about science. His offering is one of thoroughgoing Calvinist elegance and the natural beauty of holiness. Torrance begins this inquiry by refuting the concepts of deism and dualism, which seem to him incompatible with what we know about God and the world. If God is the creator of all things "visible" and "invisible;" if God is the author of the History of Israel within which Jesus arrives as Messiah—*Logos* incarnate—then the inherent or breakthrough knowledge of God, given as revelation (Word) and incarnation (Son), must be manifest within this world, thereby repudiating Cartesian, Newtonian and Kantian dualism. With Calvin and Barth, Torrance maintains that the Word upholds the world, so that a unitive view of the reality of God and world was necessary and where a natural theology was subsumed into a revealed theology. Just as geometry or mathematics must be joined with physics as the two dimensions of natural science, so theology and science must be conjoined in complementarity (Bohr). Shortly before Barth's death, Torrance proposed to the great teacher that just as Newton's disjunction of mathematical space and time and actual bodies in motion was repudiated by Einstein so natural and revealed theology must not be separated but be kept together. Barth's reply was succinct and unmistakable: "*Wohlverstand, Leibliche Auferstehung*" (Resurrection of the body—don't forget it!).[21]

For Torrance incarnation and resurrection can be seen as test issues for a theology of science, indeed for theology or science, per se. Incarnation is the nexus of the enfleshment of divinity, the ultimate scandal and truth of historical religion, especially Abrahamic faith, including Christianity. It is also *Logos*—the epitome of revelation—or attuning the human mind to the mind of God. Resurrection is the ultimate transfiguration of reality, where the scandal of historically presented deity, of incarnation and crucifixion, proleptically and really unites creation and creature so that the realm of nature and history becomes the "theatre of divine glory."

For Torrance, the scientific and theological world-views emerge in synchrony and synergy. Scientific worldviews, when expansive, imaginative and moral, are corroborative of theology. Similarly when theological views are faithful and hopeful, they provide a grounding and guidance for science. Science and theology are, therefore, reciprocally corroborative and corrective endeavors. Both endeavors have three dimensions: epistemological, practical and ethical. Both seek truth beyond falsehood and heresy. Indeed with their historical conjunction in the realm of magic they are both subject to superstition, distortion and deception and therefore need each other to maintain integrity. Secondly, they both seek, in the words of Karl Marx, "not only to understand the world but to change it." Applied science takes on the capacity "for relieving the human condition" (Bacon) or "attacking the evils which afflict humankind" (Boyle). To produce salutary and avoid destructive results is the purpose of both theology and science. Finally, both endeavors seek to create a better future as they embody hope and ethics.

For Torrance, the resurrection of Jesus as the Christ and the embedded (implicit) resurrection of historic humanity and renewal of creation (1 Corinthians 15) are the verification and reification of God as the Lord, the meaning and future of the natural world. Though still fallen, the world is already being renewed as *Theatrum Deum Gloriam*. As Pannenberg and Weizsäcker have shown, it is on this doctrine that hinges all the philosophical truth about humanity and the history of nature. It is within the structures of space and time the God makes Godself known, though not in the confining structures of knowledge about this world. Theological science, for Torrance as for Calvin, is the process by which God reveals Himself objectively in Himself but not as a worldly object. How does he corroborate this view through modern science?

---

[21] Thomas Torrance, *Space, Time and Resurrection* (Edinburgh: The Handsel Press, 1976) xi.

First, incarnation and resurrection in space and time imbues creation with dynamism and vitality. The mechanistic universe of Newton, though God-given in its brilliant insight into the mathematical physics of creation, remains static. The organismic concepts of biology and evolution in the nineteenth century begin to infuse vitality into our worldview. In the twentieth century electromagnetic theory (Maxwell), the uncertainty principle (Heisenberg), complementarity (Bohr) and relativity (Einstein) further the cosmic and spirited world picture of Boyle and foster a new view of creation in which creativity, Spirit, dynamism and purpose are possible. Today a synthetic theologicoscientific worldview is possible (e.g., Polanyi) where the physical level of reality is undergirded or overarched by the theoretical and metatheoretical dimension allowing a sense of transcending mystery and providential purpose. In the words of Polanyi, "We need reverence to perceive greatness just as we need a telescope to observe spiral nebulae."[22] Thus by such "spectacles" (Calvin), which view God and the world according to the Word, Torrance claims, we can "recognize God's absolute priority and actuality" as our minds reverently submit to His "uncreated light and majesty."[23]

Torrance's theology for science is built around the following elements:

*Conceptuality and experience are totally
interdependent and integral modes of knowing and doing*

* *

Theology and science together constitute one unitary science

The physicist James Niedhardt speaks of the *homoousion* of physics. This term, from the early formulations of Orthodox Christianity, which refer to Jesus being consubstantial with the Father, is seen as an analogy of the relationship of theology and science.

Relationality is essential to the universe

Just as Newton's mechanistic view of the world falters so does his notion of absolute space and time. In the theories of general and special relativity Einstein relates the dimensions of space and time, light and matter to the human observer and his frame of reference. It is the invariant nature of the rules of physics that renders relative all human observation. The objectivity of reality (God or nature) necessitates the relativity of our perception just as the reality of God necessitates the tentativeness and limitation of our perceptions and conceptions.

---

[22] Michael Polanyi, *The Study of Man* (University of Chicago Press, 1959) 96.
[23] Torrance, *Space, Time and Resurrection*, 193.

Mathematics is to nature as theology is to God

That the invisible explains the visible is a notion as old as Plato. Kant's noumenal realm, organizing and naming the phenomenal, continues the tradition. Behind this philosophical wisdom is the truth of theology and science that the reality of God and the reality of the world abide in a dialectical relation.

Field theory or unified theory best subsumes and explains (heuristically) reality

Heuristic theory seeks to explain, discover, and disclose ever-broadening perspectives on reality. For Torrance explanations ought to open up, relate and deepen the successive layers of insight accessible to the human mind in knowledge and faith. As Jürgen Habermas has shown, these perceptual and conceptual avenues are indispensably intertwined in any philosophy of reality. Torrance best elucidates his Boylesque doctrine of field theory as he speaks about Maxwell, Einstein and Polanyi.

We begin with Polanyi, with whom Torrance finds a philosophy of science kindred to his own dynamic theology of providence, incarnation and resurrection. Polanyi, a philosopher and scientist like Stephen Toulmin, adapts philosophical theory to the new world of electromagnetic, relativity and indeterminacy theory formulating a system compatible with what Einstein calls "the free creations of thought which cannot rise inductively . . . from sense experience, what accords with a kind of wordless thinking that goes on when the scientist is caught up in wonder and in the indefinable acts of intuitive apprehension upon which his creative structures rest."[24] On the basis of his reading of Polanyi, Torrance believes that Einstein did for natural science what Barth did for theology in joining conceptual systems with actual experience. This new intellectual act collapses what the ages have called the unbridgeable chasm between *Theoria* and *Praxis* Torrance calls "geometric physics." Mathematics is natural science.

Torrance on Einstein

In the spirit of Polanyi who showed the centrality of "ultimate beliefs" in scientific thought, Einstein would refer to "God" as the spirit and impulse behind all space and time. For Torrance this is "the intuitive grasp of the structure of reality" imbedded in faith/knowledge. Quoting Isaiah 7:9, "unless you believe you cannot understand," Torrance shows how Einstein is appropriating a theological heritage from Judaism, through Christ and Paul to Augustine and Anselm, where faith and reason are codependent functions of human perception and conception, all within an ethical and elpistic (hopeful) purview.

In *Einstein and God,* Torrance quotes Einstein:

[24] Thomas Torrance, *Transformation and Convergence in the Frame of Knowledge* (Grand Rapids, Mich.: Eerdmans, 1984) 108.

> Science can only be created by those who are thoroughly imbued with an aspiration toward truth and understanding. This source of feeling springs from the sphere of religion . . . To this there also belongs the faith in the possibility that the regulations valid for the world of existence are rational, that is, comprehensible to reason. I cannot conceive of a genuine scientist without that profound faith . . . Science without religion is lame, religion without science is blind.[25]

Ideas for Einstein come from God. Light, for example, is a theme he absorbed from scripture. His study of Jesus and Spinoza is a symbol or intimation of the divinely established beauty, harmony and purpose of the world. One finds in Einstein a mind informed by monotheistic glory and splendor with Abraham Heschel's prophetic sense of wonder, great sympathy and ethical yearning. Torrance is an exemplum of this synthetic sense of science and theology found in his mentor, James Clerk Maxwell, whose portrait hung in Einstein's study. The glory of God radiates the creation and is seen by science.

Torrance believes, with his scientific mentor, Clerk Maxwell, in the necessary complementarity of natural (physical) and theological theory about the universe. The physical perspective will always be partial because our perceived reality is contingent (a theological assumption), it is derivative: "The world was created by the Word of God" (Heb 11:3). Similarly the theological perspective will always be partial because its *via media*, knowledge of the world, is derivative of science, especially science which is grounded in and animated by faith. The unified theory of everything—envisioned by Einstein and approximated, for example, in Stephen Hawking's synthesis of thermodynamics, relativity, mathematics and black holes—is, in the estimate of Torrance, unattainable in a contingent universe even though such is assumed in his view of reality as a complementarity of theological and natural science. Such a unified vision is implied, indeed is imperative, in his view of how theology and science will proceed unilaterally and bilaterally in the future.

The clarity and certainty of this conviction is, for Torrance, built upon his theology of the truth and faithfulness of God as received in the eternal Word and in the absolute reliability of the universe, expressed, for example, in the constancy of the speed of light. From the theological side we can trust the eternal being and continuing "Way" of God. Correlatively we can trust the "objective" (knowable) dynamic arrangements of physical law.[26]

My critique of Torrance would find in his work too much scientific and theological objectivism. My own system, based more on thinkers like Hawking and Kierkegaard than Maxwell and Barth, entails a greater dimension of what I see as inevitable subjectivism and more Abrahamic venturism (into the unknown

---

[25] Albert Einstein, *Ideas and Opinions* (New York: Crown, 1954) 46. Quoted in *Einstein and God* (Napoli, 1998).

[26] Thomas Torrance, *The Christian Frame of Mind* (Colorado Springs: Helmers & Howard, 1989) 89.

and uncertain). With Schweitzer I do not find the degree of metaphysical and ontological certainty that Torrance finds in God, Jesus and the world. Rather than ontic clarity I resonate with the more Lutheran and Pascalian Barth in their deontic conviction about the "Way of God" (truth, justice and peace). We know (technically and theistically) as we obey and follow. This is what Torrance calls "scientific conscience." God, truth and right impose correlated obligations on us. He confirms Schweitzer's understanding of the eschatological vector in truth claiming with Einstein that the ultimate purpose of "field theory" is to "know why nature is what it is and not something else."[27] The 'why' is the ultimate form of the question 'how.'

Finally, Torrance offers corroboration of the leitmotif of my thesis that Akedah, the moral crux of Abrahamic theology and history is that which binds theology to science and ethics to technology. The radical Christocentrism of Torrance, derived from Barth, Calvin, the church fathers and Paul, prompts his formulation of the theme of atonement as grounding the "reordering of creation."[28] Taking Prigogine's idea that "unstable and disorderly states" lead to "richer patterns of order," including change, spontaneity and openness of future,[29] Torrance claims that upon the cross of Jesus Christ actually hang "the disorders, contradictions and evils of this world" and in the completion of the redemptive suffering in resurrection the world is proleptically (for sure, but not yet) redone and renewed. Just as in space/time godlessness and inhumanity all "hang upon the cross," so in the cross/resurrection the world is "recapitulated back through space/time to its original (or ultimately culminating) conditions."[30] Akedah, the groundwork narrative of the love, forgiveness and redemptive purpose for the wayward creation, is the narrative of resurrection and renewal—of new creation (Isaiah 65, Rev. 21:5).

Excursus: A Scientist for Theology: Karl Friedrich von Weizsäcker

Being back in Edinburgh, Scotland for a fortieth reunion with my dear Sara (whom I met here in *Auld Reekie* when we were students) reminds me of the blessing I have had being trained by a series of Bible-expositor-preachers. Here at Edinburgh it was James Stewart, recently voted by a prestigious magazine "the

---

[27] Torrance, *Christian Frame of Mind*, 90.

[28] Torrance, *Christian Frame of Mind*, 102.

[29] Torrance, *Christian Frame of Mind*, 103.

[30] Torrance, *Christian Frame of Mind*, 103, 105.

greatest preacher of this century." Stewart was my New Testament professor at New College, and a deep devotion to Christ and the messianic mission to the world marked his lectures. I vividly remember his reporting of the departure of Eric Liddell, the Olympic Champion (Chariots of Fire) from Waverly Station to become a missionary in China, where he would lose his life under Japanese occupation. The candlelight procession wound up around the Mound from Princess Street, described Stewart, as the whole city began to sing Isaac Watts' missionary hymn:

> Jesus shall reign wher'ere the sun, does his successive journeys run
> His Kingdoms stretch from shore to shore, till moons shall wax and wane no more.

My homiletical treasure house continued with George Buttrick and Paul Scherer at Princeton and Helmut Thielicke, my *doktorvater* at Hamburg. The age of these brilliant exegete-preachers seems to have passed—especially among Scotland's "trainspotting" youth culture and with our Western culture of mingled blithe secularism and bland religious sentimentality. But I believe that some new age of biblical seriousness, searching faith and compelling witness is soon ready to emerge.

In addition to working with Thielicke in systematic theology at Hamburg I was also privileged to study with the physicist-philosopher, Karl Friedrich von Weizsäcker. As a young physicist during the Second World War, his work at Göttingen with Heisenberg, Planck, Oppenheimer and others became the pretext for the U.S. to build the atomic bomb, as we wrongly assumed (as we have with "weapons of mass destruction" in Iraq) that Hitler had the bomb since Weizsäcker's father was Hitler's Ambassador to Denmark. As a youth Weizsäcker had asked the elder Heisenberg what he should do "to study philosophy." "First, study physics" was Heisenberg's reply. Weizsäcker went on to establish the Kant-Laplace theory of the origin of the universe—the "big bang"—and was rescued from Germany and taken to England by the Allies. After the war he returned to his first love of philosophy—teaching at Hamburg fundamental philosophy of science, in addition to courses like Peace, Food and Ethics for Science. After my dissertation at Hamburg we worked together again in Starnberg where he was the first Director of the Max Planck Institute for Peace Research (*Friedensvorschung*). He presented the Gifford Lectures (1959–1960) and has become to my mind one of the most profound scientist-theologians of the twentieth century. Born the year before Torrance (1912), their century-spanning careers have crafted indispensable insights into the conjunction of theology and science.

Weizsäcker writes the Gifford Lectures to respond to what he feels is the "dangerous ambivalence of our present-day scientific civilization."[31] As Torrance has shown, Weizsäcker affirms that modern science is inexplicable apart from the history of Christianity. A disciplined historian and philosopher, Weizsäcker

---

[31] Karl Friedrich von Weizsäcker. *The Relevance of Science* (London: Collins, 1964) 16.

wishes to be precise about the events and ideas that have shaped current developments. Concepts like Time, Being and Truth emerge out of a concrete history. The history of the 'history of nature' as an interpretive human activity is basic, in his mind, to what we are describing as an evolving theology for science.

Weizsäcker begins his inquiry by acknowledging that we live in an age of secularism where science is a predominant faith and technology a pervasive work. The displacement of the traditional faiths of Judaeochristianity and Islam by a secular Faith (see Nasr, Ch. 1) has left the world with a sense of anxiety and ambiguity. We have comprehended and conquered the world in awesome ways but when we look to the spiritual and ethical foundations of culture for guidance, we come up empty. Miracles, what since Newton we call "laws of nature," are now the presumed provisions of food, health, security and freedom. These benefits are now the expected yield of science and technology. The high priests who conduct the hocus-pocus of miraculous provision today are scientists, politicians or therapists. With the collapse of traditional *exousia* (authority) on the part of traditional providers and the shift of the locus of recipient expectation to others a new priesthood has arisen. While this arrogation may reflect what Torrance calls humans as "princes of the creation" it often fails by reason of its inability to satisfy insatiable desires on the part of consumers and of the positive danger of harm and destruction when technologies—for example, nuclear or genetic—are put to wayward purpose. In the Royal Museum in Edinburgh stands Dolly, the stuffed, cloned sheep. She was a pioneering, yet aberrant creature—a sacrificial lamb to our inquisitive and acquisitive manias. Weizsäcker writes:

> Much that is done technically in our time is in no way better than black magic. It is not worthy of a mature technical age. We still live more in a time of technical ritual than technical ethics.[32]

Science and technology, he continues, is of the order of creative blessing or curse. It gives life or takes life.

> Medicine and hygiene have saved thousands of millions of lives . . . Yet world population has doubled in the last century (1950) and doubled again in the last half-century . . . It becomes more and more evident that war must be abolished . . . Scientific knowledge means power. Power ought to mean responsibility.[33]

Recalling that the beauty of the world and of human endeavors is marred by pride and violence, Weizsäcker recalls the remorse of Oppenheimer: "We physicists have known sin." Yet surely we have a continuum of sin and guilt. Politicians, whose vow is to protect the security of the nation made the decision to use nuclear power to prosecute and hopefully conclude a war. The populace yearned for an end to the war. The web of hope and horror was intricate. Like his contemporary,

---

[32] Weizsäcker, *Relevance of Science*, 17.

[33] Weizsäcker, *Relevance of Science*, 18–23.

Torrance, and his predecessor by four centuries, Boyle, theology and science were integral endeavors, intellectual achievements, they entailed ethical responsibility and the beauty of holiness was manifest in the realm of nature. We now transit to the modern world of science and technology with representatives from middle Europe—Teilhard de Chardin and Albert Schweitzer.

3 Pierre Teilhard de Chardin
the etiologic vector

Introduction

As WORLD WAR I smoldered to its tragic conclusion, Albert Schweitzer was exiled from Lambaréné back home to Strasbourg. It was a somber Noel/*Weinachtzeit* of 1918. In the small Jesuit seminary near the halls where Schweitzer lectured and preached, a young scientist-priest penned words about his growing perception of reality. In a note on *"l'élément universel"* appended to a document entitled *Forma Christi*, he reflected:

> He to whom it is given to see Christ more real than any other reality in the world, Christ everywhere present and everywhere growing more great, Christ the final determination and plasmatic principle of the universe, that man indeed lives in a zone where no multiplicity can distress him and which is nevertheless the most active workshop of universal fulfillment.[1]

From Strasbourg across France through Vosges and Champagne, Gay Paris would become a blessing for Schweitzer, her Bach society would build his tropical piano, and her missionary society would undergird his envisioned work in Africa. But she would become a bane for Teilhard. A controversy to his visionary cosmos arose among his superiors and officials at the *Institute Catholique*. He was removed from his position as instructor in science. As Glaucon knew in Plato's *Republic*, the world will try to silence and blind the person of goodness and truth.

Today Teilhard's work is celebrated and heralded as fully in keeping with the creative organic theology of Thomistic Catholicism. He also enjoys Renaissance among those in the scientific community who are concerned with issues of ultimacy and normativity. His thought has resonated

---

[1] Henri de Lubac, *Teilhard de Chardin: The Man and his Meaning* (New York: Hawthorne Press, 1965) v.

as well with the emerging processional science of evolutionary anthropology. His *oeuvre* resonates with our thesis as with Schweitzer he develops an etiology and eschatology—beginnings and endings—requirements of truth and beauty in forming worthy and excellent science. Though close neighbors in Strasbourg, we know little about any personal interaction between Teilhard and Schweitzer. Schweitzer, as we shall see, was being led from the pathway of eschatological, post–liberal, Reformed and Lutheran thought to convictions similar to those of Teilhard. Together they affirmed a mystical and an empirical epistemology and a moral utility about the technical yield of that science, as had our pioneer philosopher-scientist, Avicenna, and our Puritan patron of early modernity, Robert Boyle.

Père Teilhard may have learned from Schweitzer a cosmic epistemology, eschatology and ethics that would mark his theology and science. In *La Mystique de l'Apôtre Paul,* Schweitzer had written: "Pauline mysticism is historical—cosmic, and looks towards the end of all time." This spirit and impulse of Schweitzer's Paul is always felt in Teilhard.[2] Charles Raven goes so far as to find this Pauline influence the key to Teilhard's work:

> As his knowledge of cosmology, biology and anthropology deepened, it merely expanded his sense of the universalism, personalism and consummation that is guaranteed by a full understanding of the cosmic Christ as St. Paul came to declare it in his three last great epistles Philippians, Colossians and Ephesians[3]

The decade of 1916–1926 would produce some of Teilhard's most salient writing on science and technology. Here, before his fruitful paleontological work in China and the discovery of Peking Man (*Sinanthropos*) he penned *La Vie Cosmique* (1916), *Forma Christi* (1918), *La Messe Sur Le Monde* (1923) and *Le Milieu Divin* (1926). Teilhard's early and later work all expresses the aspects of that viable theology for science we elucidate in this study.

In claiming *Logos* as "the plasmatic principle of the universe," Teilhard accomplishes the following:

1. He affirms the wisdom of Plato and Aristotle—mediated through Abrahamic religion and monotheism, entrusted to modernity by Avicenna, then scholastic philosophy, that matter and spirit—ordered ethically and proleptically co-constitute reality.

---

[2] de Lubac, *Teilhard de Chardin*, 43.
[3] Charles Raven, *Teilhard de Chardin: Scientist and Seer* (Evanston: Harper and Row, 1962) 160.

2. He knows with Robert Boyle that within divine governance, form and fire (energy) structure and animate this reality.

3. With Albert Schweitzer, following the critical transcendental reason of Kant, the spiritual idealism of Hegel and the ethical critique of Nietzsche and Marx, he espouses a theistic epistemology and a reverential ethics. He consistently calls for an access to that providential truth and good for science and technology.

4. At the heart of Teilhard's own work he sustains the Pythagorean, Aristotelian, Augustinian and Kantian premise that *Nous (Logos)* informs both human mind and physical nature, connecting these two realms in science and conscience. He holds that *Noosphere*, the realm of interpretive value and transformation is tangential and epiphenomenal to the natural *Biosphere*.

5. Teilhard, especially in critical dialogue with Hans Jonas, further provides foundation for Leon Kass' formulation of ontic and telic normativity in natural history and deontic responsibility for biomedical endeavors (such as stem-cell research); he also affirms the agapic energy that animates the world.

6. Finally he anticipates Amartya Sen's reading of both political and natural history and economic endeavor as activities empathetic to freedom and justice and accountable for advocacy for the poor. Teilhard's erudite system therefore encompasses the tableau of principles which I set forth in this study to describe a theological science and a concomitant ethical technology.

Akedah as Presupposition

The theological ethic that I call for in this book and the resonant spiritualities and sciences is grounded in the phenomenon of Akedah. I ground the ethics of the proposal in the *Decalogue*. Hereafter I will speak of an akedic and decalogic science and technology. These two metaphors for spiritual and moral normativity therefore commend themselves to a truthful science and a helpful technology.

A word about this undergirding and overriding premise: It informs the worldview of each of the scientist-theologians that I review in this study, but none more than Père Teilhard. When he claims that even in the view of the mere biologist, "the human epic resembles nothing so much as a way of the cross,"[4] he is touching on Akedah. Akedah is a referent to the "why" in nature and the history of nature. Why in the world is there suffering and renewal? Why does temptation (chance and choice) inform all reality? Why is being drawn from non-being? Akedic and decalogic themes pervade all reality where the human spirit is put to intellectual query and moral test. Present in all religion, Akedah focuses in the Abrahamic faiths epitomized by the Isaac (Ishmael) narrative. It becomes the interpretive saga of Judaism, Christianity and Islam—the tale of suffering, of moral travail, of death and resurrection. It speaks of the cosmic realm of order, loss, degradation and renewal.

Philosophically conceived, Akedah and *Decalogue* are the ontic and deontic charters—the manifestation of epistemology, ethics and esthetics—the transcendental sciences of the true, good and beautiful. These deep idioms, paradoxes and symbols thus pertain to knowledge and technology—to our project.

Science for Theology

Standing in the traditions of the knowledge and technology which we trace from Aristotle and Aquinas, the nature philosophers and the monastic *Orare et Laborare*, Teilhard insists on an empirical foundation and inductive direction in all that we think and do. In the mature years of his work he claimed retrospectively:

> I shall, as is proper, stick to the terrain of facts, i.e., to the realm of the tangible and to that which can be photographed. Discussing scientific perspectives I must and shall restrict myself to the investigation of the arrangement of appearances, that is, of "phenomena." Since my concern is with their connections and with the succession manifested by these phenomena, I shall not deal with their underlying causalities. Perhaps I may go so far as to hazard an "ultraphysics." But no one should look for metaphysics here.[5]

But it is not physics and nature that finally intrigues Teilhard. As a physician or physicist in the ancient Greek sense, he is fascinated by the appearance and future—the phenomenon of man. In lectures at the Sorbonne he claimed that "the human element can legitimately be viewed

---

[4] Pierre Teilhard de Chardin, *The Phenomenon of Man* (New York: Harper & Row, 1961) 311.

[5] Quoted in "*La place de l'homme dans l'univers: reflexions sur la complexité.*" Claude Tresmontant, *Pierre Teilhard de Chardin: His Thought* (Baltimore: Helicon Press, 1959) 14.

by science as a prolongation and the crown, at least provisionally, of the living element."[6]

In placing the human element within the living element within the cosmic element, Teilhard reverses the Copernican and Galilean redirection. No longer relegated to the margins of reality, à la Schweitzer, the glorious human is now exalted within the glorious cosmos. Pauline cosmology is reasserted—the divine milieu. The world—physical, natural, historical, yes, but exquisitely divine—proceeds from and toward God in holy agony and fulfillment. In origination and destination the world in iconic purpose guides human insight and imperative. "This is not metaphysic . . . or a theological essay," he writes in *Phenomenon of Man*. It is a "scientific treatise. I have chosen to write about the phenomenon of man. Man as the center of the manifest reality of the world."[7]

Unified field theory, the presumption of modern science, becomes the starting point for Teilhard. All facts and data established in investigations relate to all other facts, forming a matrix of truth about the evolving world. Through knowledge and technology concerted human minds construe and construct reality so that this human imposition itself becomes part of the scientific and technical process. Take genomics and proteonomics for example: These accumulations of knowledge, always interwoven with technology, are formulated today with reference to human dispositions and desires. Like Lysenko or Mendelian genetics, today we see and do what we want to see and do. Teilhard is correct. Science is a human endeavor—an anthropocentric project.

Evolution

Divinely animated emergence theory (evolution) was one of the important (though reluctant) gifts afforded science by theology. Though bureaucratic church politics often obfuscated the matter, the best theological thought always saw the divine hand in cosmic and earthly beginnings. Just as scientific and technological theories and projects are saturated with human values so the theological and philosophical etiologies and explanations of those sciences and technologies are also anthropocentrically derived and therefore provisional. Simply put, religious ideas do not refute continuing creation or evolution any more than scientific theories refute religious notions. It is their reciprocity or complementarity that I explore in this essay.

---

[6] Tresmontant, *Teilhard de Chardin*, "La place," 16.
[7] Teilhard de Chardin, *Phenomenon of Man*, 29.

A transcending mystery, purpose and wisdom lies beyond both science and theology calling each to humility, co-operation and reciprocity.

Teilhard was one of the first to see this truth. He was one of the first to see that in the Pope and the Inquisition and in Galileo and the new-found cult of empiricism, both the fundamentalists and the Darwinists were in error. He saw that evolution was "creation expressed in time and space."[8]

While the creationists felt it necessary to reject the modern sciences, especially those who conceived creation in terms of metaphysical ontologies (Thomists) and static forms (Fundamentalists), rather than in the terms (Robert Boyle and the Puritans) of experimental dynamics and while scientific positivists felt it necessary to repudiate faith, both camps missed the truth of Teilhard's insight, so obvious in retrospect, that evolution is the divine miracle of *creation continuo*. Science and evolution and theology and faith together, in synergy, have it right.

Now at the dawn of the twenty-first century of the Christian era we see more clearly that the dramatically instantaneous "big bang" cosmos is also a process of rapid instantaneous expansion and corresponding fading entropy in accord with Teilhard's description of a "process of being born, of being created all around us."[9] Meanwhile it lurches entropically toward consummation.

Creation

Two features of a theology for science proffered by Teilhard's thought are understandings of creation and of evil. His biography spans these themes as he probes the wonders and intricacies of creation in his scientific work and suffers the agonies of rejection, misunderstanding, war, international injustice, sickness and death in his priestly and personal life. His 50 years of journaling chronicles this paradoxical and probing tale, which always remains majestic and instructive. His rumination on life's mystery is much like that of his companion from the French countryside, Georges Bernanos (see *Cure à la Campagne, Diary of a Country Priest*; see also Robert Bresson's brilliant film, based on the book). Teilhard's *oeuvre* tells the same tale.

---

[8] Tresmontant, *Teilhard de Chardin*. *"La place,"* 17.
[9] Tresmontant, *Teilhard de Chardin*. *"La place,"* 19.

Pierre Teilhard de Chardin: A Selective Bibliography

1909 *The Miracles at Lourdes*
1916 *Cosmic Life*
1918 *The Form of Christ*
1923 *Mass Upon the Earth*
1927 *The Divine Milieu*
1930 *Sinanthropos Pekinensis*
1932 *The Place of Man in Nature*
1936 *We Must Save Mankind*
1937 *Early Man in China, Human Energy*
1940 *The Phenomenon of Man*
1947 *Faith and Peace*
1953 *The Idea of Fossil Man*
1958 *Building the Earth*[10]

Teilhard is offering a call of theology toward science and science toward theology in his doctrine of creation. Utilizing Teilhard's writings, *Comment je vois* (1948) and *L'union créatrice* (1917), Tresmontant capsules his theology of creation:

> In the very act by which He poses Himself, God opposes Himself trinitarily to Himself. (my note: In my perspective monotheism best grounds a theology for science and trinitarianism, though theologically valid, presents unnecessary complication). God Himself "exists only in uniting Himself" (to unify and sanctify the name/*hashem*) But by the very fact that He unifies with Himself in order to exist, the first Being causes *ipso facto* another kind of opposition to spring up, no longer at the heart but at His antipode. This is the pure Many or "creatable nothingness" which is nothing, but which, however, through the passive virtuality of arrangement (i.e., of union) is a possibility, an imploration to be *(Comment)*. The fundamental vision is that of plurality and the multitude *(Union)*.[11]

In laying hold of a theology for science, Teilhard ventures the risk of monotheism and heterodoxy, the radical skepticism which alone can envi-

---

[10] See also Robert Francoeur, "Bibliography," in Tresmontant, 112ff.
[11] Tresmontant, *Teilhard de Chardin*, 89–90.

sion truth and beauty, the behind and beyond justice and love. Amartya Sen puts it this way: "It is not held to see that the possibility of scientific advance is closely connected with the role of heterodoxy, since new ideas and discoveries have to emerge initially as heterodox views."[12]

Teilhard is struggling mightily with a key theological issue that arises in the dialogue with science. Some see trinitarianism as a stumbling block to the dialogue since the unity and singularity of God has had such a profound impact on the rise of science. While Trinitarian doctrine seems important to me, even in the articulation of a scientific world-view, I remain skeptical of a non-monotheistic, non-Hebraic construal of the doctrine in the thought forms of Greek metaphysics. It is true that Tom Torrance in his neo-Calvinist construal of theology (and science) sees trinitarianism as essential doctrine. In citing the work of Clerk Maxwell, one of the pioneers of the sciences of electricity, magnetism and light, Torrance claims that the doctrine of Christ and the Holy Trinity, especially in the aspects of person and relationality, was conducive to thinking to a post-Newtonian concept of the continuous dynamic field which Einstein claimed, "marked one of the greatest steps forward in the whole history of physical science."[13]

Given the irascibility of Trinitarian doctrine through the ages and the fact that its obfuscations and subtleties are unnecessary for the progress of science I side rather with Thomas Aquinas in locating the pertinence of monotheistic, Abrahamic faith and its proclamation: *The Lord Our God is One*. Thomas was therefore drawn to the Jew, Maimonides and the Muslim, Avicenna, for a theological charter for science. The profound relevance of the Trinitarian formulation is seen when the Judaic impulse to "unify the Name" (*Hashem*) and the theistic imperative of the *Shemah* is related to the diversification/unification and the manifestation/satiety aspects of the very nature and activity of God. According to Teilhard this divine reality corresponds to the world that science presents to our consciousness.

Two themes will be emphasized with reference to trinity and Christology in this theological *apologia* vis-à-vis science which I am proposing. To the central biblical themes of unification of the Name, creation and incarnation I will add the convictions of Jesus as Messiah and Wisdom (the Hebraic bases of theological Trinitarianism) as parts of the theological matrix that undergirds useful science and helpful technology. New research points in this direction.

---

[12] Amartya Sen, *The Argumentative Indian* (New York: Farrar, Straus & Giroux, 2005) 26.
[13] Torrance, *Christian Frame of Mind*, 150ff.

Theology for Science: Recent Work on Teilhard

From the 1965 collection, *Science et Christ (Editions du Seuil, 1999)*, which assembled Teilhard's own reflections on science down to the recent renaissance of attention to his thought,[14] theology and science has been a guiding theme of research in philosophy, science and theology centering on his work. Some of the issues highlighted in this work can be reviewed to capture his central convictions:

In August 1919, on the eve of the first World War, Teilhard writes on the "human body."[15] Of course, he notes, we are constituted and composed of the physical (chemical) elements. We are also animated and organized by the nerve system (*fibres nerveuses*). We also associate with and love one another so as personal beings we become communicable beings. This description and analysis of the human body and its *alterité* is then quite naturally, albeit mystically gathered up in the issue of Christ's body which is held to be the essence of the collective corpus. Cells, though singular and autonomous, relate beyond themselves into a body and ultimately into The Body.

On 27 February 1921 he comments on "scientific study"[16] and on the connection between science and Christ. When one seeks to analyze or synthesize reality through either the inductive or deductive act, "breaking down" or "weaving together" the data of knowledge, one is driven to associate science and Christ. Teilhard is here not only drawing on his understandings of the Sacré Coeur and the empirical love that holds and weaves reality together but on the great Hebraic/Hellenic heritage of Logos as the informing rationality of all nature. It is in our very nature and in the inclination of our minds not only to describe "what is" superficially but to "penetrate the heart of the world" (*"trouver le Secret, la Source, pénétrer au Coeur du Monde"*).[17] When we delve into the miniscule details of the world—the forests, the bugs, the waters—we ultimately face the phenomena of love and of God.[18] Through the energies of the world, like electromagnetism (light), gravity and the vitalities (e.g., biochemical pro-

---

[14] See Edith de la Heronnière, *Teilhard de Chardin: Une Mystique de la Traversée* (Paris: Ed. A. Michel, 2003), and Jacques Arnould, *Quelques pas dans l'univers de Pierre Teilhard de Chardin* (Paris: Aubin Imprimeurs, 2002).

[15] "*En quoi consiste le corps humain?*" in Teilhard de Chardin, *Science et Christ* (Editions du Seuil, 1999) 33.

[16] Teilhard de Chardin, *Science et Christ*, 47.

[17] Teilhard de Chardin, *Science et Christ*, 50.

[18] Teilhard de Chardin, *Science et Christ*, 51.

cesses), natural process moves forward. The world and all in it seems to move 'from' and 'toward' a divine center (*au centre divin*). "*Le Christ n'est pas un accessoire surajouté au Monde. Il est celui qui consomme—l'alpha et l'oméga.*"[19]

In the same vein of philosophy of science, in November 1946 he comments on scientific certitude and the idea of evolution.[20] As scientific theory (i.e., concepts) interprets the data the universe gives us, it organizes that data into explanations of the greatest whole—"*organicité*." These concepts are now more or less valid because of their comprehension. Indeed they gain precision and credibility as they embrace more of the data (i.e., of the evolving phenomenon of life). The complexity and the long "*histoire*" of life bestow greater certitude on concepts of greater grasp. The minute and detailed aspects of nature themselves verify the grand theory.

Finally, as a sample of his specific theology for science, on 3 August 1948, he records a note/memento on the biological structure of humanity.[21] Reaching for what his contemporary, Albert Einstein, sought as "unified theory," Teilhard seeks to build an analysis of the psychic life, mental and moral, on the basis of the foundations which describe and organize the material bases of life. The amazing yield of his research is a unified theory that is at once rudimentary on the physical level and sublime on the theological. An interpenetration of the material and the spiritual is achieved which had been sought ever since Aquinas took the body/soul unity of Avicenna and Maimonides thus affirming the "*valeur organique du phénomène social.*"[22] While automaticity and necessity dominate life process at the fundamental level—freedom and creativity predominate at higher levels. Overall and throughout, however, a creativity and ingenuity prevail.

This direction of recent Teilhardian studies is corroborated by the comprehensive (50-volume) *Oeuvres Complètes* of Cardinal Henri de Lubac (1896–1991), who championed Teilhard's wisdom through the years of wiles and maneuvers, commendation and censure. He summarized the contemplation of his *frère Jesuit* as an exquisite synthesis of science and theology, nature and grace. Through the "christification" of humanity in the life-world of nature the natural powers (*puissances naturelles*) are being

---

[19] Teilhard de Chardin, *Science et Christ*, 62.
[20] Teilhard de Chardin, *Science et Christ*, 235.
[21] Teilhard de Chardin, *Science et Christ*, 257ff.
[22] Teilhard de Chardin, *Science et Christ*, 260.

transmuted into *puissances surnaturalisables*. The movement of nature is ultimately gracious and transformative.

If de Lubac is correct, Chardin's message for our time is one of heightened human responsibility for the development and enhancement of life in the world. He as much as says that the world will become what we humans make of it. Though God is all in all (*'Dieu tout en tous'*) and though the final end is God (*Cette fin dernier est divine*) it is human effort, individual and collective, which will procure the good future of God's intention.[23]

Science is one realm of that cooperative endeavor. Here humans probe the etiology, essentiology and eschatology of the world. *What the world is* is ultimately grounded in where it has come from and where it is going. Now we discover how things (structures and processes: Peacock) are constituted and how they can be appropriated and applied. Here in decisive action we work with what the world has been, what it now gives and what future it allows and invites. An example: Both cloning and parthenogenesis of the human organism is now being stimulated by scientific/technological initiative.[24] This profoundly ambivalent and morally freighted activity (see chapter on Kass) is derived from precedents in nature, is allowed by the conditions of possibility but is not presently being done for human reproduction, as it probably could, but rather for the potential production of stem cells to ameliorate human impediments and illnesses such as Parkinson's disease and diabetes. There is a pathway of potency and power inherent in nature itself—and within the imagination and ingenuity (e.g., in science and technology) of humans—which channels human initiatives. Teilhard's great contribution to a theology for science is to find within the deep streams of meaning in the faith the impulses for scientific endeavor.

The Etiological Dimension (Creation)

In summary and synthesis we find in Teilhard an articulation of an etiological and evolutionary concept of theology for science. Science is best served and secured by a theology which affirms the lordship of the One God who is creator, sustainer and redeemer of heaven and earth. Most salutary for science is a faith in creation, which finds it orderly, predictable, disclosingly creative and blessed. These derivative axioms of the Hebraic divine thrones (Psalm 84) from which exude law, order, justice, mercy and serendipity establish the spirit of culture, including science. This theol-

---

[23] Henri de Lubac, *Oeuvres*, v. 23 (Paris: Cerf, 2002) 169.
[24] *The Economist*, Jan. 3–9, 2004.

ogy is insured when the biblical view of creation in Hebraic (and Islamic) goodness, power and shalom is conceived together with the creative energies of Trinitarian Christian thought. Creation is a dangerous theological doctrine. The constant temptation of pantheism, cosmolatry, fertility worship, even idolatry positioned on particular creatures—sun, mountains, water, humanity itself—frequently shipwrecks a belief system.

Teilhard himself floundered on this shoal. By reason of this temptation rigorous biblical, philosophical and theological groundwork is required before a theology for science can be established. The etiological dimension, which religion must formulate about beginnings and causation in creation, has often been obstructive not only to science, but to theological belief itself. Bad music often drowns out the "music of the spheres." In 1934, Teilhard sought to win belief from a skeptical-scientific community by offering the following *apologia*. It infuriated the religious guardians of the faith otherwise known as the inquisition:

> If, as a result of some interior revolution, I were successfully to lose my faith in Christ, my faith in a personal God, my faith in the Spirit, I think that I would still continue to believe in the World. The World (the value, the infallibility, the goodness of the world): that in the final analysis, is the first and last thing in which I believe. It is by this faith that I live, and it is to this faith, I feel, that at the moment of death, mastering all doubts, I shall surrender myself. . . . I surrender myself to this undefined faith in a single and Infallible World, wherever it may lead me.[25]

We must understand that Teilhard here is seeking to win over the "unbelieving scientist" with this unfortunate text, which yields to the temptation of a system of cosmic etiology (which is based more on Aristotle's *Metaphysics* than on the monotheistic rigors of biblical faith). All the same we still see, with the benefit of 70 years 20/20 hindsight, that Teilhard was right and the detractors were wrong. The passage indeed expresses a certain wisdom grounded in creation and incarnation somewhat in the mood of his contemporary, Dietrich Bonhoeffer, who affirmed that only when one loved the earth so that without it everything would be lost and gone that one could believe in the resurrection. The passage also has some of the anti-other-worldly sting of one who delights in God's good world as Zorba the Greek's creator, Nikos Kazantzakis, who had inscribed on his tombstone near Athens: "I love the earth, I have no hope, I am free."

---

[25] Henri de Lubac, *Teilhard de Chardin: The Man and His Meaning* (New York: Hawthorne Press, 1965) 132.

The coherent composition and creative energy of the Cosmos provokes, if not adoration, such responsibility, love of creation and respectful stewardship not nature—worship or geodolatry. The doctrine of creation itself flows, as Carl Friedrich von Weizsäcker argues, from the history of nature, which is subsidiary to and derived from the nature, and history of God. God radiates and reflects divine glory on to the earth as the moon reflects sun.

Alfred North Whitehead begins his study of *Science and the Modern World* with the conviction that the origin of modern science arises from "the medieval insistence on the rationality of God, conceived with the personal energy of Jehovah and with the rationality of a Greek philosopher." The genius of the Earth in a resplendent doctrine of creation is that the order of nature is contingent upon the divine Will."[26]

This reciprocal glorification of God and creation is the prime dimension of monotheistic theology and the essence of Trinitarian doctrine, which identifies and extols God as creator, redeemer and sustainer of creation. It is what Père Teilhard is reaching for in the controversial passage in the 1934 essay (*Comment je crois*) for Teilhard his words are addressed "*ad gentiles*"—to nonbelievers. This is Christian apologetics—reaching out by virtue of the glory of the world ("The heavens proclaim His handiwork.")

Teilhard's creation theology as the "panorama" or "theatre" of God's glory and grace rather than being heterodox or heretical is fully in keeping with Christian orthodoxy. Faith in the world (psalmic faith) is what Teilhard calls "initial faith." From this beginning point or foundation it leads ". . . successively to faith in the Spirit—then to faith in a personal God—and finally to the threshold of faith in the personal God revealed in Jesus Christ."[27] While this sequence and continuum may betray a religious system more kindred to "natural theology" (Aquinas, Brunner) than to Kierkegaard and Barth, it does affirm the primacy of God, Jesus Christ and the Word. It is fully orthodox in accord with the definitions of theology I offer in this essay. It adheres to Abrahamic monotheism, venturism and akedic theodicy. It reflects the ethical matrix of decalogic Torah. It expresses the doctrines of creation and incarnation.

Any theology conducive to sound science and salutary technology will accent this etiologic (creative) dimension. Creation theology anchors science into cosmic origins as eschatology anchors science in cosmic destinations.

---

[26] John Baillie, *Natural Science and the Spiritual Life* (New York: Charles Scribner, 1952) 22ff.
[27] de Lubac, *Teilhard de Chardin*, 136.

Tom Torrance and Creation Theology

Among contemporary theologians subsuming science into their purview, Calvinist-Barthian Tom Torrance best articulates this etiologic dimension. We have considered his contributions in an excursus in our chapter on Robert Boyle. Torrance's pertinent works include:

1981   *Divine and Contingent Order*

1982   *Reality and Evangelical Theology:*
A Dynamical Theory of the Electromagnetic Field
(by James C. Maxwell, 1865; edited and with an
introduction by Torrance, 1982)

1984   *Transformation and Convergence in the Frame of Knowledge*

1985   *The Christian Frame of Mind:*
Reality and Scientific Theology

1988   *The Trinitarian Faith*

Torrance was my teacher in theology in Edinburgh, Scotland in the early 1960s. True to his mentor and New College colleague, John Baillie, Torrance built on the Reformation implication of Baillie's thought that "creation of the free, Divine will" was what Whitehead meant when he referred to "the personal energy of Jehovah" as the root impulse of modern science.[28]

When we opened our reflection with Avicenna and Maimonides, the signature theologians for Thomas Aquinas, we noted the firm grounding that Abraham (including Akedah), the way of Israel, *Torah*, covenant and the *oneness* of God provided as a foundation for medieval science. Along with Greek and medieval logic which provided rationality, this Semitic framework provided the directionality for the scientific quest and project. "It was the Hebrews," writes Baillie, "who first conceived man and man alone as having been made in God's image and having been given dominion . . . over all the earth."[29]

As we have shown in our study of Robert Boyle and the Puritans, even Frances Bacon and the empiricists, as they repudiate Aristotle, affirm

---

[28] Baillie, *Natural Science*, 24.

[29] Baillie, *Natural Science*, 29. See also my dissertation with Helmut Thielicke, *Subduing the Cosmos: Cybernetics and Man's Future* (Atlanta: John Knox Press, 1970) and Thielicke's *How the World Began* (Harper).

the fact that primary and secondary causes in the creation point clearly to "providence and deity."[30]

In resonance with Alfred North Whitehead in *Science and the Modern World*, Torrance sees a reciprocal relationship between science and theology finding in the latter a sustaining impulse for science. He finds (as this study does) key elements for the scientific revolution and its concomitant ethical guides and safeguards in the Hebraic (Abrahamic, Akedic, Decalogic) heritage:

- In Hebraic thought the concept of the human being as personal was found in the biblical teaching about God and the interconnection between the commandments to love the Lord God and to love one's neighbor.[31]
- The decisive Christian doctrine of incarnation is itself based in "the Old Testament unitary view of man" where "the wholeness and integrity of our human being (is affirmed) as "body of our soul and soul of our body" (p. 39).
- Further Hebrew thought and incarnation "has to be thought of as the decisive intervention in our midst by the love of God (Akedah, crucifixion), the ultimate power of order, not to suspend the rational order of things at any point, but rather to restore it (p. 40, 41).
- "Newton was indebted to the Judaeo-Christian concept of the contingent universe" for his belief in *creatio ex nihilo* (which insured the mechanical-causal order). Judeo-Christian creation belief is also the ground for the sequellae to Newtonian mechanics in quantum, relativity and indeterminacy theory (p. 50).
- All of this is transformed by "Judaeo-Christian monotheism which gave rise to a unitary conception of the universe of heaven and earth which rejected all forms of cosmological dualism and polymorphism" (p. 50).
- This is assured by a new construal of "natural law" whereby the human mind intuits "natural truth" (a concept of the Puritans) where to "know and understand" requires that we behave "in a

---

[30] Baillie, *Natural Science*, 38.
[31] Torrance, *Christian Frame of Mind*, 37.

true and faithful way according to their (objects) natures effecting a scientific conscience" (p. 53).

- Now humans (at the boundary of divinity and materiality) are "priests of Creation and mediators of order." The human mind not only grasps and construes the order and possibility of material reality but in that very epistemic act it confirms inherent and eschatic ethical direction (p. 59ff.).

In sum, Torrance's view of creation theology and science takes the wisdom of the Church Fathers, St. Anselm, natural law theology (Thomism) and Reformation insight and contends that science is woven into the activity of "faith seeking understanding" and that we therefore enjoy a profound interdependence and inseparability between faith and science.

To achieve such monotheistic clarity and conviction and to avoid metaphysical obfuscation Teilhard steeps his thought not only in the theological heritage, as does Torrance, but in the tradition of empirical observation of the world. Tresmontant summarizes Teilhard's view referring to *La Lutte Contre La Multitude* (1917):

> The working energy of the world, in the beginnings, must be pictured as at grips with an infinite pulverization [entropic deterioration, Vaux adds] a thing which by its very nature (and therefore by tendency) is infinitely disunited, a kind of pure Many. The problem and secret of creation consisted in reducing and reversing this power of disunion in such a manner as to obtain monads of a more and more synthetic kind.[32]

Again the power of multiplicity, disintegration (disunion) and deterioration amid a contrary direction of unification, concentration and intensification poses an akedic (paradoxical) view of creation. Although Teilhard is doing nothing more here than importing a classical Christian view of creation, fall and redemption into his "empirical observation" he does come to terms with the harshest of "stubborn facts"—the phenomenon of evil. In his theologico-empirical view the dissolution of the world itself contains sublime mystery. The ashes of Isaac become the phoenix of resurrection. Creation therefore is the ambiguous complex of realization and erosion—of organization and entropy. In this anticipation of the problem of evil Teilhard offers what he sees as the secret meaning—the very genius of creation. Teilhard's view of discord is more a view of dissonance or creative tension, one, which portends not failure or destruction

---

[32] Tresmontant, *Teilhard de Chardin*, 90.

but accomplishment and ameliorative advance. At root, this is a theological conviction that when and only when creation has consummated its purpose will it roll up, shake down and pass away. Raven finds in Teilhard the paradoxical (akedic) confidence that "history will remain a struggle of good and evil till the day God chooses to complete His purpose and bring all things to their end."[33] Entropy will be the reabsorption of space and time back into eternity and infinity.

It is proliferation of "the many," the inevitable consequence of freedom and dynamism in the creation that constitutes the problem of evil. Early in his career as a stretcher-bearer in World War I he had learned of the reality of evil. At Ypres and Arras, at Chemin des Dames and Verdun, he sees the inevitability and irascibility not only of willful violence but also of ignorance and the vicissitudes of freedom and chance. With Platonic and Aristotelian eyes Chardin sees evil as not ultimately defeating of good and God, but as part of the creativity of creation, a structure and impulse without which creation could not exist.

Not at all because of impotence . . . but by virtue of the very structure of nothingness over which He leans, God, in order to create, can proceed in only one way: namely by arranging and gradually unifying, under His attractive influence, an immense multitude of numbers which are at first infinitely numerous, extremely simple and barely conscious, then gradually more rarified and more complex, and finally endowed with reflection. Now what is the inevitable counterpart of any success obtained from a process of this kind, if not that of having to pay for a certain proportion of waste? Among those we might number: physical disharmonies or putrefactions in the domain of the preliving, suffering in the domain of the living, and sin in the domain of freedom. There is no order in the process of formation, which at all stages does not imply disorder. And there is nothing in this ontological condition (or more exactly ontogenic) of the participated being that detracts from the dignity or limits the omnipotence of the Creator. Finally there is nothing at all here that "smacks" of anything like Manichaeanism. In itself the pure unorganized Many is not evil. But because it is multiple, that is to say subject essentially to the play of chance in its arrangements, it cannot progress absolutely toward unity without engendering evil here or there—through statistical necessity. *[Necessesarium est advenient scandalas.]* If, as I believe must inevitably be admitted, there is with respect to reason but one possible way only for God to create, namely

---

[33] Raven, *Scientist and Seer*, 74.

evolutionally, by means of unification, then evil is an inevitable by-product, it appears like a penalty inseparable from creation.[34]

Just as the fall, in biblical perspective, in an uncanny way becomes the precondition of ascent (knowing good and evil, life and death), so ensuing wrong seems to become the inevitable consequence of creating humanity with freedom. Yet there remains something ungrateful in such conjecture. In his inimitable ire at such idle speculation Martin Luther answered one who asked what God was doing before the creation, with the reply, "making hell for those who ask too many questions." Yet speculate we must and will, not only because it is irresistible but also because it is imperative as we ask after ameliorating the world's wrong in resurrection authority—assessing and undertaking our tasks of knowledge and technology.

Considered with reference to science and technology—construals and constructions within the realm of nature—these three dimensions of evil offer intrigue.

- Physical disharmonies—dismorphologies or disfigurations, perhaps (my suggestions), or "putrefactions in the domain of the preliving"
- Suffering in the domain of the living
- Sin in the domain of freedom

These value considerations, superimposed on the realm of natural occurrence in what Teilhard has already identified as a sphere of evolutionary necessity, even redemptive possibility, raise the issue of whether humans should undertake preventive or interventive action (science and technology) or accede to these disharmonies. As we visit this afternoon a second young cousin struck down with a lethal and mind-devastating brain tumor (*glioma*) and as we ask whether likely futile and caustic interventions ought to be employed, Teilhard's quandary hits home.

Intellectual freedom in explaining physical (i.e., natural) processes (implying the intent to do something in the face of the deleterious), and technical freedom to do those very things, are both morally ambiguous endeavors. Knowledge and technology are always fraught with potentials of good and evil. The knowing and doing can help or harm. These powers provoke unforeseen and unintended consequences. The inevitability and inescapability of knowing about and working with nature always carries the possibilities of mistakes. "We physicists have known sin" wrote a re-

---

[34] Teilhard de Chardin, "*Comment Je Vois*," Oeuvres de Pierre Teilhard de Chardin, v. 10 (Paris: Editions du Seuil, 1948) 442–43.

morseful Robert Oppenheimer when remembering the Manhattan Project on nuclear fission and the building of the atomic bomb. Even though it was the politicians who dropped the bombs on Hiroshima and Nagasaki the knowledge prior and requisite to that act was their responsibility and when this knowledge was fatefully connected to the "weapons of mass destruction" and the release of such terror into the world, Oppenheimer could only comprehend this evil in light of the predictive horror of the Vedas which perceived a supernal conflagration "brighter than a thousand suns."

Natural evil, suffering and human sin, as Teilhard rightly suggests, are intertwining and continuous phenomena. A web of guilt, complicity and inaction colors all human comprehension and ingenuity. It is the fractures, multiplicities and multipotencies of the natural world that translate this human malevolence and violence into suffering of fellow creatures and destruction of the world itself. While Marxist and other philosophers criticize Teilhard for the cosmic breadth of his view of evil and his failure to distinguish natural from moral evil, his reflections are in perfect accord with the biblical conviction that in human sin the world's own order and goodness is affected and it recoils in animosity.[35]

The Bible, from Torah to Paul in Romans 8, knows of a cosmic transgression—originating and continuing in humanity—and extending into nature itself. Yet in the enduring love and will of God for the creation, grace and new opportunity overwhelms this flaw and fault. The God of Abraham and Torah, of the Prophets and Wisdom, the God and Father of the Lord Jesus Christ is a God ever-seeking to redeem this world according to that grace. This God has disenchanted the world in the consummate victory of the cosmic Redeemer over the "elements and powers" (Colossians 1). In this disenchantment creation has been severed from its divine and demonic potency. Now in severe, faith driven iconoclasm, humanity receives and cooperates in a world now presented to human inquiry and ingenuity as serenely supplicant and splendidly plastic to its endeavors. This is its resplendent glory and provocative terror.

Nikolai Berdyaev boldly asserts:

> However paradoxical it may seem, I am convinced that Christianity alone made possible both positive science and technics. As long as man found himself in communion with nature and had based his life upon mythology, he could not raise himself above nature

---

[35] See Jacob Milgrom's monumental commentary on Leviticus in the *Anchor Bible* (2002) and Robert Jewett's commentary on Romans in the *Hermenia* series (2004).

through an act of apprehension by means of the natural sciences or technics. It is impossible for man to build railways, invent the telegraph or telephone, while living in fear of demons. Thus for man to be able to treat nature like a mechanism, it is necessary for the demonic inspiration of nature and man's communion with it to have died out in the human consciousness.[36]

Teilhard's Vision of the Cosmos

To summarize our treatment of Pierre Teilhard de Chardin's illustration of a theology for science we may note his vision of the cosmos. On April 15, 1929 he writes:

> I now find that I can no longer envision the world otherwise than in the form of an immense movement of Spirit . . . I am rediscovering the personality of God and the immortality of the soul as elements essential to the structure of my universe.[37]

The organic, evolving substance of the world is diffused with a divine essence and salience—ever distinct and ever-present. Avicenna, Averroës and Boyle reappear in Teilhard's contemplation. Here rehearsed we find the biblical vision:

> He who maketh the Pleiades and Orion, and turneth deep darkness into the morning . . . who calleth for the waters of the sea . . . Jehovah is His Name (Amos 5:8).

> O the depth of the riches both of the wisdom and of the knowledge of God (Rom 11:33ff).

What Teilhard finally wishes to say is that the cosmos is more, is greater, is beyond all that science or theology imagines it to be. When we most think that we are "grasping" the world—scientifically or spiritually—we must remember that God and His manifest world (time and space) is always "ahead of us" (*L'Esprit de la Terre*). This prolepsis—this pending and impending reality of God—in mystery somehow implicated and intricated in the future of the world—is the ultimate binding ligature between theology and science. As our search takes a proleptic direction we now turn to Albert Schweitzer.

---

[36] Nikolai Berdyaev, *The Meaning of History* (New York: Meridian, 1962) 113–17.
[37] Picht, *Man and His Work*, quoted in Tresmontant, *Teilhard de Chardin*, 97.

4 Albert Schweitzer
the eschatologic vector

Introduction

OF LATE, OUR FAMILY has grown fond of wild and natural things. Rather than rooting out the great Virginia bluebells that have overgrown our backyard, we let them push out the geraniums and the Rose of Sharon. We are "letting the Prairie back," as we say in Illinois. Like Albert Schweitzer, we have decided to "live and let live." Though, like him, we may not yet have sparing sympathy for the rampaging hippo or the aggravating mosquito, especially in this season of West Nile virus and avian flu, we too seek to "reverence all life." We recently prevailed on mother and wife to "tough out" Rottweiler fang wounds in her arm after an attack back of our house, rather than report the beast to authorities, for the compulsory "put down." As if it too contained consciousness or preciousness, in our romantic excesses we even grieve with Schweitzer's "roadside primrose thoughtlessly cut down."[1]

Before we adjourned our study leave in his university town of Strasbourg as we were first-drafting this chapter, we heard a Bach-*Todestag* organ concert at St. Thomas Church, a series Schweitzer inaugurated fifty years ago. Now, today, as I cross the avenue from the Ecumenical Institute where we live and work, past the serene, bird-spattered, whitewashed statue of Goethe, beneath the formidable carvings of Luther, Leibniz and Kepler on the capital of the great facade, I look up at the second East windows of the *Palais der Universitat*. Here Schweitzer lectured as a young theologian and grieved when he took his leave for Africa. To truth, beauty and initiation we now add "consummation" to our criteria for a theologically derived science. Schweitzer may be history's best spokesperson for eschatological science.

So I wonder. Did the 37-year-old present his recently found, untranslated lectures on theology and natural science here at Universität Strasbourg? Can I find some way to summarize them, as that is the thrust

---

[1] Schweitzer, *Animal World of Albert Schweitzer*, transl. Charles Rhind Joy (Boston: Beacon Press) 19ff.

of this essay? Was he still pondering the theodicy of his first book, written as a young man just for his friends, of the untimely death of his organ teacher Eugene Munch in Mulhausen. As he completed medical school in this *annus horribilis* of 1912 how had the *Souffrance* and jubilant pathos of his masterpiece on Bach tempered his clinical work? How would I articulate his vision of a theology of science and a civilized ethic so as to form a keystone for this present study? Schweitzer often formulated the conviction that science and technology without faith was dangerous and religion without science was fanciful. Only eschatological healing (*shalom*) could restore the integrity of each endeavor and their complementarity. He wrote of the divorce of the two cultures:

> Today, thought gets no help from science, and the laity stands facing it independent and unconcerned. The newest scientific knowledge may be allied with an entirely unreflecting view of the universe. It maintains that it is concerned only with the establishment of individual facts, since it is only by means of these that scientific knowledge can maintain its practical character; the coordination of the different branches of knowledge and the utilization of the results to form a theory of the universe are, it says not its business. Once every man of science was also a thinker who counted for something in the general spiritual life of his generation. Our age has discovered how to divorce knowledge from thought, with the result that we have, indeed, a science which is free, but hardly any science left which reflects.[2]

> Western thought is not governed like mystical thought by the idea that the one thing needful is the spiritual union of man with infinite Being, and therefore (if it is obliged to renounce the hope of attaining to a knowledge of the universe that corresponds to ethical world- and life-affirmation), it is in danger of saying it is satisfied not only with lowered ideals, but also with an inferior conception of world-view. That is the tragedy that is being enacted before our eyes.[3]

To approach the challenge of this estrangement, we have taken a brief summer research leave, having exchanged our Victorian Evanston home for the elegant nineteenth-century house of the Ecumenical Institute. Actually, I was surprised this week to read that our Evanston home was

---

[2] Albert Schweitzer, *Decay and Restoration of Civilization* (London: Black, 1932) 72.

[3] Albert Schweitzer, *Indian Thought and its Development* (London: Hodder and Stoughton, 1936) 253ff.

probably visited in the 1940s and 1950s by an effort centered in Alsace and Paris, radiating to the United States, where it was centered in Evanston, as children sang Christmas carols and collected "Soap for Schweitzer." For decades Chicago has been home to the Albert Schweitzer Foundation. The research for this chapter was written while I stayed in Albert's bedroom in the old Schweitzer parsonage in Günsbach, Alsace.

Purpose

The logic and sequence of our inquiry into useful science now continues, with a consideration of the Alsatian polymath. We have seen the way in which the membrane between science and theology has become and remains permeable through the pathways that navigators of faith and philosophy have made. The bridge has become passable in the brilliance and goodness of Hebraic and Hellenic *phronesis* (practical wisdom).

We saw the expression of such science in the illustrative work of Muslim physician-philosopher Avicenna, and Anglican physicist-theologian Robert Boyle. We now contemplate the insights of two early twentieth-century figures who will build the keystone of our arch—the Roman Catholic paleontologist-philosopher, Père Teilhard de Chardin and the Protestant Reformed Pastor-Physician, Albert Schweitzer.

Finally, we will consider two contemporaries: Amartya Sen, son of Hindu sages, Nobel Laureate in Economics and now Director of the Institute of Economics and Justice at Harvard; and Leon Kass, the Jewish philosopher-physician, director of the U.S. Commission on Bioethics and Stem Cell Research.

To rehearse the thread of the thesis that weaves together this study, I have sought to establish a theologically-girded and ethically-guided mode of knowledge as:

- Avicenna shows how the mystical is manifest substantively in matter and formally in mathematics—*aletheia*
- Robert Boyle shows the eternal and ethical salience and beauty of the atmosphere and the earth—*aestheia*
- Pierre Teilhard de Chardin projects a physicospiritual cosmos where finitude, chaos, even evil is sublimated into ultimate meaning—*aetioloia*
- Albert Schweitzer formulates an eschatological Christology, which prompts a reverential zoology, anthropology and sociology—*aeschata*

- Amartya Sen affirms an enveloping sacredness and calls for human sacrifice and justice in the global *oikomene—aethica*, and
- Leon Kass finds awe, duty, and love in macroscopic and microscopic phylogenesis and evolution—*agape*.

My Thesis

The persistent *Weltanschauung* which I offer in these pages is one where the obvious kinship of science and theology is evidenced as knowledge is claimed from the unknown, and as meaning and satisfaction is wrought from the chaotic and merciless void and reality wrested from the hoped-for future. Together this epistemology and ethics fashions a knowable and livable universe. This realization—scientific and ethical—is accomplished through what I call akedic redemption and what Schweitzer calls the "fellowship of those who bear the mark of pain." In a sympathetic assertion, Teilhard testifies that "even from the perspective of a mere biologist, nature resembles nothing so much as the way of a cross."

Schweitzer's Empathy

To Schweitzer's soul, the suffering of humankind, even of the world of living animals and plants, became intolerable. He had read about the miseries of Africans in the primeval forests. The missionaries went out, we recall, with the two-fold ethical mission beyond salvation to educate and end the slave trade. Education and edification were somewhat at odds with the colonial impulse.

Since these African regions had opened up to European and American consciousness and conscience in the nineteenth century, Schweitzer felt acutely that teachers and doctors were obliged to go out to help. "Society in general must recognize this work of humanity to be its task."[4] Whatever it takes must be given. He believed that all who had been blessed with "civilization" and "Christendom" must answer the call. Like *Médecins Sans Frontières*, Oxfam or World Vision today, Schweitzer believed that this opportunity was an obligation. We must go to teach and heal.

But the biblical vocation "to whom much is given, much will be required" had sadly reverted to the Pagan maxim "by those to whom much was given, much more was taken." Regrettably today we reap the bitter harvest of a century of neglect of Africa, the Americas and Arabia as these lands of poor peoples rise up in violence and vengeance against the affluent

---

[4] Albert Schweitzer, *On The Edge of the Primeval Forest* (London: Fontana, 1959) 9.

and blessed West for both its humanitarian neglect and for her colonial and capitalist exploitation. Now as the West circles the wagons in *Heimat*, homeland protection and security, it aggresses with more preposterous, imperious and disproportionate power. At the same time we slowly but inexorably withdraw from effective aid to the poor and suffering of the world as it arms itself in provocative brutality against "terrorist" attacks. We now realize in Dives-Lazarus' regret the terrible cost of the failure to heed Schweitzer's summons.

Dives and Lazarus

Schweitzer framed the world's plight of the haves and have-nots perceptively and eschatologically as the once wealthy and competent Dives cries across the chasm of time and eternity back to earth to the still-there and still-suffering Lazarus. From his now-neglect-induced torment, incompetent now beyond the pale to help poor Lazarus, he now realized what he could and should have done in the providential realm of real history.[5] The work of "healing the world" (*Tikkun Olam*) or "building the earth" (Chardin) was the work of humans in the world. Salutary science and efficacious ethics, knowing and doing well, was the essence of humanity's vocation. Rather than extending the useful gifts of science and the helpful healings of technology, the West had chosen to inflict on Africa the decimating scourge of slavery, the enervating affliction of alcohol and drugs, the dehumanizing forces of colonialism and the exterminating plagues of disease and now, HIV/AIDS. Though the issue of the injection and transference of the HIV virus is complicated, it is clear that this stigma culminates a long saga of violence, neglect and manipulation of African peoples by Euro-American geopolitics and the global economy.

W.E.B. Du Bois

Perhaps the most vivid and stringent commentary on the work of Schweitzer is that of W.E.B. Du Bois. Contributing to Schweitzer tributes as a young Harvard graduate in the 1920s, then in the 1960s as a 95-year-old and wise professor he writes in apocalyptic wrath:

> Of the debt which the white world owes Africa, there can be no doubt. No black man can recall it without a shudder of disgust and hate. The white followers of the meek and lowly Jesus stole fifteen million men, women, and children from Africa from 1400

---

[5] Schweitzer, *Primeval Forest*, 9.

to 1900 A.D. and made them working cattle in America; they left eighty-five million black corpses to mark their trail of blood and tears; then from 1800 to this day their scientists, historians, and ministers of the Gospel preached, wrote and taught the world that a black man was by the grace of God and law of nature so evil and inferior that slavery, insult and exploitation were too good for him.[6]

Yet Du Bois goes on to celebrate the salutary thrust of Schweitzer's ethically animated medical science.

> I know of the fine efforts of Dr. Schweitzer to rid Africa of disease—that Africa which my friend, Sir Harry Johnston rightly called "the chief stronghold of the real Devil—the reactionary forces of Nature hostile to the uprise of Humanity. Here Beelzebub, King of the Flies, marshals his vermiform and arthropod hosts—insects, ticks, and nematode worms—which more than on other continents . . . convey to the skin, veins, intestines, and spinal marrow of men and other vertebrates the micro-organisms which cause deadly, disfiguring, or debilitating diseases, or themselves create the morbid condition of the persecuted human being."[7]

Plan for Life

Schweitzer's life plan was animated by this apocalyptic grievance and ameliorative command. He resolved as a young man in his twenties to think, write and talk for 30 years. After this, he would go silent—and only act—act out this discrepancy between gift and need in God's good world. By his thirtieth birthday, he had completed amazingly penetrating theological doctorates on the Lord's Supper and the historical Jesus; a philosophical doctorate on scientific and ethical knowledge (*Reine, Praktische Vernunft*) in Kant and a landmark musicology dissertation on J.S. Bach. Then he undertook medical training. He took the knowledge of his day to its epistemological apex in several fields. He lived out the ethical mandate implicit in this composite realm of knowledge.

Was he, in the words of his most masterful intellectual biographer, Werner Picht, "making atonement by his own behaviour for the crimes of the civilized world"?[8] Or was he, like his protégé in music, Johann

---

[6] See W.E.B. Du Bois, "The Black Man and Albert Schweitzer" in *The Albert Schweitzer Jubilee Book*, ed. A.A. Roback, Greenwood Press.

[7] Du Bois, in *Albert Schweitzer Jubilee,* 247.

[8] Werner Picht, *Albert Schweitzer: The Man and his Work* (London: Allen and Unwin) 22.

Sebastian Bach, simply taking the intellectual, aesthetic and moral trends of his time on to their next natural stage? As the nineteenth-century progressivist paradigm began to fade, was he already on Thomas Kuhn's cusp of a new paradigm? In his apocalyptic consciousness was he in some way the first post-modern, the first radically orthodox thinker?

Interdependence of Science and Theology

Somewhat after Kuhn's notion of paradigms, science is, in my conviction in this work, that intellectual and theological development which emerges under the influence of concrete historical events. The ethical concomitants of intellectual advancements correlate with that same *Zeitgeist* of history, science, technology and faith.

Comprehensive scientific knowledge (what we today call unified field theory), emerges historically with and in turn influences philosophical and theological liberalism. Parochial neo-orthodoxy arises simultaneously with post-modernism. Conceptually, I draw on the work of John Polkinghorne's *The End of the World and The Ends of God*, and on Wentzel van Huyssteen's *Postfoundational Rationality* and *The Shaping of Rationality* (Grand Rapids: Eerdmans, 1999). Also relevant to my thesis is the notion in the radical orthodoxy of John Milbank, Catherine Pickstock and D. Stephen Long that the natural and supernatural cannot be sharply separated in knowledge or action.

Schweitzer's scientific endeavors and conscientious efforts, and the ethical convictions behind those actions, were made possible by emergent twentieth-century science and technology. Later thinkers in this study will depend on developments in modern surgery, anesthetics, antibiotics, retrovirology, genetics and biotechnology.

Sickness in Africa

What was the affliction that challenged Schweitzer's mind and heart? Like river blindness, which in recent decades has afflicted millions in the tropical world, sleeping sickness was a plight that struck the Bach chords of *"Christ lag in Todesbanden"* and wrought akedic agony in Schweitzer's soul. He lived eschatology. The choral chords of efficacious hope and possible help also sounded in Schweitzer's heart. He lived at the dawn of our age of ambiguous dread and hope, which today takes hope from the conquest of smallpox and polio, yet remains in dread over HIV and SARS. From ancient times, sleeping sickness seemed to have stricken countless persons in Equatorial Africa to lifeless lethargy and death. In six years it had carried away two thirds of Uganda's population.

It was the genius of French and English microbiology early in the nineteenth century that discovered the boring organisms that caused the disease. The names of Koch and Le Boeuf, Ford and Dutton first saw the *Trypano somata* through the awesome technology of Leeuwenhoek's microscope. Like bubonic plague with its vector sequence of filth, rats and fleas, here lack of hygiene, puerile water and *Glossina palpalis*, a form of tsetse fly, were the culprits.

Just as what W.E.B. Du Bois would call the demonic sequence (Beelzebub) was present in causation of the specter of disease he described, so too the preventive and ameliorative sequence that Schweitzer brought involved belief and action, science and technology.

One other formative experience for the young man Schweitzer seemed to move his knowledge from abstract conceptualization to active amelioration. While home on leave forced by World War I, his mother was knocked down and killed by cavalry horses on the road between Günsbach and Weier-im-Tal. The strife between Germany and France, his two *Väterländer* in the Vosges and Alsace, as well as in the gruesome carnage of Verdun, engraved in his heart the passion for healing and world peace. Though cautious of the coercive rationality and the impiety of Kant's *Perpetual Peace*, he knew that such strenuous commitment to justice was required in the bloody twentieth century that unfolded during his adult lifespan.

In order to explore the building block which Albert Schweitzer fashions for a useful science, we need first to describe what Picht calls "his greatest scientific work . . . *The Quest for the Historical Jesus*."[9] Here we will find the foundation of his eschatological/scientific perspective on reality. Here is the basis of his ethical mysticism, from which we can derive the zoology, anthropology and sociology of his science.

The Quest

In all of Schweitzer's work—intellectual and practical—we see the working-out of his self-acknowledged "enthusiasm for the true and serviceable."[10] Even as a child, he recognized not only the intellectual dishonesty in church teaching about Jesus, but also how it was impractical and a stumbling block to faith. When he was seven years old, his father gave him

---

[9] Picht, *Man and His Work*, 13.
[10] Picht, *Man and His Work*, 34.

a New Testament, which he proceeded to study assiduously. He stumbled on the nativity narratives. Where did the gold gifts go? Why didn't the wise men return? The critical mind was sharpened in school days, in his early theological studies (*Hebraicum* and *Graecum*), and most surely during his philosophical studies on Kant. By then, his mind was tuned to tackle the Jesus question. Initially, he was astonished and offended by the way that scholarship had obscured for believers the clear and moving biblical portrait of Jesus.

His first theological exam took one precise moment in the Jesus teaching—the Lord's Supper. Prompted by Schleiermacher, he asked how the elaborate Eucharistic theology had emerged when Jesus had simply enacted the Passover meal? How had the metaphysical obfuscations of real presence, symbolic transfiguration and the like, corrupted theology?

We must recognize at this point that these thoughts were not just the sophistry of an overgrown adolescent or a churchly skeptic. He found genuine issues of science and truth in the prevailing Jesus appraisal. *The Quest* is a book of cool objectivity and vehement passion. Readers over the century, I'm sure, have, like myself, often put the book down trembling and in tears.

Schweitzer utilizes all of the tools of historical and scientific research. In this rigor I believe he achieves the first totally scientific faithfulness to scripture in the Abrahamic heritage. Judaism has known the illumination of rabbinic reasoning and Islam the ardor of devout repetition, but Schweitzer culminated the Enlightenment age of higher criticism and made it irresistible to the modern mind. In some ways he is the first scientific evangelical after Augustine, Aquinas and Calvin.

Here the modern intellectual crisis of humanity—the crisis of reason and faith, science and revelation—sharpens on acute focus. And Schweitzer prevails! After Schweitzer, the calamities of Galileo and Darwin are obsolete. Theology in the Schweitzerian mode has committed itself irrevocably to truth!

We have seen how Avicenna submits both religious and scientific truth to the achievement of Aristotle and Greek thought. Averroës and Maimonides, Albertus Magnus and Thomas Aquinas had followed this path. Schweitzer culminates this process (before the chaotic subjectivism of post-modernism) by not only requiring the intellectual rigor of the prevailing thought forms of modernity, and by lifting up the higher standard of objective, universal truth. He remained aware, however, that truth must always be elusive and humanly refracted.

For Schweitzer, the nineteenth century of German and French critical thought—especially *Jesusvorschung*—Reimarus, Schleiermacher, Strauss, Hegel, and Wrede, among others—was the finest historical achievement of the human intellect. It had liberated the "greatness of Jesus" from encrusted, incredible traditions and had made redeeming knowledge at last possible.

Jesus, according to Schweitzer, really did believe that he was the messiah in terms of the prevailing Jewish apocalyptic expectation of the period of the Second Temple. All of our attempts to demythologize and make Jesus relevant for ". . . our time are riveting him to the stony rocks of ecclesiastical doctrine."[11] In accepting this eschatological vocation, Jesus became God and Lord for all history. His Spirit now mediates and radiates that divine salience—that power (*exousia*) and that ethic—into all subsequent time.

On superficial reading, Schweitzer seems to be saying that Jesus' deluded and misguided apocalyptic consciousness (the immanently coming Davidic messiah) insured his validation in the hearts of disciples (and the believing world) and his perpetuity as the eschatological messiah ("He who comes"). In reality, Schweitzer is saying that allowing Jesus to be who he really "was" and "is," rather than tied to our orthodoxies, proffers faith. Only by accepting Jesus for who he "was" can we know him for who he "is." Two magnificent passages from *The Quest* reflect this paradoxical truth:

> He comes to us as One unknown, without a name, as of old, by the lakeside, He came to those men who knew Him not. He speaks to us the same word "Follow thou me!" and sets us to the tasks which He has to fulfill for our time. He commands. And to those who obey Him, whether they be wise or simple, He will reveal Himself in the toils, the conflicts, the sufferings which they shall pass through in His fellowship, and, as an ineffable mystery, they shall learn in their own experience Who He is.

> There is silence all around. The Baptist appears, and cries: "Repent for the Kingdom of Heaven is at hand." Soon after that comes Jesus, and in the knowledge that He is the coming Son of Man lays hold of the wheel of the world to set it moving on that last revolution which is to bring all ordinary history to a close. It refuses to turn, and He throws Himself upon it .Then it does turn; and crushes Him. The wheel rolls onward, and the mangled body of the one immeasurably great Man, who was strong enough to

---

[11] Albert Schweitzer, *The Quest for the Historical Jesus* (Minneapolis: Fortress, 2001).

think of Himself as the spiritual ruler of mankind and to bend history to His purpose, is hanging upon it still. That is His victory and His reign.[12]

The second passage throbs with beauty and has provided inspirational closure for many a sermon. The first passage is more complex, but more telling. The assertion that Jesus' failure is his victory, his defeat is his kingdom, takes us into the labyrinth of akedic philosophy. If the Kierkegaardian paradox (after Luther and Paul) is true, then the true hero is the defeated one, and somehow the crisis of Abraham's vocation is borne out. Abraham knew God in the unknown. He followed God, he knew not where. He found faith in total exigency. As biblical study is showing in our time" either/or" rather than black and white captures the reality of God with this world. Abraham was fruitful (rather, Sarah was) in barrenness. He was called to kill the beloved son to vivify the son and perpetuate all humanity (seed) in him. Verity, at day's end, is "topsy-turvy." This paradox will become the Pauline mystery of mystical knowledge and redemption of humanity and the cosmos. "Though rich . . . He became poor . . . though in the form of God, He emptied Himself . . . for the joy before Him . . . He endured the cross." (Phil. 2:6–7). Perhaps the best recent exposition of this theology is found in the two books of Jack Miles, *God: A Biography*, and *Christ: A Crisis in the Life of God,* and in James L. Kugel's *The God of Old.* Turning a Pauline phrase, we can only know Christ "in the flesh" (2 Cor 5:16) as we know Him "in the spirit."

To be perfectly candid, we must say that Jesus himself was mistaken, as were the evangelists who recorded their recollections of his words: "I say you shall not have visited all of the cities of Israel before the Son of Man will come" (Matt 10:23). Miles argues the provocative notion that the God of Israel and Jesus actually changes his strategy from the warrior king to the existential and eschatological redeemer. In my view, scientific scrutiny requires only that we see the refracted truth of the hopeful followers. We need not advance the absurd proposition that Jesus, even Godself, was mistaken. The "Holy War" construal was wrong.

Schweitzer has a glorious image to convey this truth:

> The situation may be likened to the course of the sun. Its brightness breaks forth while it is still behind the mountains. The dark clouds take color from its rays, and the conflict of light and darkness produces a play of fantastic imagery. The sun itself is not yet visible" it is there only in the sense that the light issues from it. As

---

[12] Schweitzer, *Quest,* 70, 219.

the sun behind the morning glow, so appeared the personality of Jesus of Nazareth to his contemporaries in the pre-Messianic age.

At the moment when the heaven glows with intensest coloring, the sun itself rises above the horizon. But with this the wealth of color begins gradually to diminish. The fantastic images pale and vanish because the sun itself dissolves the clouds upon which they are formed. As the rising sun above the horizon, so appeared Jesus Christ to the primitive Church in its eschatological expectation.[13]

Proper understanding of Jesus' life and words emphasizes, according to Gunther Bornkamm, his "utter concentration on the kingdom of God."[14] Jesus' life and work point, not to himself, but to this immanent and impending kingdom. In Kierkegaardian cryptography Jesus comes as "one unknown" to be known. His fellowship is akedic, that's to say, it comes in the temptation, in the command, in the act of decisive obedience. He makes himself known in the "toils, conflicts, and sufferings which we pass through" as companions bearing the "sign of pain."

What is this kingdom if not that of the physical-historical overlord of Jewish apocalyptic? Jesus is God's Messiah. "Follow me," it must be, is rather Jesus' rendition of *Adonai*'s call to Abraham. Though Schweitzer's Judaic sources are scarce, prejudicial, and not nearly as rich as those which we possess today, he knew that Jesus' message was Judaic. It was Toric and akedic in a thoroughgoing way:

> For him (Paul), there was only one religion: that of Judaism. It was conceived with God, faith, promise, hope and law.

Even for Paul, Schweitzer continues:

> Christianity is not a new religion, but simply Judaism with the center of gravity shifted in consequences of the new era. . . . It professes to be nothing else than the true Jewish religion, in accord both with the time and with the Scriptures.[15]

Torah is that path of witness, of suffering, through death into life. It is the joy, the light of life (Psalm 139). The commandments "follow me" are echoed in the calls of the Sermon on the Mount and Plain—the Beatitudes—which are irresistibly ethical in their eschatological spirituality and which form the great measure of Schweitzer's Lambaréné teaching.

---

[13] Picht, *Man and His Work*, 61.
[14] Picht, *Man and His Work*, 63.
[15] Schweitzer, *Mysticism of Paul the Apostle* (New York: Seabury, 1968).

This martyrial summons was understood by Schweitzer's contemporary and soul mate, Dietrich Bonhoeffer: "When Christ calls a person he bids him come and die."[16]

The Quest in Scientific Purview

Picht locates the radical uniqueness of Schweitzer's research when religion submits itself to the scrutiny of scientific method, no matter how relativistic a post-Humean, post-Kantian, post-liberal world knows science to be:

> A religious self-examination such as that represented by historical dogma research . . . canonical writing and . . . the utterances of a founder of religion regarded as a divine being, is unique in world history."[17]

The Quest begins in the eighteenth century as radical Lutherans rejected the arid fields of orthodoxy and proposed sharply critical investigations. While some, as Schweitzer stated, hated Jesus and the church, others responded through faith. The great German playwright, Lessing, pioneered such bold thought. In words that Dostoevsky would later turn into the memorable "if I was shown that truth was one thing and Christ was another—I should choose Christ."

Lessing wrote: "If God offered me all for the truth in his right hand, and in the left the constant urge to truth, even on pain of repeated error, I would in all humility indicate his left hand and beg that he might give me that."[18]

This was all the more surprising, coming from Schweitzer who believed that "religion must have a metaphysic, that is to say, a fundamental idea concerning the nature and significance of being, which is completely independent of history and verbal tradition."[19] Schweitzer is contemporary in that he sees faith as valid, irrespective of any verification in historical or scientific method.

For Schweitzer, only strenuously critical work on Jesus and Paul can release the eternal Jesus. Only thus can we know his companioning life spirit and follow his commanding way.

---

[16] Dietrich Bonhoeffer, *Cost of Discipleship*, transl. R.H. Fuller (New York: Macmillan, 1963). See also Clemens Frey, *Christliche Weltverantwortung bei Albert Schweitzer, Mit Vergleichen zu Dietrich Bonhoeffer*, Albert Schweitzer Studien (Bern: Paul Haupt, 1993).

[17] Picht, *Man and His Work*, 203.

[18] Quoted in Picht, *Man and His Work*, 205.

[19] Picht, *Man and His Work*, 71.

The Quest is therefore a liberating iconoclasm—truth. In terms of Hebrew theology, the pursuit of other gods and the construct of idolatrous structures and systems—false knowledge—are forsaken. The vertical God association is sustained so that the horizontal interhuman imperatives may succeed—truth in order to goodness.

As the Quest clears the debris of tradition and wishful thinking in the early church, Jesus appears as the Son of Man who realized that he misperceived God's will when he sent out the first disciples in Matthew 10, sure that they would not return as they absorbed in persecution and death the "messianic tribulation"—the precondition of the new age. Now Jesus realized that he himself, not the commissioned ones (Matt 10:23), was to be God's offer to the evil one.

The "temptation" or akedic confrontation with the justice and goodness of God and the allure of evil is the sign of ultimate confrontation with the powers opposed to God.

Schweitzer writes: "The Lord's Prayer, which is a prayer about the Coming Kingdom of God . . . bids God to not lead the believers 'into temptation (but) to deliver them from the Evil One' . . . This (feared) persecution would be God's action in the Times of the End . . ."[20]

Now Jesus realizes his freedom to be "the Son of Man" and in self-chosen death to be the atonement made for believers, sparing them pre-messianic tribulation by accepting, as Isaac did, before Abraham the redeeming suffering and death of the "only beloved Son" (Genesis 22, Isaiah 53, John 3, Rom. 8:23). Kingdom is now released into the world.

In Schweitzer's insight we see in this Jesus research (*Jesus vorschung*) the conjunction of epistemological, theological and ethical dimensions of divine and natural reality and of human perception (*Wissenschaft*).

Knowledge (both Jesus' self-cognizance—perception—and Apostolic hermeneutic construal—apperception) has uprooted the unethical untruth, the unknown has been discovered and salvific efficacy has ensued. Now the just and good—the Kingdom—is released into the world.

Picht finds this awakening, which Schweitzer consummated already in Reimarus, professor of Oriental languages in Hamburg (died 1768), in Lessing's posthumous publication of his *Wolfenbuttel Unknown*.

> He recognized that Jesus lived in Jewish ideas. . . . He recognized that the ideology of Jesus was eschatological. Justice in view of the coming Kingdom of God was the innovation in his teaching. Justice according to the Law was no longer sufficient because the

---

[20] Schweitzer, *Out of My Life and Thought* (New York: Mentor, 1949) 35.

Kingdom of God was at hand. A new more profound morality was needed. He (Reimarus) confuses the messianic idea with the political-Davidian idea which expected the Messiah as a worldly liberator.[21]

Physicalizing or materializing the spiritual disturbed and impeded the power of the ethical, just as science without technology would become demonic.

To continue the akedic/decalogic analysis of Schweitzer's project to unite the intellectual and the ethical—to overcome the Cartesian and Kantian split—to restore the integrity of knowledge and techne—let us consider another enigmatic section in *The Quest*.

> There came a Man to rule over the world; He ruled it for good and for ill, as history testifies; He destroyed the world into which He was born; the spiritual life of our own time seems like to perish at His hands, for He leads to battle against our thought a host of dead ideas, a ghostly army upon which death has no power, and Himself destroys again the truth and goodness which His Spirit creates in us, so that it cannot rule the world. That He continues, notwithstanding, to reign as the alone Great and alone True in a world of which He denied the continuance, is the prime example of that antithesis between spiritual and natural truth which underlies all life and all events, and in Him emerges into the field of history.[22]

The first commandments require that we not fashion other Gods, including intellectual formulations of truth or ultimacy. Schweitzer's phrases—"He destroyed the world into which He was born; the spiritual life of our own time seems like to perish at His hands . . . and Himself destroys again the truth and goodness which His Spirit creates in us so that it cannot rule the world"—seem to be sublime iconoclasm. Iconoclasm is the first stage of scientific and spiritual investigation. It is the precursor and precondition of all truth. We persist in idolizing our beliefs and thought forms which prevent us from knowing ever-unfolding truth, justice and love. He elaborates later in *The Quest*:

> The general affirmation of the world . . . if it is to be Christian, must in the individual spirit be Christianized and transfigured by the personal rejection of the world which is preached in the sayings

---

[21] Picht, *Man and His Work*, 206.
[22] Schweitzer, *Quest*, 2.

of Jesus. It is only by means of the tension thus set up that religious energy can be communicated to our time.[23]

Science itself and appropriate technological application (e.g., using our knowledge of microbial disease to eradicate river blindness in the tropics rather than manufacturing piles of antibiotics for the deleterious consumption of Western people and livestock) and theology-ethics are countercultural phenomenon. They offend and grate against the Spirit of the age. In Schweitzer's iconoclastic concept, spirit rejection is required for spirit release. Resisting such release and reifying either science or theology is demonic as it intensifies messianic tribulation.

Eschatology and Natural Science

A season of research in Strasbourg and Günsbach in Alsace, Schweitzer's *heimstadte,* in Weinachtzeit 2003, enabled me to formulate the critical connection between his science and theology by reviewing four unpublished lectures given at the Theological Faculty in the Winter term 1911–1912 on the theme: *Die Ergibnisse des historische-kritische Theologie und die Naturwissenschaften fur die Wertung der Religion* (the relationship of historical-critical [scientific] theology and natural science for the value of religion). These lectures attempt to reconcile the concepts and convictions of the religions of the world (especially Christianity) with the findings of natural science.

These lectures were given at a critical moment in Schweitzer's intellectual and vocational life. Six years earlier he had vowed to give up the "word-life" and take up the "work-life." He had spent his first thirty years learning, speaking and writing, now he sought "hands-on-service." As the theme his beloved Franz Schubert had sounded in *An Die Musik* he sought now to still and center the soul through the deep wordless silence of Georges Bernanos—*Le Sante Agony*. During these two years, at the conclusion of his medical studies, he also revised *The Quest*, wrote on Paul and co-edited, with Charles-Marie Widor, the edition of Bach's preludes.

Now he himself must engage in the "messianic tribulation"—the precondition of "Kingdom come." This conviction he had found in his study of Jesus' ministry to the destitute. A child of great blessing he had studied medicine and was now ready to go out to equatorial Africa. Here he would serve the sick and wounded "without a word" (*muet comme une carpe*). Now he would live out what he discovered in his Kant research for the

[23] Schweitzer, *Out of My Life and Thought*, 83–84.

philosophy thesis that knowledge "intelligible" must become "supersensible" and ultimately ethical. He had discovered that secret of ethical/eschatological knowledge known in the more biblical moments of the work of Hegel and Marx that "knowledge is not only meant to understand but to transform reality."

During the years of medical education and practice Schweitzer was given "the increase of knowledge I had longed for." Natural science was "to me a spiritual experience."[24] With this exaggerated sense of the "truth" accessible to "exact science," Schweitzer found an epistemology resonant to his Jesus and Paul mystical perception and incorporation. "Knowledge of Being without entailed that of Being within."[25] Natural science would now corroborate his theological science becoming together a unified eschatological apperception. The beyond space (here) and time (now)—the mystical realm of God—was integral to all knowledge of this world, and further, that knowledge was best formulated and implemented in ameliorative and saving action.

It was during the year of his practical volunteer service of the poor and sick in the *Charité hôpital* in Strasbourg, while he was composing his medical dissertation on "Jesus and mental derangement" that he presented his four lectures on natural science and theology. The lectures dealt with:

- The conflicts and complementarity of theological and scientific views of human being
- The development of the human body and of the human species
- The will of humanity and the direction of the world through ethics
- The ethic of freedom and humanity in the convergence of theology and science

Before we explicate his thesis we must take note of how this moment in Schweitzer's *Lebenslauf* has given shape to these lectures, forming what I have called an eschatological epistemology, binding theology and science in a unified *cooperatio dei*. It begins with the doctor of medicine thesis. Now dealing with psychiatry this surgeon-to-be asked if Jesus was paranoiac, possessed of delusions of grandeur and persecution complexes—popular analyses in that dawning age of Freudian psychology. Schweitzer offers an emphatic *NEIN!* Jesus expected the coming messianic Kingdom,

---

[24] Schweitzer, *Out of My Life and Thought*, 84.
[25] Schweitzer, *Out of My Life and Thought*, 85.

yes. Being in the Davidic family line, he would have been looking for the new inauguration, perhaps even through himself. Tellingly, however, Schweitzer goes further and points to the near necessity of this awareness in Jesus' self-understanding by virtue of his upbuilding in Torah and the prophets, his association with what we now know to be the Ben Johanan (John the Baptist) and Essene community and foremost by the presence of the ethical and the eschatological in his very being as that unfolded in his work. Jesus, for Schweitzer, allowed himself to be the "Son of Man." Two passages document these claims:

> The real Jesus is convinced of His being the coming Messiah. Because, amid the religious ideas then prevailing, His powerful ethical personality cannot do otherwise . . . By His spiritual nature He was in very fact the ethical ruler promised by the prophets.[26]

And again the familiar passage from *The Quest* lifting up the mystical eschatology:

> He comes to us as One unknown, without a name, as of old, by the lakeside, He came to those men who knew Him not. He speaks to us the same word "follow thou me" and sets us to the tasks which He has to fulfill for our time. He commands. And to those who obey Him, whether they be wise or simple, He will reveal Himself in the toils, the conflicts, the sufferings which they shall pass through in His fellowship, and as an ineffable mystery, they shall learn in their own experience Who He is.[27]

Initially Schweitzer finds in natural and medical science an ethical dimension, which resonates with his Christological epistemology. While we may question the necessity he finds in Jesus' personality, especially in light of the fact that knowledge and moral intuition (*scientia* and *conscientia*) arise together in all human beings, his conviction is an outgrowth of his philosophical and scientific study where he finds, even in Kant, an ethic of love constituting the absolute (categorical) imperative. Critical (scientific) and ethical thought are synthetic (cognate) in Kant. This synthesis becomes the enduring mark of Schweitzer's theology for science.

The passage from the *Quest* is even more telling, validating in Schweitzer's thought the ethical dimension of knowledge. Here in the midst of his most formidable scientific work we find this awesome mystic logic and episteme-logic. In the toils of the divine work in the world (cf.

---

[26] Schweitzer, *Out of My Life and Thought*, 89.
[27] Schweitzer, *Quest*, 74.

Boyle) the truth of God—ultimate reality—becomes known. As Kepler discovered from his own theological tradition, similar to that of Schweitzer, contemplation (*betrachten*) and adventure (inclination) are features of all human knowing and doing. Schweitzer, the prodigious scholar, has grown impatient with *theoria* divorced from *praxis*. He has come to believe, as Kepler believed, that insight into truth was opened to the caring and reverent mind.

These lectures were delivered in the weeks Schweitzer was raising money, purchasing medicines and getting his belongings and the provisions for the hospital ready for the ship that would leave Bordeaux for Lambaréné. Together with other writings from his myriad corpus, especially on matters on science and technology, they constitute the body of his thought on theology for science. The controlling theme of an eschatological and ethical epistemology guides the content of the lectures:

- Natural science has shown that the truth and meaning about human emergence in nature comes not from history or science but from the inner reality of human being.
- This inner impulse (*"Ehrfurcht vor den Leben"*), a biological and spiritual impulse, animates vitality and sacrality—two primal energies.
- Where religion is still primal and biological—e.g., India and some Islamic cultures —people live by this impulse.
- Human development, including reason and ethics rises higher than the chemical and animal ground (Teilhard). Though we share the physical dimension of life, and are woven therefore, thoroughly into earthly life, our destiny and very nature lifts us beyond time and space.
- In the physical realm the experiences of suffering, infection, aging and death convey a grand affinity of humanity with nature and a call to use the full powers of mind and heart in helping all others in the creation. This is humanity's cosmic purpose.
- The energy of the will (Schopenhauer) toward freedom, altruism and life gives rise to culture and religion as part of the response of theodicy (explaining) and technology (ameliorating) the enigmatic pains of life. The phenomena of guilt, wonder, prayer and hope (e.g., for a newer or better world) are responses to what we recognize as inherent in the presence and will of God.

- Resisting resignation faith rises to absolute dependence and through love and hope responds in justice and care to human and world need.

- The philosophical heritage of Socrates, Kant and Nietzsche show the possible paths of critical thought—of altruism and egoism—framing human existence under God as freedom fashions the ethic of reverence for life.

- The higher cultural development in the world is the Will of God- the Kingdom of God attested and embodied by Jesus (Ritschl). This eschatological existence (living out now a world not yet) is a world of justice, peace and love through vigorous and ubiquitous help for one another. The transcendental will is here expressed fully in and through the will of the world.

Schweitzer celebrates the synergy of insight afforded by natural science and theology as both infuse meaning and direction into the activity of the human family in the physical world. It is here within the emergence and future of humankind that religion proffers helpful "whys" and "wherefores" as we seek our purposes in the world. For this reason this book focuses its concern on life science and biomedicine as one aspect of the broad realm of science.

Because of his passion for the "not yet," the "beyond" and the "coming" Schweitzer helpfully furthers our inquiry and commends the dimension of eschatology as an indispensable feature of a theology for science. We now further explicate this dimension.

Eschatologic Dimension

Schweitzer leaves us therefore with what we have called useful knowledge and helpful technology. This is best fathomed when we accept as we have seen, the scientific insight of Schweitzer's research concerning the inescapability of eschatology. Only an eschatological purview can soundly ground ethics. Schweitzer has thoroughly synthesized theology and science. He is a voice at the bridge. Science in his case is biblical, eschatological Christology.

Princeton's Walter Lowrie, the great Kierkegaard scholar, once told Amos Wilder (brother of Princeton playwright Thornton), that Schweitzer thought of his work in Africa as "eschatology in Action." The science of Gospels research would break down and splinter in our time. The absurd and offensive residue of fundamentalist literalism and the Jesus movement are all that remain. A shred of light proceeds from the Jewish-Christian collaboration on texts such as the Sermon on the Mount. Only in the mind of Paul, says Wilder, do eschatology and ethics remain associated.[28]

The formulation of the bond between eschatology and ethics is, for Schweitzer, found in the exposition of religious existence under God in the work of the Apostle Paul. Here the love command (the ground of reverence for life) is linked to the historical manifestation of Spirit. Here in Paul's great exposition of divine and human reality in Romans, Corinthians, and Galatians, for example, we find the confrontation of world-spirit and the demonic with the Christ-Spirit, which is love and justice. Through travail and tribulation, the Kingdom of God proleptically prevails as human justice and service overwhelms wrong.

Paul's scientific *Weltanschauung* is focused on his eschatic and proleptic discovery that "the Spirit is the manifestation of all the radiations which pass from the super-earthly to the earthly . . ." The purest and brightest of these radiations is "the unsensational ethical guidance of the Spirit wherein love is recognized as the gift in which the essential nature (of the spirit) becomes reality within the temporal."[29]

Put simply, in the enduring Christ presence which threw him from his horse on the road to Damascus, Paul mystically perceived and received (as now any person can) the suffering, dying, rising and eternally redeeming One whose "way" in the world is the "way" of Israel—the way of Spirit—the way of the Kingdom—the way where knowledge overcomes ignorance, love overcomes evil and life overcomes death. Eschatology has become ethics.

Die Geschichte der Paulinischen Forschung (*Paul and His Interpreters*) obviously continues Schweitzer's *Jesus Forschung*. This work was delayed by his first tour in Africa (1913–1917), his incarceration in France (1917–1918) and serious illness (with dysentery) requiring two operations. Completely broke, he began work as a medical assistant at *Burgerspital* (Strasbourg public hospital) and as the vicar of St. Nikolai parish. It was not until December 1929 that he finished *The Mysticism of Paul the Apostle* "on board the river-steamer which was taking [us] to Lambaréné."[30]

Now 55 years old, the work bears the mark of one who has known the pain of the world. Perhaps only one who has struggled with the historic and living Jesus—one who has heard that call and followed—can

---

[28] Amos Wilder, *Eschatology and Ethics in the Teaching of Jesus* (New York: Harper, 1950).
[29] Schweitzer, *Mysticism of Paul*, 380.
[30] Schweitzer, *Out of My Life and Thought* (1933) 251.

comprehend that theoethical construal of Paul that will become the foundation of the Christian faith.

It becomes evident at this point of the biography that Schweitzer contemplated a life's work of what could be called a "history of the Kingdom of God." This exploration would span from the Hebrew tradition with parallels from China and India, through the Jesus work, on to Paul and through the early church to the present age. The *Kingdom of God*, his last work, reflects this ambition that has been lost in the corridors of missionary service.

The work on Paul is monumental. Though we wish for detailed textual commentary, theological hermeneutics and studies of contemporary relevance in Romans, Corinthians, Galatians and Philippians, what we have is highly instructive. Picht sees this study as the bridge between Schweitzer's Christology and his ethics.

Though Schweitzer rightly demurs given the many problems involved in bringing Paul to contemporary comprehension:

- the *sitz-im-leben* amid the first century Jew/Gentile controversies
- the juridical/soteriological tension on issues like justification and salvation
- the concentrated distorting and historically justificatory use of Paul in the politics and ecclesiology of the European Reformation

He cuts through to the theological, cosmological, metaphysical and ethical genius of the man of Tarsus. In Paul, Schweitzer found insight amplifying that of the cross-Logos found in Jesus, of the power and wisdom of God amid the terror, the chaos, the anguish and the hope of this present age. Like his contemporary, Karl Barth (*Romerbrief*), he knew that Paul's fathoming of the Gospel in the Apostolic Age was the only sure diction and direction for contemporary history.

Paul, writes Schweitzer, "becomes a thinker of elemental power . . . by recognizing the special character of the period which interposed itself between the resurrection and return of Jesus."[31] As such a spirit, gripped by the meanwhile before *parousia* and delayed *parousia*, one aware of the "here and not yet there" and the "now and not yet then," Paul could wisely formulate the character of a tentative knowledge and an interim ethic. Could this perspective fashion a way to know and do in the playground of time and space in the world and cosmos?

---

[31] Schweitzer, *Mysticism of Paul*, 140.

Paul's answer is the new being, *kaine ktisis, en christou*, the creature grasped by the presence of the infinite while yet in the mundane—one caught up in eternity while still in time—all this occurring in the world body and community. The new being—anticipated in Judaism, foreshadowed in China and India—a Kingdom being is made possible. Now knowledge and technology can now be responsibly animated and activated. An eschatological or future being is now fashioned. Paul fathoms the oppression of the creation, as in Romans 8 he sees the futility of the creature, not yet released, still in bondage, but thrilled by the foretaste of being set free. Like Nelson Mandela in his island prison, he knew Him, who was the One to come. Like C.S. Lewis described in *The Lion, the Witch and the Wardrobe*, endless winter is now punctuated by the promise of Christmas.

This new being, world existence in Christ, is set free in love: set free from old forms of through to new possibilities, set free from gnawing desperation from life conditions, diseases, and unknowns to insights useful and actions helpful; set free from "that's the way it is and it must be" to "that's the way it could be." Paul came to know One in whom all the experiences of exigency—refracted knowledge, persecution and torture, sickness and dying, frustrated projects—became the fellowship of His sufferings and the participation in His resurrection.

Music

Schweitzer best understood this expectant, eager waiting, this vibrant hope and joy amid apparent hopelessness, when he played the music of his beloved Johann Sebastian Bach. Whether at the organ of Thomaskirche, Strasbourg, or at the old zinc-lined tropical organ at Günsbach, sent to Lambaréné by the Paris Bach Society, he found solace in music from the world in order that he might serve the world. *Insouciance*, blessed serenity, he found in Bach, even in the Jaws of Death.

Last evening at Strasbourg's great Reformed church, St. Paul, at the foot of the main canal through the city, François Menissier of Rouen Cathedral presented the organ concert. The program concluded with a *Messe* by Cesar Franck, a work Schweitzer mastered with the repertoire while in Lambaréné. The majestic orchestral symphony ends with a serene and stately church hymn. My mind journeyed to the pew where St. Paul parishioner and philosopher Paul Ricoeur often sat. From here he rose to offer a lecture on his 80th birthday! The pew hymnal begins with the simple yet elegant psalm texts and tunes set by Jean Calvin and Martin Bucer when in 1538 they led the reformation movement in Strasbourg.

The evening vesper moved the soul as fading twilight illumined the haunting glass windows of the old church. At the center and apex of the dark blue glass designed by Eric de Saussure—of the Taizé community—is Christ in glory, his face cast in the likeness of Christ's in St. Priscilla's catacomb in Rome. Above the glory of Him who conquered death is the Lamb to whom resurrected bodies arise. Like the *Finsternis*—the ominous closing hours that gripped the world in Paul's days—now on these days—Israeli F-16s rocket an apartment in Gaza killing nine children, global stock markets collapse in the wake of corporate fraud in America —one knew that even earth's last tremulous hours—were a bestowal of the hand of God—another annunciation of the kingdom at hand—lifted to the glorious, reigning, akedic lamb of God.

Schweitzer actually saw the psalm song tending toward the plodding and pedantic (at least in contrast to the Luther tunes and Paul Gerhard hymns). Schweitzer is no Francophile on this issue. He finds a more jubilant idiom across the Rhine. "Germany, in its bitterest need, created a religious poetry to which nothing in the world can compare and before which even the splendor of the psalter pales."[32]

"The German Reformation," Schweitzer continues, "had this advantage over the French, that it found a spiritual song." The sacred folksong had withered away in Romanesque countries. Luther eschewed the puritan impulse. "Luther would not permit the old wood to be cut down."[33] We remember his gruff *tischrede* as he composed hymns on the recorder. "Why should the devil have all the good tunes?" he asked.

Schweitzer's greatest jubilation and exaltation is reserved for the chorale. Before he embarked on his medical studies, Schweitzer had researched and was prepared to write a study on Schubert, whose accompaniments to the *Lieder* he found as "the nearest thing to Bach's Cantata. The playfulness of *La Fiorella* as well as the profound tension of *Die Winterreise* were dear to the *Grand Docteur*. He loved the deep purple hues and the bright yellows in Bach's "*Well-Tempered Clavier.*" The pathos of the *Prelude in E-flat minor* from Part I and the jubilant *Prelude in G Major* from Part II, were as dear to him as the preludes and organ fantasies on the chorale melodies. Here Schweitzer found Bach at his philosophical best. Here thought preceded technique. Here technique enhanced and expressed thought.

---

[32] Schweitzer, *Johann Sebastien Bach*, v. 1 (London: A. C. Black, 1938) 10ff.

[33] Schweitzer, *Bach*, 7.

Here again is the heart of Schweitzer's achievement *vis-à-vis* our thesis. Knowledge true is careful.

Schweitzer once confessed to Widor (organist at St. Sulpice in Paris, and teacher, mentor and colleague to Schweitzer) that he could not comprehend the musical logic of Bach's chorale melodies. This comes only, responded Widor, as one interlaces thought and tune, text and melody. From that moment, Schweitzer translated all of the chorale texts into French and then committed them to memory.

In the chorale, for which Schweitzer wrote the definitive edition of the Preludes, he found the brilliance, the utility and the help of the Protestant liturgy. Here was *foi et vie*, faith set to life. Here was the work of belief. The chorale reaches into the Latin Middle Ages for its spirit and form. Charles Joy writes, "sinking his (Bach's) roots in the Twelfth Century, he establishes vital contact with a great past. . . . now the aspirations, striving, even the soul of former generations live again." (*Anthology*, p. 294)

Bach, wrote Hindemith in his landmark lectures, probed the curtain of infinity and eternity. He took the form and substance of classical music and lifted them to their ultimate virtuosity. Yet, he could not penetrate the veil. But rather than despair, like Schweitzer, he fell back into serene acceptance and the impulse to simply serve human need.

This brief interlude on music readies us to approach the heartland of Schweitzer's work—his ethics. We have seen that he sees the distillation of Jesus' life and message and Paul's mystical vision as love put to action in the life situation. Schweitzer's vocation patterns this conviction. To his ethics we now turn.

Schweitzer's Ethics

Schweitzer's position on scientific investigation and technological application ultimately rests on his ethics. Ethics is about what we do with what we know. His ethics emerged from a composite source: 1) His investigations about Jesus, Paul and the Kingdom of God, 2) his philosophical training, 3) Africa, and 4) his duty as a world statesman and citizen. The central ethical principle is *Ehrfurcht vor das Leben*, Reverence for Life, *Respect de la Vie*. Though he recalls morally formative childhood experiences, this student of the Apostle has his Damascus road experience in the Ancient East. The epiphany comes on the Ogowe River sailing upstream on a mission of mercy.

> Slowly we crept upstream, laboriously feeling—it was the dry season—for the channels between the sandbanks. Lost in thought,

> I sat on the deck of the barge, struggling to find the elementary and universal conception of the ethical which I had not discovered in any philosophy . . . Late on the third day, at the very moment when, at sunset, we were making our way through a herd of hippopotamuses, there flashed upon my mind, unforeseen and unsought, the phrase, "Reverence for life." The iron door had yielded: the path in the thicket has become visible . . . life affirmation and ethics were together founded in thought.[34]

Was this warmed-over Bergson or Schopenhauer? Was it an answer to Descartes' "oven," with C*ogito,* now become *vita ergo sum*? Was it a throwback to the childhood "birds and bees" (*double entendre*)? Was it the Hebraic *l'chayim,* "choose life," a wisdom he strangely ignores until he is an old man writing of the kingdom of God? Then, at last, he consults the kings, poets and the prophets of Israel?

The principle of "Reverence for life" was so thoroughgoing and life-transforming for Schweitzer that it deserves serious attention. Which, after all, is what he always asked, that we stand at awe, at attention (*achten, achtung*), before the mystery of life in humble respect. The doctor or pastor at the birth table or death bed knows what it is to bow down in respect.

This is especially true today when we dismiss as collateral damage innocents sacrificed in war—the nine children this week in the bombing of Gaza, with sanctions in Iraq, or as environmental side-effects in the profligate pillaging of natural resources. Hitler, and today's fascists in the Middle East and yes, in the Wild West, also speak of collateral damage —"*lebensunwerten lebens.*" "Human trash" is always the phrase of scoundrels. In crisis times as well as in the commonplace, I have found the concept—reverence for life—very useful and helpful across my career in bioethics. Jean François Collange of Strasbourg employs it in his ethics of medical and human rights. Many scholars have pointed up the ethical ambiguity of a radical principle of vitalism. Peter Singer's utilitarian critique may be exaggerated, but it raises the key issues. When life prolongation becomes artificial and technological, it can be ethically problematic. Insisting on the sanctity of life at both thresholds of birth and death can become inhuman.

In my view, Schweitzer's principle is generally useful and helpful especially when chastened by his corroborating akedic principle of the fellowship of the mark of pain. To review his ethic, let us first delineate the notion, then analyze its value and disvalue, then compound its meaning in

---

[34] Schweitzer, *Out of My Life and Thought,* 185ff.

the light of Schweitzer's fellowship of those who "bear the mark of pain" (*Der Dienste den Barmherzigkeit*). Finally we can apply it to some contemporary problems.

Reverence for Life

Here is the primary text:

> Ethics is nothing else than reverence for life. Reverence for life affords me my fundamental principle of morality, namely, that good consists in maintaining, assisting and enhancing life and that to destroy, to harm or to hinder life is evil. Affirmation of the world, that is to say, affirmation of the will-to-live which appears in phenomenal form all around me, is only possible for me in that I give myself out for other life . . . in world and life affirmation and in ethics I fulfill the will of the universal will-to-live which reveals itself in me. I live my life in God, in the mysterious ethical divine personality which I cannot discover in the world, but only experience in myself as a mysterious impulse.[35]

First, note the residue of universal, Christian and Kantian ethics: "Do unto others as you would have others do to you." Only in altruism is self-affirmation possible. Only *altérité* discloses selfhood. Note secondly that faith corroborates reason. Schweitzer seems to be affirming not only the common ground of rational and revelatory ethics, but also the thesis I propound in this study that theological grounding and bearing is conducive to an effective science and a salutary technical ethic. Assurance of scientific truth and ethical implementation of knowledge are enhanced by religious perspective. For Schweitzer, not only is ethics the fulfillment of the Jesus, Paul and Biblical heritage, it is the culmination of the rational quest.

The meeting ground of sacred and secular ethics is the phenomenon of love. As Teilhard will show in relation to cosmic structure and evolutionary process, love is the primal, binding substance of reality. "Ethics," writes Schweitzer, "is the maintaining of life at the highest point of development—my own life and other life—by devoting myself to it in help and love, and both these things are connected."[36]

For Schweitzer, the impetus to love is only possible in a kind of ascetic disdain—if one dies to life and to this world. "Only he who experiences inner freedom from external events in profound surrender to his own will-to-live, is capable of the profound and permanent surrender of

---

[35] Schweitzer, *Decay and Restoration of Civilization*, xvi.
[36] from *Christian Century* article in *Anthology*, 237.

himself for the sake of other life."[37] Here again we see the sacrificial and akedic note. Love is a rational, Kantian imperative, yes, but ultimately it is a matter of the will and heart—the impulse of mercy, sympathy and kindness. Love is the heart of Schweitzer's decision to stop talking and start doing. Fortunately for the world, he continued the academic career of reading, thinking, talking and writing—now all in the context of philanthropic action.

Another window on the ethics of active service is related to technology. By virtue of the fact that the West has developed technology, in ways, as Max Weber suggested, which were disproportionately intense and accelerated in contrast to Islamic, African, Indian or Asian culture, it now had the obligation to utilize that technology in justice. Western visualization, causation and therapeutic medicine quite outstripped that of the medicine man in the ability to outwit the sleeping sickness, the microorganism *Trypano somata* and the tsetse fly. Muslims cried foul when Christian evangelists came to Africa in the nineteenth century in the guise of medicine. But despite this there was a unique convergence of the needs of poor and sick in Africa and Western medical and surgical skill. For Schweitzer, this confession of need/profession of ability matrix formed an imperative and obligation. He framed this coincidence in the eschatologic and akedic imagery of Dives and Lazarus.

> I gave up my position of professor in the University of Strasburg, my literary work, and my organ playing, in order to go as a doctor to Equatorial Africa. How did that come about? I had read about the physical miseries of the natives in the virgin forests; I had heard about them from missionaries, and the more I thought about it the stranger it seemed to me that we Europeans trouble ourselves so little about the great humanitarian task which offers itself to us in far-off lands. The parable of Dives and Lazarus seemed to me to have been spoken directly of us! We are Dives, for, through the advances of medical science, we now know a great deal about disease and pain, and have innumerable means of fighting them: yet we take as a matter of course the incalculable advantages which this new wealth gives us! Out there in the colonies, however, sits wretched Lazarus, the colored folk, who suffers from illness and pain just as much as we do, nay much more, and has absolutely no means of fighting them. And just as Dives sinned against the poor man at his gate because for want of thought he never put himself

---

[37] Schweitzer, *Decay and Restoration of Civilization*, 258.

in his place and let his heart and conscience tell him what he ought to do, so do we sin against the poor man at our gate.[38]

Though Nietzsche understood and sought him, Schweitzer had faced the defaced and deformed, the beauty and goodness, of Isaiah's Suffering Servant (Isaiah 53), "One in whom there was no comeliness or attraction." Nietzsche's ethic more resonates with Aristotelian teleology and entelechy and with the aesthetics of German idealism. Goodness, as Wesley would say, is moral perfection; or as the Greek that Nietzsche extolled over Christian masochism would contest, moral excellence is uprightness, symmetry, fulfillment—*mens sane in corpore sano*. This passage makes all the more remarkable the wisdom and great love that Schweitzer found in poor, wounded, suffering Africans:

> The essential nature of the will-to-live is found in this, that it is determined to live itself out. It bears in itself the impulse to realize itself to the highest possible degree of perfection.
>
> In delicate blossoms, in the manifold wondrous forms of the jellyfish, in a blade of grass, in the crystal; everywhere it strives to reach that perfection which is implicit in its own nature. Imaginative power, determined by ideals, is at work in all that is. The impulse toward perfection is innate in us—beings, as we are, endowed with freedom and capable of reflective purposive action—in such a way that we naturally aspire to raise ourselves and every portion of existence affected by our influence to the highest material and spiritual degree of value.
>
> We do not know how this aspiration came to be in us and how it has developed itself in us. It is an intrinsic part of our being. We must follow it if we will not be untrue to the secret will-to-live which is rooted in us.[39]

Reverence for life flows from Schweitzer's Christological eschatology—to an anthropology—to a zoology—to a no longer so eschatological concern for the whole earth—a geosociology—searching for justice and peace in the concourse of traumatic world history. From an epiphenomenon of vitality itself—from a primal yearning and urge and yearning to live and become in all creatures—from a passion to render the world a loving community after so much brutality and sheer inertia, agnosis and futility—to a prayer for a nuclear-imperiled earth—Schweitzer here expounds the core principle of his ethics.

---

[38] Schweitzer, *Primeval Forest*, 1ff.
[39] Schweitzer, *Decay and Restoration of Civilization*, 222.

In the presence of the cacophony of human need from the angered buzzing bees, the shriek of frightened birds, the bellow of the threatened hippo, the warning clatter of the pelican, the groan of the starving child, the deep howl of the native wailing through the jungle (with a strangulated hernia), to the sigh of the burned civilians of Hiroshima, to the hope for a better world, Schweitzer offers the silent power of his ethic.

The final characteristic of that ethic is sacrificial service. I latch onto this quality from my own research, which sees the ground of both parochial and universal ethics in the *Torah*-Akedah complex of Abrahamic faith. This ethic, which embraces Jewish *Torah*, Christian ethics and Muslim submission, bears out value and vision into communities of faith as well as to secular social and global structures.

Living out the law of life in this ethical understanding provokes tribulation, temptation in the Spirit-sent and demon-resented freedom wherein individuals and collectivities make decisions. The Decalogue is the essence of this value matrix. Here in Schweitzer's words, we challenge world spirit and *Zeitgeist* by Logos-spirit. We live out the way of God which he called, after Siddhartha and Moses, Jesus and Paul, Luther and Calvin, Francis and Gandhi, "the Fellowship of those who bear the mark of pain."

The Fellowship of Pain

The normative crux of Schweitzer's akedic (i.e., crucifix) conviction, in ethics, is found in the context of this work.

- When contemplating Bach, he wrote chapters on Bach's *Schmerzmotif und freudenmotif*
- He pondered the crisis (decay and restoration) of civilization
- He vowed to *live* in the mode of life and world affirmation
- While pondering the vital energies and weariness of Western thought (including reflections on world religion), the experience on the barge came upon him in the very act of caring for the sick
- While delivering the Goethe address in Frankfurt in March 1932, on the 100th anniversary of his *Todestag*—he extolled the infinite respect for the individual as the only redemption in the Faustian drama enveloping Europe

Werner Picht, Schweitzer's most reliable biographer, argues that "Reverence for life" is a "voice of the jungle." He hears it near what Schweitzer called the three islands of "reverence for life" near the village of Igandja in the area of the Ogowe River. Here in dense, uninhabitable forest, he contemplated the elemental "life force" that he found in the African—even in the midst of "sickness, pain and death." Against the kind of primal curse of disease the responsive cure and care through compassion was the gesture of reverence. As with Isaac to Abraham and Sarah, or Jesus to God his father, the beloved son is given over only to be received back as in the presence of love suffering becomes healing, death becomes resurrection.

It was a contradiction—Kierkegaard's paradox—that sounded the call. It was in the pain of life—the terror of the unknown, the dread of that which is inimical to being and well-being—even in a resplendent world which present itself as provident—this paradox grounded reverence for life. In Rudolph Otto's and Schleiermacher's commingled lure and dread of the "Holy" (*Das Heilige*) and of *äbhängigskeitsgefuhl* (feeling of absolute dependence) one was drawn to the abyss, which was rescue. Schweitzer comprehended this perception in the imagery of Goethe's *Sorrows of Werther* and *Weltschmertz*. Werther, remember, was the tender one grieved by the mechanical world of "Modernity." Like Jesus in the *Quest* being crushed on the wheel, here at the edge of the primeval forest, away from orderly and organized Alsace, Schweitzer found moments when he was "glad to be alive."

Akedah, that intricate symbol of the cross fertilization between early Christianity and Judaism—perhaps most poignantly embodied in that life-child of both faiths—Islam—lies behind Passover, Exodus, New Year, Jubilee and ultimately, the suffering, death and resurrection of Jesus.

In Reverence for Life doctrine, we realize the sacrifice entailed in the gift of life. Life can only exist at the cost of other life. Here Barth's treatment of Schweitzer's concept is instructive, especially on matters like suicide, abortion and accepting death. V*eneratio vitae* is liturgy and sacrament. "Greater love has no one than this, that one lays down his life for his friends. You are my friends if you keep my commandments" (John 15:13–14). The threshold of life is the fellowship, the *koinonia* of the cross. It is the fellowship of "those who bear the mark of pain."

Schweitzer keenly felt the pathos of the mark of pain against the panorama of providence:

> I saw a man lying on the ground with his head almost buried in the sand and ants running all over him. It was a victim of sleeping sickness whom his companions had left there, probably some days before, because they could not take him any further. He was past all help, though he still breathed. While I was busied with him I

could see through the door of the hut the bright blue waters of the bay in their frame of green woods, a scene of almost magic beauty, looking still more enchanting in the flood of golden light poured over it by the setting sun. To be shown in a single glance such a paradise and such helpless, hopeless misery, was overwhelming . . . but it was a symbol of the condition of Africa.[40]

Schweitzer intuited that what he called the "child of nature" felt these agonies more acutely than Westerners so protected by pain.

> The natives who live in the bosom of nature are never so ill as we are, and do not feel pain so much." That is what my friends used to say to me, to try to keep me at home, but I have come to see that such statements are not true. Out here there prevail most of the diseases which we know in Europe, and several of them—those hideous ones, I mean, which we brought here—produce, if possible, more misery than they do amongst us. And the child of nature feels them as we do, for to be human means to be subject to the power of that terrible lord whose name is Pain.[41]

Pain is not only afflicted, it is inflicted. This intensifies the responsibility for amelioration and alleviation.

> Ever since the world's far-off lands were discovered, what has been the conduct of the white peoples to the colored ones? What is the meaning of the simple fact that this and that people has died out, that others are dying out, and that the condition of others is getting worse and worse as a result of their discovery by men who professed to be followers of Jesus? Who can describe the injustice and the cruelties that in the course of centuries they have suffered at the hands of Europeans? Who can measure the misery produced among them by the fiery drinks and the hideous diseases that we have taken to them? If a record could be compiled of all that has happened between the white and the colored races, it would make a book containing numbers of pages, referring to recent as well as to early times, which the reader would have to turn over unread, because their contents would be too horrible.
>
> We and our civilization are burdened, really, with a great debt. We are not free to confer benefits on these men, or not, as we please; it is our duty. Anything we give them is not benevolence by atonement. For everyone who scattered injury, someone ought to go out to take help, and when we have done all that is in our

---

[40] Schweitzer, *Primeval Forest*, 168–69.

[41] Schweitzer, *Primeval Forest*, 168.

power, we shall not have atoned for the thousandth part of our guilt.⁴²

Bearing and sharing suffering, therefore, is the explanatory and expiating mystery of life.

> The Fellowship of those who bear the Mark of Pain. Who are the members of this fellowship? Those who have learned by experience what physical pain and bodily anguish mean, belong together all the world over; they are united by a secret bond. One and all they know the horrors of suffering to which man can be exposed, and one and all they know the longing to be free from pain. He who has been delivered from pain must not think he is now free again, and at liberty to take life up just as it was before, entirely forgetful of the past. He is now a "man whose eyes are open" with regard to pain and anguish, and he must help to overcome those two enemies (so far as human power can control them) and to bring to others the deliverance which he has himself enjoyed. The man who, with a doctor's help, has been pulled through a severe illness, must aid in providing a helper such as he had himself, for those who otherwise could not have one. He who has been saved by an operation from death or torturing pain, must do his part to make it possible for the kindly anesthetic and the helpful knife to begin their work, where death and torturing pain still rule unhindered. The mother who owes it to medical aid that her child still belongs to her, and not to the cold earth, must help, so that the poor mother who has never seen a doctor may be spared what she has been spared. Where a man's death agony might have been terrible, but could fortunately be made tolerable by a doctor's skill, those who stood around his deathbed must help, that others, too, may enjoy that some consolation when they lose their dear ones.⁴³

Conclusion

In highlighting this eschatic dimension of reality⁴⁴ and in accenting the ethical dimension in his active program in science and medicine as gifts in world healing and development Schweitzer sets the stage for our contemporary voices in a theology for science.

---

42 Schweitzer, *Primeval Forest*, 171–72.
43 Schweitzer, *Primeval Forest*, 287.
44 see Kenneth Vaux, *Birth Ethics*.

5 Amartya Sen
the axiologic vector

RIGHT OFF ONE MIGHT ask how a practitioner of the "dismal science" gained access to our company of searchers in theology and science. Certainly economics is more a human science (in the European sense) than a natural or physical science. But with this writer's bias toward life science and with most of our exemplars of the bridge being physicians, we have positioned this project well within the purview of "human science." Though economics has become a mathematical and computational science and technology, at least in comparison to the heady philosophical days of Adam Smith and Karl Marx, even John Maynard Keynes and John Kenneth Galbraith, her purposes remain profoundly moral, even theological, as she serves as the steward of norms for exchange in our common life in the "world house" (*oikos/nomos*). In addition to this justification for inclusion, Amartya Sen has become one of the most important philosophers of science and religion in the modern world.

Recent books by Stephen Long, Douglas Meeks and Max Stackhouse[1] have reiterated the connections made early in the century by Max Weber and R.H. Tawney between theology and economics. Amartya Sen himself is quite at home with philosophers and theologians including Kenneth Arrow, John Rawls, Robert Nozick and Martha Nussbaum. Sen's elders were sages and teachers in the Hindu faith tradition. For these reasons I am persuaded that he can play a crucial role in this study. Like our other scientist-theologians he takes a global and ethical view of the knowledge and technology that is unfolding before us.

Sen is more reticent than our other exemplars of theology and science to own a religious commitment, though his faith and ethics are evident in person and in his expressed work. Since he, however, has witnessed, first hand, the sectarian brutality of Hindu and Muslim in his native Bangladesh and India, like Boyle and Kass he wants nothing to do with

---

[1] D. Stephen Long, *Divine Economy* (London: Routledge, 2000); Douglas Meeks, *God: The Economist* (Minneapolis: Fortress, 1989); Max Stackhouse, *Christian Ethics and Economic Life* (Nashville: Abingdon, 1996).

dogmatic sectarian animosity and the disorientation and disgrace which those distorted religions bring to the human and divine project on earth. He doubts the helpfulness of simplistic designations like "culture wars," "Islamic civilization," "Hindu India" or the "Christian West." One who celebrates pluralism, diversity and toleration, he has moved from the spiritual persuasion of his family to a more secular outlook. Yet his theological seriousness and ethical outlook, residual from an intense theocentric background, shines through.

Amartya Sen: A Selective Bibliography

1968 *Choice of Techniques*
1970 *Growth Economics: Selected Readings*
1971 *Behaviour and the Concept of Preference*
Crisis in Indian Education
1975 *Employment, Technology and Development*
1980 *Levels of Poverty: Policy and Change*
1981 *Poverty and Famines*
1982 *Utilitarianism and Beyond* (ed. Sen and Bernard Williams)
1984 *Resources, Values and Development*
1985 *Commodities and Capabilities*
1987 *Food, Economics and Entitlements*
Hunger and Entitlements
On Ethics and Economics
1988 *Gender and Cooperative Conflicts*
Africa and India: What Do We Have to Learn From Each Other
1989 *Hunger and Public Action* (with Jean Drèze)
1991 *Money and Value: On the Ethics and Economics of Finance*
1992 *Inequality Reexamined*
1993 *Quality of Life* (edited with Martha Nussbaum)
1995 *Choice, Welfare and Development* (Festschrift ed. Basu, et al.)
India, "Economic Development and Social Opportunity" (with Jean Drèze)

1997 *Social Choice Reexamined*
Resources, Values and Development
Choice, Welfare and Measurement
On Economic Inequality
1999 *Reason Before Identity*
Development as Freedom
Economie est une Science Morale
2000 *Amartya Sen on Keralla*
Beyond the Crisis: Development Strategies in Asia
2002 *India, Development and Participation* (with Jean Drèze)
Rationality and Freedom
2005 *Argumentative India*

Famines do not occur in democracies

Sen's work is gathered around the poles of several simple theses. One is that *famines do not occur in democracies.* Here Sen shows himself to be the heir of the Puritans whose Cambridge University College, Trinity, he recently mastered (2003). The first thesis also shows the complexity of his thought, which is parcel of his genius and wisdom. Democracy (a sociopolitical modality) and famine (supposedly an "act of God"), like freedom or faith and science, on first glance seem to be unrelated phenomena. Yet from the outset of our pathway in this study, when Maimonides, for example, binds together spiritual and mental perplexity, or when he links personal and political *shalom* together as interrelated realities, we see this uncanny ability to tie disparate things together into what then becomes an obvious whole. Creative imagination has become a revelatory mark of truth and goodness.

In the mid-1970s when the International Labor Organization (ILO) invited Sen to look into the cause of famines, he began to research the great Bengal famine of 1943, in which three million people had perished. The then-nine-year-old Bengali youth had experienced in person the suffering caused by that famine. Unlike Siddhartha, the pain and death fashioned in him a resolve not to escape but to try to ameliorate this agony. Using careful historical, empirical and statistical work, Sen discovered that it was not a collapse of the food supply (carrying capacity of the environment) that caused the catastrophe. The food supply actually increased during this period. The real cause was that economic and political systems failed as distribution, compensation and access mechanisms broke down so that poor rural workers could not obtain food. A fresh epistemology, a different look and a justice perspective enabled Sen—the ethicoeconomist—to see and solve a most perplexing issue. Why on this provident earth had this lethal scarcity arisen?

This led to a study of a sequence of famines: Ethiopia, Bangladesh and China (1958–1961) in which 30 million persons had died. In his 1981 book, *Poverty and Famines*, Sen added complex political, philosophical and ethical values to explain the enigma of China's famine—also amid plenty—within a totalitarian-Maoist state. Now it became clear that issues like education, free press, opposition political parties and free speech were co-etiological factors in the occurrence of famine. The libertarian philosopher also noted the failure of justice and compassion—theological vectors.

Freedom enhances capability

Another simple maxim emerges, again as fundamental as the *Tao* or *Torah*, that *freedom enhances capability*. In *Democracy and Freedom* (1999) and other recent work in economic and religious history, Sen now turns to a cache of issues which we might call social or ethical values: development, freedom, opportunity, dignity, rights, justice and concern for the "worse off" ("the least of these"). In June 2003, for example, he was scheduled to dialogue with theologian Paul Ricoeur (*Myths and Symbols of Evil*), under the auspices of the Von Hugel Institute in Cambridge. Though this meeting regrettably was cancelled, his work on philosophical and ethical issues, he assures, will continue as he returns to Harvard to direct the Justice and Economics Center.

Hinduism, Religious Pluralism and Democracy

Sen is sensitive to the fact that in our age, like the sixteenth and seventeenth centuries, interconfessional strife often obviates the credibility of religion. Muslims in Lebanon, for example, have objected to recent proposals to bring Christians into dialogue saying that "they are already Christians." Sen's appropriation of his Hindu heritage, rooted in the Vedas and the deeply salient synthetic and syncretistic and skeptical Hindu faith, follows this line. Sen's paternal grandfather was a Sanskrit master and as a young scholar Amartya set out to work on Sanskrit and mathematics. Tagore and the Master's rendition of Indian wisdom and religious pluralism influenced his early education. From this inception of his learning Sen's interests seem to have focused on the social, political and economic yield of the faith traditions within which he lived: Hinduism, Christianity and Islam.

The irrepressible religiosity of the Indian sub-continent and the natural spiritual and ethical sensibilities of the young man seemed to flourish in his first marriage to Eva Colorni, daughter of the Jewish Italian philosopher—a sagacious and activist leader—Eugenio Colorni, who was killed by the fascists. His teaching posts at Oxford, London, India, Harvard and Cambridge (and other stops along his way) also shaped him. He is assiduously studied at Louvain and other centers of Roman Catholic learning given the naturalism and justice orientation of his work. During these years he struggled with the theological and ethical thought of the likes of John Rawls (*A Theory of Justice*) and Martha Nussbaum (*The Fragility of Goodness*) as his own work took on more of a philosophical tenor. It is the view of this observer that these earlier and later associations formed a real, though subliminal theological imprint on his work and sharpened the proclivities which would train a rather unique mind and spirit in the soul of the economist.

I've chosen Sen as a capstone of this study because his spiritual tongue, Sanskrit, is the *Logos* and language of Indo-European faith, worldview and ethics. Indo-European faith, it now appears after the work of Eric Lincoln and others, lies behind Hellenic wisdom and in many ways is older and productive of Semitic perceptions of God, man and the world. The Indic "One and the Many," a primal impulse of all knowledge and technology, all theology and ethics, is difficult to discern and trace, but nevertheless it becomes the formative way for the God of Abraham, Isaac and Israel, the high sky god of Egypt and the great deity of reason and *Nous* of Plato, Socrates and Aristotle. This primal, though still impersonal, river of reality and force also joins with other streams of conviction and commitment to form Buddhism and Confucianism. So this archaic and akedic faith participates in the "plan of the ages," speaking in "diverse times and ways" (Hebrews 1,11)—the preparation for *kairos*—when the time was fully ripe—in the precise moment of Hebrew law, Hellenic culture and language and Roman peace—God sent His Son—eternal *Logos* into the world (Gal 4:4). Here in Sen's Indo-European heritage, in other words, lies the *Tao*—the milieu of origination and destination—the normative ethos of all theology and science—all construal of God and world.

The primal polytheism found in Hinduism, like the primal pantheism of the Pre-Socratic Greeks ("the world is full of god and gods"), must evolve toward monotheism, monovialism (one way) and universalism (one cosmic reality) before useful knowledge and helpful technology can emerge in world history. Before science can find its divine and humane expression and application, it remains for humanity to perceive and be grasped by the God of Abraham, Isaac and Israel, the pervasive deity of Parmenides and Plotinus, the God and Father of the Lord Jesus Christ and the continuation and mutation of this heritage in the God of Jesus—and Muhammad—*EL' LAH*—the God of *Torah* and *Prophets*—of *Taurut* and *Injil*—of law and Gospel. Only after this history thus unfolds can the world receive the gift of Avicenna and Maimonides and the subsequent theological saga, which we relate in this book.

A further word, though, is necessary as we examine the cosmos, pathos and ethos Sen embodies. It is only as the world receives Abraham's faith, Isaac's Akedah, the God of Israel and Mosaic *Torah*, that monotheistic science can take hold. Out of this Indo-European and Vedic substrate a philosophy conducive to science and an ethic appropriate to world-building (*Tikkun Olam*) can arise.

Abraham's futurity, venturism, trust and knowledge of divine promise and Isaac's transaction of the primal temptation (the risk of freedom) and his victorious transfiguration, by God, into eternal wisdom, *messias christos*, as this is capitulated in Jesus, the Lamb of God, becomes an ingredient of an adventuring science contoured by the stipulates of justice. Transmuting humanity's perennial economic ritual of appeasing the Earth Mother with sacrifice into the duty of work (worship), joy and release, creative Sabbath is proffered to the world. Humanity can now try, under responsibility, even failing, to fashion industry under this canopy of forgiveness and encouragement. As Einstein said, God isn't capricious, and therefore we can move on to the next mountain of science knowing we never need climb this one again.

Now that death and resurrection, even of life in the cosmos, is positioned in the context of God's love for the world (John 3:16) a new meaning is given to failure and triumph as hope is given to carry on. Now that Jacob (Israel) continues the Isaac/Ishmael drama finding in faith and righteousness that tribes shall transfigure into a global human family where "all the peoples on earth are blessed" as Abraham's seed of faith, hope and righteousness overcomes the bitter seed of enmity of Adam's fall (Genesis 3:15). We now know that "knowledge will cover the earth as the waters cover the seas" (Isa. 11:9). We know that a salutary human project of science and technology is possible even though the dark underside of Cain's lethal madness and humanities' deleterious mania continues to blight the earth.

Now that Moses has received and articulated *Torah* as the way of life and in Jesus' Sermon on the Mount this has become for the world the will and Word of God, we now know, as Whitehead has shown, a groundwork, ethos and directionality for science. A theology of life, of truth and goodness, a world-view and moral calling which prompts more than maintainative and decorative endeavor but now the genuinely innovative, has been injected into history. Amartya Sen's science and practical work embodies this cultural achievement.

Sen's Science

From this metaphysical heritage, in its knowledge aspect and in collaboration with colleagues who related this philosophical and theological wisdom to economic theory and action, Sen has formulated his science. He is impatient .with religion, psychology and ethics where famine, starvation and poverty are defined as matters of morals, feelings or fatalities. His work reaches for absolute and objective standards—for the truth. Like Marx he is a person of concrete action grounded in conceptual accuracy. Here I see him as a theologian in the strict pre-religious sense of that word as one pursuing the truth and justice of transcending deity within human affairs. Sen expresses this quest in terms of his economic science. The ingredients of that science are:

- SOCIAL CHOICE THEORY
- INEQUALITY THEORY *and*
- ENTITLEMENT *and* PUBLIC ACTION THEORY

Social Choice Theory

At the conjunction point of sociopolitical science, ethics and economics Sen develops a central theme of his scientific thought. At the Delhi School of Economics in the 1960s and 1970s Sen began to formulate his scientific starting point in social choice theory, reflected in *Collective Choice and Social Welfare* (1970). This conceptual model allowed him to gather into a unified field theory the phenomena of poverty, inequality, unemployment, income and living standards. In concert with the London School of Economics and growing out of the course he now taught on

"Social Justice" with Kenneth Arrow and John Rawls, this theory proved statistically and conceptually useful in looking at problems such as liberty and rights and gender inequality as these bore on economic success and deprivation. Social choice theory as defined by Sen in *The Handbook of Mathematical Economics*[2] seeks to identify the "epistemic sets" and "aggregation preferences" which coalesce when value decisions in economics are made. A variant and subset of general utilitarian theory in philosophy, this theory offers quantification models for various qualitative choice made by individuals, and especially collectivities.

An example which Sen uses is the present private and public policy of aggregating the "most vulnerable" (Rawls)—the poor and sick—into cohorts, say for welfare or health provisions—eliminating them from the pool of those provided for from the collective covenant. This occurs as insurance companies cut their losses along with state and federal governments in cordoning off the needy, say in Medicare, Medicaid and Maternal-Child Welfare support. Do such measures, supposedly "bottom-line" efficient, actually maximize benefit and minimize cost? Or do they end up costing more? These utility models do help to accurately depict these choice trees and decisional results. They possess the great truth-value of seeing the actual not hoped for results. Sen argues that the greater range of freedom and choice offered to persons and groups, the greater is aggregate health and prosperity. By constructing his research against the most radical case of deprivation and vulnerability (hunger and famine) he is able to construct models that illuminate meaningful and helpful public policy.

The science here is statistics and mathematical probability, the questionable truth matrix of modern epistemology. This form of knowing (epistemology) and doing (ethics) is common to all of the contemporary sciences especially the new, fledgling human sciences. While this mode of science may convey more ultimate resonance with the computational deity of Descartes and Spinoza, it is the construal of contemporary rationality. The inadequacy of this mathematical approach to human moral choices is highlighted by the work of Rawls and Ricoeur who show that when we ignore "the least of these" we engage in disutility. This is because in ultimate accounting *anawim* receive God's preferential option. Rawls learned this as a young theolog. Ricoeur, also a Reformed theologian, would have us acknowledge not only untoward results but the will and motivations of people, the soul impulses, as to their worthiness, their good or evil.

---

[2] K.J. Arrow, *Handbook of Mathematical Economics* (Intrilligator, Amsterdam: North Holland, 1986) 1073–1181.

Inequality Theory

> *O Roschen rot*
> *Der Mensch liegt in groster Not!*
> *Der Mensch liegt in groster Pein!*
> *Je lieber mocht ich im Himmel sein!*
> *Da kam ich auf einen breiten Weg;*
> *Da kam ein Engelein und wollt'mich abweisen,*
> *Ach nein ich liess mich nicht abweisen!*
> *Ich bin von Gott, und wieder zu Gott!*
> *Der liebe Gott wird mir ein Lichten geben,*
> *Wird leuchten mir bis in das ewig selig'Leben!*
> *Urlicht*
>
> — Gustav Mahler

A little light, like a red rose, radiates from that light beyond light and shimmers in this twilight. Realizing the insufficiency of customary economic theory Sen projects another dimension of his scientific theory, which he calls inequality theory. Sen speaks of this shift in approach as a desire to find a more "practical" and "efficacious" approach to problems. To assess poverty with accuracy, to clarify the nature of relative deprivation (e.g., "Aren't American blacks better off than those in Liberia?"), to assess the efficacy of programs of income security, taxation and enhancement, a more nuanced scientific model was needed. Sen's collaboration with Martha Nussbaum began to disclose the critical importance of the variable of "gender inequality."[3]

In *Inequality Reexamined* (1992) Sen lays out his theory. Since the processes of globalization and global market formation, at least in the tradition of Milton Friedman, do not have concern for human rights, democracy, human harms and dislocations, but principally serve the goals of efficiencies and production, there have to be companion or correlational concerns for education, public participation and "opportunities for society's underdogs" (Sen and Rawls) if those very economic efforts are not to backfire and produce negative utilities.

---

[3] Nussbaum and Sen, "Toward Developmental Ethics" in Wilber Charles, *Ecological Ethics and Public Policy* (Lanham: Rowman & Littlefield, 1989) 320. See also Sen, *Commodities and Capabilities* (Cambridge: Cambridge University Press, 1985) and his *Development and Freedom* (New York: Knopf, 1999).

Sen's science of inequality resonates perfectly with theological science in its doctrines of "preferential option for the poor," "equality," "*Imago Dei*" and "social justice" as the imperatives of *Hashem* and *Shemah,* the being and action (name) of God.

> Hear o, Israel, The Lord our God is One
>
> You shall have no other gods
>
> You shall sanctify (honor, protect and live by) the divine Name
>
> You shall do justice
>
> Recognition of the Divine is made manifest in justice and kindness to fellow humans,
>
> especially the needy.

Equality as Capability

One of the best theological treatments of Sen's economics is Douglas A. Hicks' *Inequality and Ethics* (Cambridge, 2000). Undertaken at Harvard Divinity while working with Sen, this study concentrates on this recent motif in his writing on "equality of basic capability." Whereas "ability" can mean "natural gift" or aggressive competency to get what one wants, "capability" means the actual human capacity to desire not despair, to possess the freedom to pursue one's desire rather than the customary "limited impossibilities." Capability is the enjoyment of operational success in the search for the goods of life.

While "equality" and "capability" move much more into the realm of values than of scientific fact Sen contends that these factors belong at the very core of economic theory. He uses the concept of "space"—we might say "room" to wield one's desire, through freedom into accomplishment. In Sen's Tanner Lectures[4], he uses cognate concepts such as "utility," "opportunity," "resources" (Dworkin) or "primary goods" (Rawls) to signify what seems to me to mean "commanding presence" or the German *achten*—attention. In all these concepts Sen is emphasizing that expressed need, where appropriate, must be heeded and not be denied, and that this commanded and demanded attention must be extended to all. Basic human rights and theological goods, not utopian fantasies, have now been incorporated into economics. With his Harvard colleague, John Rawls, he sees the right "to be seen, heard and answered (*verantworten*)" to extend to the weakest, the most vulnerable, those in "the original position" whose presence and cry is often invisible and inaudible.

---

[4] See Sterling M. McMurrin, ed., *The Tanner Lectures on Human Values,* v. 1 (Cambridge, 1980).

Capability means to be able to function with dignity (again standing or presence). Building on Sen's *The Standard for Living* (Cambridge, 1987) and his collaboration with Martha Nussbaum, *Quality of Life* (Oxford: Clarendon, 1993) Hicks specifies "capability" as some "functions (considered elementary) like being well-nourished, having basic shelter, escaping morbidity, breathing unpolluted air, being disease-free . . . and other (functionings) more complex . . . having self-respect, preserving human dignity, taking part in life of the community and appearing in public without shame."[5]

Sen is also aware of the perplexity of this doctrine expressed by Gilbert and Sullivan: "if everybody's somebody then nobody's anybody[6]." Because of the immense variation in cultural expectations, perceptions, and means to deliver the goods it may be the case that equality extended may mean that some are denied, especially women. Demanding equality for men's and women's restrooms in opera houses or in per capita health care coverage will simply mean less care for women because pregnancy and other gender-specific needs require extraordinary care. Science, as this case points out, is an ethical phenomenon: it draws truth from falsehood, beauty from formlessness, goodness (justice) from the amorphous void. Sen exemplifies this characteristic.

In *Women and Human Development: The Capabilities Approach*, Martha Nussbaum takes capability doctrine an important further step. Like Sen, impatient with abstractions and moral shibboleths, Nussbaum seeks concrete help for poor women in their struggles for subsistence, adequate means to live, dignity and the verve and delight of capability. As we shall see later when we discuss Sen's notions of *unfreedom*, women in the world are disproportionately harmed by being "less well nourished than men, less healthy, and more vulnerable to physical violence (including war) and sexual abuse" (from the book jacket).

Nussbaum defines "capabilities" as what a person is able "to be and do." This basic core-value, born in high religion—promulgated by Aristotle, Kant, then Marx—affirms that each person is an end in herself—not just a means to an end. When persons become tools of production (Marx), slaves (violation of the eighth commandment: 'do not steal') to anyone or anything, their God-given "capability" is abrogated.

---

[5] Douglas Hicks, *Inequality and Ethics* (Cambridge, 2000) 26, 27.
[6] From W.S. Gilbert and Arthur Sullivan's *Gondoliers* (comic opera, 1889). Recently reprinted in Ian Bradley, ed., *Complete Annotated Gilbert & Sullivan* (New York: Oxford University Press, 1996, 2001).

With disarming and provocative specificity Nussbaum identifies the following "capabilities" which ought to be sought and guaranteed in our common life in the world:

- Life (lifespan)
- Bodily health (including reproduction)
- Bodily integrity (movement, non-violence)
- Senses, imagination, thought
- Emotions
- Practical reason (freedom of conscience)
- Affiliation (self-respect)
- Other species (animals, plants)
- Play (laugh, recreation)
- Control over environment (political and material)[7]

This rich array of capabilities are held forth as worthy of recognition as universal values, global human rights, and qualities worth providing and protecting in public policy. Nussbaum is the Ernst Freund Professor at the University of Chicago, with appointments in law, ethics, philosophy and divinity—an interdisciplinary scholar like one we will later meet, again at University of Chicago, Leon Kass. Nussbaum's work in science and theology, technology and ethics speaks well to the coupled concerns of this book. Deeply steeped in pre-Socratic as well as Socratic (Plato and Aristotle) philosophy, knowledgeable in Jewish, Christian, Islamic and Indic faith and ethics, Nussbaum insists that we must "come clean," disown our worldly violence, and affirm the commands and convictions of our faith heritage. Quoting as superscript of her chapter on "the role of religion" she cites law student Heera Nawaz of the Bangalore College of Law:

> Although all religions were initially founded with the aim of purifying men and women and helping them live ethical lives through prayer, it was found in some instances that blind traditions, customs and superstition often resulted in—not the cathartic effects of religion—but the spread of communalism, fanaticism, fundamentalism and discrimination.[8]

---

[7] Martha Nussbaum, *Women and Human Development: The Capabilities Approach* (Cambridge, 2000) 72.

[8] Nussbaum, *Women and Development*, 107.

Capabilities, I would argue, are competencies (Ivan Illich) assured and secured in our creation as children of God, children of society and children of the earth. They are inalienable human endowments and rights, which therefore convey inexorable societal duties to provide and protect. Darwinian economics, prevalent from Adam Smith to Milton Friedman ride roughshod over this philosophical and theological heritage. Nussbaum and Sen vividly recall it to our lost conscience.

Drawing an ironic blessing from Hamlet's words of bitter vengeance Nussbaum and Sen draw vision of a new world:

> ... whether tis nobler in the mind to suffer
> the slings and arrows of outrageous fortune;
> Or take arms against a sea of troubles,
> And by opposing, end them.
> ... to say we end the heart-ache and
> the thousand natural shocks that flesh is heir to
> tis a consummation devoutly to be wished.

To seek a newer world, with implications of rejecting one gone wrong in injustice is a Divine and sublimely human impulse.

ENTITLEMENT AND PUBLIC ACTION THEORY

> There are more things in heaven and on earth, Horatio,
> Than are dreamed of in your philosophy[9]

Hamlet again offers an epistemic reach which characterizes Sen's work. His gravitation to more radical, even transcendent categories of knowledge and action leads him into the avenues of natural law philosophy, theology and political theory where inherent human rights (e.g., life and liberty) are seen as data of truth and experience. It also opens his thought to what we have identified as Abrahamic or Monotheistic science where a theistically grounded and ethically governed Universe is an assumption of scientific reality. Beyond such ontology Sen also defines "entitlements" in a pragmatic fashion as "bundles of goods over which persons establish ownership through production and trade."[10]

The most extreme cases of impoverishment—famines—find their etiology not in the vicissitudes of nature or in some enigmatic evil force

---

[9] *Hamlet*, 1.5. Reference is to act and scene.
[10] Sen, Tanco Lecture (August, 1990), privately provided document.

or judgment but rather in "entitlement failures." "Famines are initiated by severe loss of entitlements of one or more occupation groups, depriving them of the opportunity to command and consume food."[11] Though my interpretation goes beyond Sen's conviction I would argue that the "right to food" is a "command." The charter of all ethics—theistic and humanistic—is that ancient dictum seen on the sarcophagus of Tutankhamen and reprised in Hebrew ethics and Jesus' inaugural sermon:

> Feed the hungry, Clothe the naked, Set at liberty the oppressed, Heal the sick.[12]

Sen rightly sees the phenomenon of accessibility to food as a personal right, initiative and responsibility as well as an aggregate (community) burden and opportunity. To see it as "command" is to root it in *Shemah/Hashem*—our obedience to God in the service of humanity in the world. Sen's unspoken premises are a divinely given and guided world and the obligation of human interdependence—"the one and the many."

Sen's Ethics

Given the practical bent of his theory and the tight linkage of theory and practice Sen's ethics are almost inseparable from his science. His core ethical ideas are:

- DEVELOPMENT *and* FREEDOM
- DEVELOPMENT *and* THE COMMON GOOD
- DEVELOPMENT *and* MEANING

Just as refined utility theory marks his science a search to ameliorate harms and enlarge fulfillments and enrichments within the human condition and circumstance comprises Sen's ethics. Human development in the holistic sense—psychological, social, political and economic—is the goal of his practical proposals, his economic policies. The watchword for this cluster of convictions called "development" is first seen as a correlate and concomitant of freedom.

---

[11] Sen, Tanco Lecture, 6.
[12] Matthew 25.

Development and Freedom

For Sen development and freedom are inseparable if not conjoined realities. "Development can be seen as a process expanding the real freedom that people enjoy."[13] His view of freedom, a precondition of happiness and well-being, of delight, choice and responsibility is thoroughly Hebraic. Only in such holistic development is justice and shalom achieved. In Hebraic ethics the precondition of freedom is to eliminate "unfreedom" just as the precondition of belief is to remove idolatry. In this vein Sen begins his discussion of development and freedom with the imperative to remove the personal and structural impediments to freedom or the sources of "unfreedom"—what the Bible calls bondage or tyranny:

> Development requires the removal of the major sources of unfreedom: poverty as well as tyranny, poor economic opportunities as well as systemic social deprivation, neglect of public facilities as well as intolerance or overacting of repressive states.[14]

In positioning antagonism to freedom both in the personal apathy and will and in societal negligence and oppression Sen is echoing a biblical view of good and evil in the human condition—individual and collective. Unfreedom produces undevelopment. This, of course, is also the underlying premise of libertarian and conservative political philosophy and economics. Milton Friedman's root premise for vigorous economic vitality is "non-interference" with free markets and entrepreneurial activity. Sen goes farther linking justice and salutary (upbuilding) actions as concomitants of freedom. This we know in both Erasmian and Lutheran economic ethics—freedom is best expressed in human service.

At this point I can offer a theological perspective on Sen's starting point. What social scientists call "development" theology calls "the Reign of God." In this realm with its pristine freedom, goodness, justice and abundance flourish in and for the world. Yes, the world has been tragically reduced in "unfreedom," bondage, violence and exploitation to a sorry state of affairs. The cry of the poor, like the cry of Nelson Mandela from his island prison, reaches the feeling "heart of God." Judgment ensues. Acquisitiveness, oppression, inequality, violence and unfreedom fall under the natural and spiritual sanctions of a "Righteous God." This judgment in some way resembles the utilitarian calculus where untoward consequences weigh out, only this justice cannot be fooled or manipulated. If the poor

---

[13] Sen, *Development as Freedom* (New York: Knopf, 1999) 3.

[14] Sen, *Development as Freedom*, 3.

and vulnerable, the widow and the orphan are not served, disharmony and unfreedom ensue.

Here again, as often in this study, we face the theological issue of accountability—divine and human—in our scientific knowledge and technological application. One reason I added Sen to our roster of exemplars of efficacious science and ethical technology is that, like medicine, every thought and act is of supreme human consequence. Ethics is an indispensable dimension of knowledge. *Conscientia* is an integral concomitant of *scientia*. Sen is an admirable exemplar of this phenomenon.

The news this morning (July 9, 2003) comes from Singapore that Laleh and Laden Bijani, 27-year-old Siamese twins from Iran, have died after more than 50 hours of surgery separating the women, conjoined at the head, sharing a major cerebral artery. German surgeons had refused to do the surgery, seven years earlier, because of the high risk presented by the shared blood vessel. The cause of death was bleeding and unstable blood pressure. The young women had received full informed consent and had vigorously requested the procedure, knowing the high probability of one or both dying or being left brain-dead.

In the human application of science, in cases such as this, knowledge and technique are always fraught with the unknown and unpredicted. The knowledge and application are burdened therefore with a kind of epistemic and ethical gravitas such as that which informs Sen's work. Knowledge of subatomic matter and the composition of the atmosphere on Mars may indirectly, one day, affect the fate of the Bijani twins. But, for now, this is more humanly inconsequential knowledge. Sen, though, moves our heart and mind along the pathways of life and death, suffering and happiness, which testifies to the inescapable theological and ethical dimension of science and technology.

The "unfreedoms," which are amenable to human choice and action, are listed by Sen as "positive rights":

- Freedom from hunger and chronic malnutrition
- Freedom from inadequate health services
- Freedom from "premature ends"[15]

Science, Sen argues, is knowledge in order to development. Its very nature is active, ethical and dynamic. When we can gauge the consequences

[15] See Javier I. Echeverria, "*Development and Freedom in Sen and Guitierrez: Religious and Secular Common Grounds*" (privately distributed online; to be published as a part of symposium by University of Notre Dame Press).

of "unfreedoms" and the "De-development" this fosters we have evidence for the necessity of applied scientific action. Here we see the importance of ethical research where the sponsors demand follow-through in terms of the knowledge that comes to light through the study. Those who initiate research must be prepared to follow through with the consequences or prospects of the knowledge they uncover. Einstein and Oppenheimer, for example, called for the physicists to be accountable for the bomb they were building. When an efficacious remedy for a problem is researched and proven it must then be provided to those who need it. When pharmaceutical companies, for example, establish that medications effect persons positively or adversely they are obliged to provide or withdraw those medications. Social science research has the same societal obligation. When universities, governments, industries, the United Nations or any other party accepts or appropriates money from community resources for scientific or technological research and development they must stand accountable for the consequences and contributions of that work.

An example: Merck Pharmaceuticals, along with other drug companies, has received the benefits of societal tax incentives and has utilized publicly funded universities in its research for drugs to combat HIV/AIDS. To recoup their own research and development costs and to provide strong earnings for their owners and workers they assess exorbitantly large profits in the early phases of the medicine's distribution. If this Robin Hood measure is to meet the ethical bar it should provide these drugs for reasonable costs for the poor of Africa and Asia. Knowledge should be seen in this ethical manner even in our highly commercialized world. Again, in Sen's concept this approach must be secured in freedom not coercion.

DEVELOPMENT AND THE COMMON GOOD

Today (July 20, 2003) I visited St. Mary's University Church in Cambridge. Here Ridley, Cramner, Erasmus and Bucer preached. Martin Bucer, Calvin's mentor in Strasbourg was called here as Regis Professor of Divinity in 1550. He was buried in St. Mary's, but his remains were later exhumed and burned by enemies of the Reformation. While at the university he composed his masterwork—*De Regno Christi*—which sketches in detail the nature of the "common good" and the sociopolitical condition of the nation in terms of concrete policies on work, welfare, refugees, food, water, economics and the like. As had Calvin, then in Geneva, he subscribed to an economic theology of the world where it was seen as an organism enfolded within the Will of God wherein some were rich and some were poor, serving each other in *le mystère des pauvre et des riches*.[16]

In this sacramental/political network God makes provision for bread for the world and the goods for life, after the paradigm of *manna* in the wilderness (Exodus 16, John 6, 2 Cor. 8:13ff.). All goods are freely distributed into this world in order that the whole people and the whole creation might flourish. This reciprocal covenant of sharing and *koinonia* enlivens and ingratiates the human family, all creatures and all creation.

> He opens His hand and satisfies the desire of every living thing
> (Ps. 145:16)

The disruption of this Shalom, which is commandment, is stealing, hoarding, greed. In the manna commentary Calvin paints the scene where manna sufficient covers the ground like snow. Everyone gathers what is needed and all are satisfied. But some, like the "grab all you can while you can" herdsmen in the "tragedy of the commons" take more than their fair share, hoard it, store it under their bed in the trunk where it rapidly becomes moldy. The "common good" and its covenant have been breached and the world goes rancid.

Development and Meaning

> The land is marked for desolation
> And unless we plant the seeds of
> Cities and villages in the human
> Bosom Albion must be a rock of blood
>
> — William Blake, "Jerusalem"[17]

Our discussion now moves to the final feature of Sen's ethics. The epitome of this ethicist-economist's vision is found in the meaning with which he imbues the economic endeavor. Though he hesitates to use the language of theology he is talking of the same sphere that Calvin saw in covenantal terms as the "theatre of God's glory." The ecumenical system of the life-world with its architectural structure; its substructural foundation of the

---

[16] For some consideration of this "mystery of the poor and the rich," see André Bélier, *La pensée économique et sociale de Calvin* (Geneva: Cerf, 1965).

[17] The William Blake Trust, *The Illuminated Books of William Blake, Vol. 1* (Princeton, NJ: Princeton University Press, 1998) 271.

resources for life and its flourishing; the infrastructure of its lineaments and conduits of justice and provision and the superstructure of its consummate meaning all find expression in Sen's articulation of meaning and development. Even in his own mathematical and statistical analyses his reader feels at home and welcome as an inhabitant of an amiable worldhouse.

Sen's creativist interpretation of development—built on his affirmation of entitlement and capability—is a move beyond traditional economic philosophy's focus on wages, incomes, markets and spending. He has now gravitated to a new basis of moral economics in human virtue (transcending power) and social justice. When a servant, broken down, is seen "kneeling under the weight of work beyond one's capacity,"[18] the multiple violations of inequality, unfreedom and injustice are manifest. Meaning is the inversion of those negatives or the positive presence of the fulfilled needs, choices, aspirations and capabilities. Human development in Sen's purview is the "right to one's life."[19]

Rabindranath Tagore, India's greatest philosopher, affirms that this meaning is transcendent:

> In his experiments with creating life the Creator suddenly becomes quite daring when he comes to creating human beings. He does not confine the freedom of its soul. Outwardly the species is thrown naked, armourless and weak in all respects while its soul is freed to fly. Elated by the joy of this freedom it cries out: "I shall do the impossible!"— meaning I shall not accept that what has been happening all the time will continue to happen—what does not happen will also happen.[20]

Sen and the Ethical Dimension of Theology for Science

Of our exemplars Amartya Sen best represents the ethical dimension of a theology for science. This claim is not based on any moral superiority found in the man, although, like Schweitzer, we find a compelling witness to social and global justice in his work and a passion for the poor and downtrodden. I choose him rather to illustrate the ethical dimension because he is able to restore the science of economics to this valuational

---

[18] Amartya Sen, *Jibanjatra o Arthaniti, Arthaniti Granthamala* 7, Ananda Pib. Translated from Bengali by Anisur Rahman (Calcutta, 1990) 105.

[19] Sen, *Jibanjatra*, 105.

[20] Tagore in Rahman, "Amartya Sen and the Search for Meaning." Unpublished paper provided by Sen.

construal. Though his 1998 Nobel Prize was highly controversial, especially among the more libertarian economists in the University of Chicago tradition, his honor was well earned and perhaps more worthy of Nobel's stated purpose ("to acknowledge service to humankind") than other recent laureates. Sen shows in the very nature of his understanding and practice of economic science what we wish to show as a theology for science and an ethic for technology.

Economics, of course, has a very close affinity to ethics itself. The words are almost synonymous. *Economics* literally means the norms or rules for the house. The word *ethics* derives from *ethos* meaning stable, *habitus,* or house where the salience for manners or mores is habituated. In the study of the disciplines—their nature and distinctiveness (*Der Grenze der Wissenschaften*)—Weizsäcker taught that all of the sciences, including economics, took definition and substance from one or another aspect of the substance of reality. Yes there is the human and Kantian truth that all disciplines of knowledge and technology (*reine und praktische Vernunft*) are constructs of the human mind with, at best, only explanatory success (or failure) in describing or defining reality. Causality, certainly, is a construct of the human mind making some sense in explaining natural processes. Weizsäcker, the modern formulator of the Kant-Laplace theory of the origin of the universe, is well aware of this philosophy of science. Still he argues that just as the very nature of the discipline of physics is defined by the phenomenology of matter and energy as these realities (concepts) continue to be defined and refined, economics inheres in the very moral substance of making the world work for the good of her inhabitants. This is done by the discovery (and invention) of laws which pertain to transactions in the world (house rules).

Not only does economics relate with profound affinity to ethics, it is also a moral art that transcends the structures and dynamics of the exchanges of life. Sen's writings of 1971, 1982, 1984, 1987, 1989, 1991 and 1999 (French), listed at the beginning of this chapter, all grapple with the issue of whether norms (*nomos*) inhere intrinsically in natural processes or supervene, overarch and undergird as extrinsic judgments. The word *nomos* or norm implies an objective, non wavering standard among the changeability of natural phenomena—the data of economics.

My thesis contends that science, to be true to its theological source must be resolutely ethical. Goodness (justice) is of the order of truth. This characteristic of true and good science can be illustrated by four examples beginning with economics and proceeding to nuclear energy and weaponry, ecology and biological genetics.

Ethical Economics

Sen's entire life's work struggles to show moral parameters in the very warp and woof of economics. Letiche's assembly of his ethical writing *On Ethics and Economics* (Blackwell, 1989) and volume II of his collected works (Belknap, 2003) exhibit the necessary connection. Without the ethical dimension economics becomes a loose cannon on the ground of human endeavor. Norms, we will contend, inhere in the very thought/act of the discipline. Despite the self-evidence of their value-laden nature some still argue that economic patterns are value-free, functioning in their own autonomy. Markets, for example, are said to move by the pseudo-theological concept of an "invisible hand," like something from Dr. Strangelove. Demand controls price and supply, it is held, with inexorable fixity and predictability. In my view there is a natural law that normatively guides economic activity, but that direction comes through responsible human action. Societies may choose to follow Darwin, Malthus or Sen.

Nuclear Energy and Weaponry

On the eve of a missile attack of Israel (with America's blessing) on an alleged "Hamas" training center south of Damascus (October 6, 2003) the world seems dangerously close to the three previous instances of earth threat from nuclear "weapons of mass destruction:"

- US and Hiroshima/Nagasaki
- US/Soviet Union and the Cuban missile crisis
- Israel in the 1967 war with Syria and Egypt

Does nuclear knowledge and capability have an ethical dimension? Robert Oppenheimer, after serious study of Sanskrit and the Vedas, lamented: "we physicists have known sin." An interesting phrase! Is their culpability, complicity or neutrality found in the basic knowledge of physics—atomic structure, nuclear fission and fusion—quarks, subatomic particles or black holes? Boyle and Newton would object. After all, is not all human insight the afterthought of divine wisdom? Or is it only as scientists (and engineers) build bombs, and as politicians order their use against enemies, and as pilots and bombardiers drop them (think of the conscientious objection of Israeli pilots to bomb civilian targets in Palestine), that ethics come into play? In this thesis I hold that responsibility is implicit in the knowledge itself, in the scientific endeavor (and I say this as an emeritus faculty at the University of Illinois, winner of two Nobel Prizes in science—medicine and physics—in 2003) and in the technological application. One could argue that the pure abstract formula, $E=mc^2$, is ethically neutral. If it is never utilized in any endeavor or is never intended to be used (in the design and formulation of the knowledge), it may be ethically benign. Mind games and fantasies are often spun out free of will or desire but for the most part the pure mathematical act of formulation leads inevitably, even necessarily where it is intended to experimentation and validation. Even though we must acknowledge the salutary ambition for the peaceful uses of atomic energy (as in nuclear medicine or electricity generation) we must concede that knowledge itself is *techne*—to know is to do.

Ecology

Ecology is a cognate science to economics. They are sciences of the *oikos*—the earth house. Indeed in today's frontiers of theology concerns of place and resources have blended (Moltmann) to inform a new conceptual basis for this scientific realm. The study of living systems—Edwin Wilson's *Sociobiology or Consilience*, paul Ehrlich's *The Machinery of Nature* or Freemon Dyson's *Imagined Worlds* all call our attention to the intricate web of all living things and to the values of sustenance, maintenance, equilibrium and flourishing and the disvalues of extinction, destruction, overuse and stress. The study of the black crow population in Chicago after the West Nile virus or toxic mold pulmonary hemorrhaging in Northern England exhibits conclusively the connection of knowledge and ethics in the felicitous and deleterious aspects of environmental action. That harm may rise to the level of legal action although the rapidly deteriorating ozone layer gives scant comfort to the promise for corrective public action. An insult may take years of legal activity (cigarette smoking) before even modest public response occurs. With Sen's unfree or exploited issues may never reach the level of alarm and preventive or corrective action—lead poisoning or toxic waste dumping in poor neighborhoods. As the sciences fragment into more and more minute specializations and as new cross-disciplinary fields of knowledge and action emerge the connection of science with ethics will become apparent.

Molecular (Genetic) Science

If the ethical parameter is evident in the nuclear (cosmic) economic and ecologic realms it is profoundly evident in the molecular realm of bioscience. Knowledge about how life works could not help but be morally provocative even at the purely conceptual level. When knowledge of how cells are constituted and how they function moves to the level of alteration, manipulation, cessation or renovation, "all hell and heaven breaks loose." The age of Darwin to Dawkins, of Mendel to Genome, becomes so overwhelmingly controversial, especially when science and theology are involved, that science sometimes stops (recombinant DNA moratorium) or technology is put on hold (stem cell research and implementation). This zone of human ethical concern is so poignant and important that we devote our entire last chapter to the matter by viewing the work of Leon Kass, M.D., Ph.D., Director of the U.S. Presidential Office on Stem Cell and Bioethics Policy.

While physicians and economists have been reluctant to concede ethical implications to their work the biologists and physicians, in particular, like the ecologists, seem kindly disposed to this consideration. Indeed they have opened up major efforts of exploration, research, teaching and consultation within the domain of biomedicine.

Celia Deane-Drummond, a scientist-theologian and Director of the Center for Religion and the Biosciences at Chester College, University of Liverpool, illustrates such work going on to probe, promote and elucidate the ethical dimension of bioscience. For example, *Reordering Nature: Theology, Society and the New Genetics* (London: T & T Clark, 2003) has Templeton Prize winning chemist-theologian Arthur Peacock 'relating genetics to theology on the map of scientific knowledge'(p. 122ff). Peacock uses the scheme of W. Bechtel and A. Abrahamsen, philosophers of science in their book *Connectionism and the Mind* (Cambridge: Blackwell, 1991) to chart such connectivity. This chart shows, as the Weizsäcker illustration did earlier, that all human knowledge is interrelated and that any singular piece of knowledge spreads ramifications across the entire spectrum of human comprehension and utilization. Ethics, therefore, is a rudimentary assumption of all knowledge and technology.

Figure 5.1 *The relation of disciplines (an elaboration of Figure 8.1 of W. Bechtel and A. Abrahamsen, Connectionism and the Mind (Oxford and Cambridge, MA: Blackwells, 1991).*

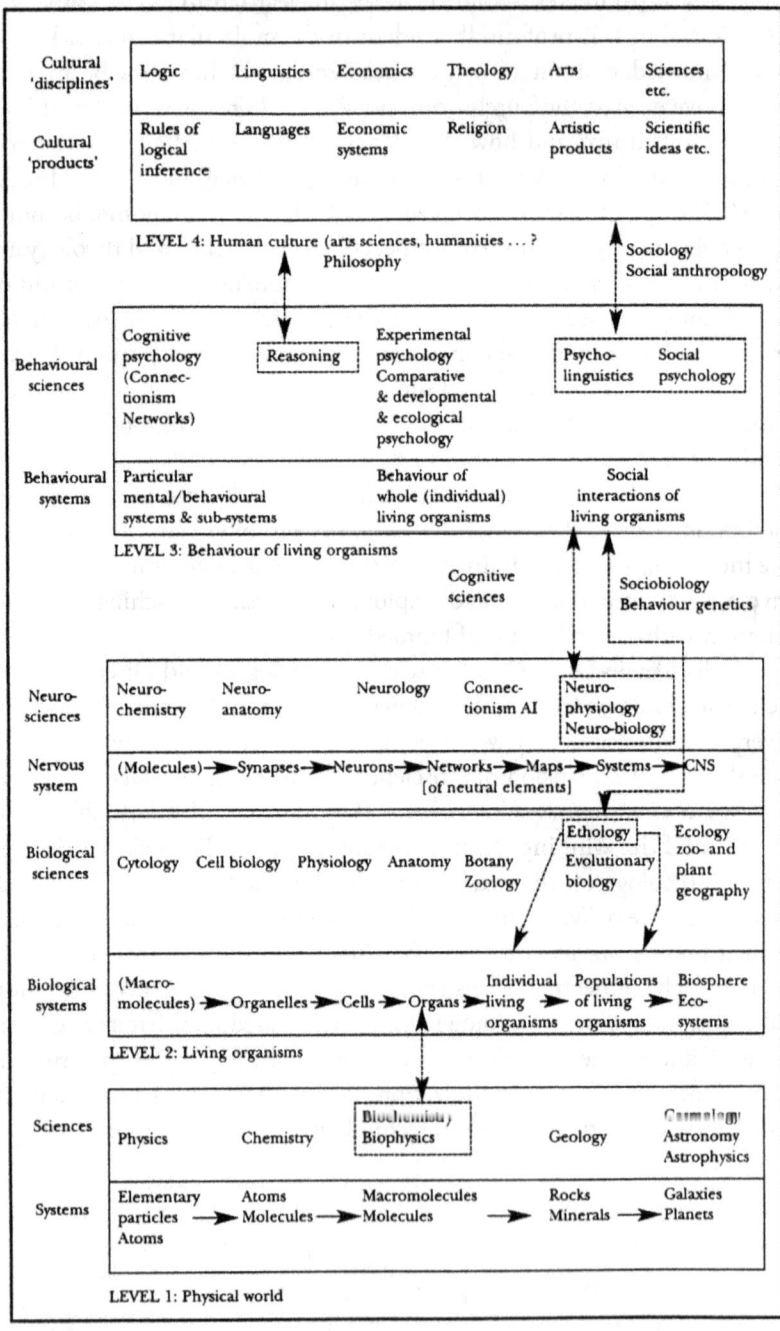

Excursus: Jürgen Moltmann, Science and Wisdom

The foregoing analysis of the political theology of Amartya Sen with focused attention on the vector of ethics as an accent of his work invites us to consider the resonating theological work of one who has been called the preeminent theologian of the late twentieth century. Moltmann's book on *Science and Wisdom* further commends him to our attention in this book. He becomes a natural, almost compelling correlational thinker to Sen as Torrance and Weizsäcker do with Robert Boyle. Moltmann's life work corresponds closely with the theological impulses of the project. The leitmotif of his thought is Akedah—the crucified God. The reader will have traced this interpretive theme from the beginning of this book in the work of Abrahamic thinkers like Avicenna and Maimonides, through Schweitzer and Teilhard and on to Kass. A constant theme in Moltmann is iconoclastic truth and radical justice—a strong theme in this study. Finally, he projects a future where religious eschatology, human political planning and technological possibility unfold in synchrony as the divine and human spirit interplay and collaborate.

Theology of Hope (Theologie der Hoffnung) appeared in the turbulent year of 1965. Student unrest against stifling authoritarianism, social oppression and the Viet Nam war gripped society. The book shook the world with its focus on the God of history who was champion of the oppressed of the world. The strong influence of Marxist philosopher Ernst Bloch was felt throughout. The enduring power of the book was a reassertion of the message of Schweitzer, 60 years earlier some miles down the Rhine, of thoroughgoing eschatology which encouraged Jews, Christians and secularists (Jürgen Habermas) to confront the crises of world history within the impulse of a hope that will not put up with the world as it is because of the divine promise of the redemptive future which judges every unjust and unfulfilled present.

Theology of Hope was followed by *The Crucified God* (1972) where the pivotal theme in Luther's "theology of the cross" (*Der gekreuzte Gott*) is elaborated as the companioning, liberating, evil-confronting and evil-overcoming One who in suffering has sympathized with and has undertaken the human plight. In resurrection He has released overcoming redemptive power into the world in order that God be glorified, creation be liberated and humanity be made well and whole. This proleptic achievement grounds present protest, constructive hope and creative planning.

It was from Moltmann that this young pastor first developed what I have called an akedic theology. From my work-bench and bedside setting in the world of biology and medicine in the 1960s and 1970s, this theocentric cosmology and philosophy offered a broad-band interpretive mechanism to explain (make plain and show the way) the phenomena of life and death, health and suffering, disease and pain, healing, caring, restoration and resurrection.

Through my work as a biblical theologian, one for whom biblical interpretation was the central axis of theology, I tried to follow Barth and Moltmann in making exegesis fundamental to the formulation of religious philosophy and ethics. The dynamic realities of the history of God and of the travail of the human condition were well fathomed and formulated by this motif. Here was a metaphor, grounded in the architectonic event of Abrahamic faith and testing which comprehended:

- Love and creation
- Temptation and Fall
- Sacrifice and Forgiveness
- Resurrection and New Life

Moltmann amplified Barth's biblical theology with an even more celebrative view of Creation, a more positive rendering of human initiatives and tasks and a more explicit and clear political format. It was working toward a theology for science in his mind—a course which I would follow.

In recent years Moltmann has written books such as *Hope and Planning* (1971), *The Experiment Hope* (1975), *Future of Creation* (1979), *God in Creation* (1985), *The Spring of Life* (1992) and *Science and Wisdom* (2003). All of these studies deepen his consideration of theology and science. Many secondary studies have attended to this phase of his work including Celia Deane-Drummond's *Ecology in Jürgen Moltmann's Theology* (Edwin Mellen Press, 1997). Far from just "jumping on the bandwagon" this turn in Moltmann's research grows naturally out of his early Christological theology. Science itself, as we attempt to show in this study, is an attempt to fathom the human predicament, to ameliorate the human plight, to heal the sick and create a better future. The future and direction of science is therefore an inescapably theological-messianic and eschatological matter—thus Moltmann's concern. The advance of science is therefore a fundamental challenge to theology just as the scientific advance of theology is radically important to science.

Monotheism, Tritheism and Trinitarianism in Moltmann's Theology for Science

The apologetic task—interpreting science to theology and interpreting theology to science—thus becomes vital for the truth claims of both realms. For Moltmann this hermeneutical endeavor begins with a reenacting of Augustine's *De Trinitate*—the rehearsal of the Trinitarian formulation. Part of the dynamism of Moltmann's theology is the active pursuit of the Living God of Israel, Jesus and the Spirit active in the world. This pursuit entails the quest to discover the energy of Jehovah, the movement of the Abrahamic (Akedic) impulse, the directionality of Mosaic and prophetic covenant, the transformative messianic redemption and the release of spirit renewal within the very knowledge acquisition and historical (technical) process unfolding in today's world. As with Thomas Aquinas' awakening within the insights of Avicenna and Maimonides in the early medieval world Moltmann finds the recovery of an Hebraocentric theology, a vivid Christology and a dynamic pneumatology a precondition for the arrival at a true and good science.

He elucidates this probe first in an early exploration on *Jewish Monotheism and Christian Trinitarian Doctrine: A Dialogue by Pinchas Lapide and Jürgen Moltmann* (Philadelphia: Fortress, 1979). It continues through his monumental work on the trinity and the Spirit in the 1990s. Lapide, an Orthodox Israeli Jew, engaged Moltmann in dialogue on these crucial issues in a West German parish in 1978. The dialogue presupposes an openness of insight such as that exemplified in Maimonides' parable about various sages in *The Guide for the Perplexed* (3:51) where Rabbis, philosophers and Christian teachers all approach the same king. Lapide extols the glory and triumph of God as revealed in Judaism (perfected in truth) and Christianity (commissioned to fulfill the "Way" in the world). Moltmann, with help from Abraham Heschel, draws on the "suffering God" who in *Shekinah* and *Sophia*—companioning compassion—visits the sick and shares the anguish of His exiles in the world.

"The Jew," writes Lapide, "recognizes the 'One God' in all His raiments" (p. 26). Rejecting polytheism and henotheism under the authority of *Shemah* and C. 1 & 2, only the unity of God can assure unity of faith, which alone can secure unity of knowledge and truth about reality. The *Shemah Israel* and derivative Decalogue is on the lips of every observant Jew (including Jesus and Paul) five times during each day and on the lips of each son and daughter of Israel in the hour of death. Not only will the consummation of earth history be seen when the world community of all faiths acknowledge "The God of Abraham," but also penultimate concord, justice and truth are only known within the unity of God. This is the ground of any concomitant comprehension of the universe. As the flesh was being flayed with an iron comb from the body of Rabbi Akiba his last words were *Echad*—"oneness"—as his soul breathed its last (p. 29). As Akedic Passover hovered near the body of Jesus at the moment of the sacrifice of the lambs Jesus prayed "that they may be One . . . as you Father and I are One" (John 17). The receipt, enrichment and relinquishment of life on this earth ("our reasonable sacrifice") are in the "Oneness" of *Hashem*—the One Name that is above every Name. Maimonides' second article in the Thirteen Truths of Faith is "that the Creator is One, and there is no Oneness that is in any way like God and that 'God was . . . is . . . and will be'" (p. 30). This assertion is the precondition of our being and of life in the world. This *unificatio* is linked to wisdom (*Sophia*)—which is Messiah. It gathers the one human family and the *uni-verse* of all creatures into the divine family. It signals the direction for the universe and the theology for science.

Defending and articulating a Catholic, Orthodox or Protestant doctrine of the Trinity is a work to affirm and preserve monotheism. As with Augustine in *De Trinitate*, Moltmann points to Book 12 of Aristotle's *Metaphysics*, where a "philosophical monotheism" (recall Thomas Aquinas on Avicenna and Maimonides) of the "one simple, unmoved, apathetic, immortal divine being monarchically constituted the one reality: One God, one law, one world" (12:1072b4–1073b14). Both Israel and the Church adopted this philosophical monotheism, monarchism (one God and King) and ethical monolatry as they submitted their revelations to the thought forms of Roman-Roman culture. This, of course, was an ambiguous commitment since the biblical disclosure is Asiatic and European, Oriental and Occidental—indeed a universal concept. For this reason these faiths saw beyond Aristotle to another aspect of the unified divine nature that transcended the brilliance of Greek philosophy. This was the aspect of adventurism and passion overwhelming the "unmoved and apathetic" divine ontology of the Greeks. God as an outgoing, pathos animated, collaborative presence with oppressed and suffering humanity is derived more from the bible than philosophy, more from the creating and incarnating One than *demiurgos*. Building on Maimonides then Spinoza, Heschel postulated this divine quality as that which animated the risk of the creation; which suffered through the anguish of akedic sonship —Abraham and Sarai, Isaac and Ebed Israel.

This One God, now a sympathetic partner with Exile Israel (whom that God had subjected to exile) and with the messianic (anointed to regality and suffering) people of *Judentum*, *Christentum* and *Dar al Islam* fashions covenant with Abrahamic humanity, Israel, the Church and the whole world, now exuding aspects of Lordship, Sonship and Spirit at the point where entry into and absorption of historical humanity has made the human plight and prospect forever the divine project. Heschel sees this "divine abasement" as the outgoing love of God for His people and His creation. Science and technology can now be seen as a work of unifying and glorifying *Hashem*—the Name. The irradiation of God into the history of nature (Weizsäcker) both in epistemological disclosure and ethical direction is the matrix of science.

Monotheism therefore and its Hebraic unification and Christian triunification are formulations and construals of the singular reality of God an of His bestowed world which is received through the grace and love of the One God who is "given over" into and to that world and who, in partnership with the households of faith and with greater humanity, is seeking messianically to heal and restore creation (*Tikkun Olam*) to its original and ultimate Oneness and Shalom.

Moltmann's theology of Hope, of Akedah ("crucified God") and his teaching about theology and science come together in his book *Science and Wisdom*. Here are some of the convictions that he offers:

- Wisdom signifies "insightful" and "guidance-full" knowledge
- Wisdom is about the paradoxical Akedah where ignorance is knowledge, simplicity is profundity, weakness is power, suffering is strength, death is life.
- Wisdom is the Word of God crying out in the creation for searchers and understanding.

- "Fear of the Lord" (see *Fear and Trembling*, Kierkegaard's study of Abraham and Isaac) is "the beginning of wisdom."[21]
- Wisdom discerns the limitation of knowledge and the necessity of faith. Just a tiny bit (mustard seed) is an enormous (sufficient) amount.
- Theology abandoned metaphysics (certainty) when it turned to the God of Abraham, Isaac and Jacob and the God of Christ.
- Wisdom's hope for the future (Messiah's resurrection and embedded redemption of cosmos) is hope for the world and its salutary future—therefore science.
- Wisdom posits fullness in partiality—"now we know in part, then fully, as we have been fully known" (1 Cor 13:12).
- *Phronesis* entails knowledge and ethics. It is practical wisdom knowing "what," "why," and "what for" in our knowing and doing.
- Natural science is a *sapientia practica*.
- Reverence for life (however small, Schweitzer might add) is the foremost commandment of the "right to life."
- Kenotic theology (Philippians 2) sees glorification and fullness of God in creation in "self-restriction," in love giving over life to and for the creation. God dwells in the midst of his exiled, suffering, world-placed and world-bound creatures. Science and its correlative wisdom is "living well" within this frame and condition.[22]
- God creates in love, in self-limitation, in order to allow room for human freedom and flourishing.
- Wonder (*thaumazein*) and wisdom (*hokma, sophia*) constitute the origin (Plato) and condition of all knowledge.
- Wisdom brings about creation. Through wisdom (Logos) the world was called into being from that which did not exist (Rom 4:17). There is something and not nothing because of the Word (wisdom).

She is a breath (*nephesh*) of the power of God

She is a reflection of eternal light

A spotless mirror of God's works

An image of His goodness

— Wisdom 7:24ff

---

[21] Søren Kierkegaard, *Fear and Trembling* (Oxford University, 1946; Penguin, 2006).

[22] See my book on the theological history of science—*Being Well* (Nashville: Abingdon, 1977).

- Beyond refracted light, broken image and marred goodness is perfect wisdom. Science and technology is transforming the former toward the latter.
- Lao-tzu's *Tao Te Ching* is a primal articulation of this wisdom which is the way of this knowing which is to do, of this adventure which is to follow.
- The wisdom (Logos) of God upholds the universe (Robert Grosseteste) . . .
- *Supportari ab aeterno Verbo*

In these recent years of his work, Moltmann wants to note a shift (or expansion) of his work from political theology to ecological theology, from an emphasis on historical and eschatological matters to concerns of space and place. The God of History and liberation is also "the indwelling God." In this mood he has formulated his Trinitarian treatise with special emphasis on the divine spirit active in the world. This trinitarianism has encouraged the emergence of a theology based less on obedience and judgment than on relationality, network and freedom. In a somewhat Judaic turn Moltmann speaks of God's *Shalom* and *Shabat*, the interruption of *Chronos* into *Kairos, Shekinah* now radiates within the creation. The light or fire of *Shekinah* is a radically ethical phenomenon (theophany) "the indwelling glory of God present with His exiled people." Sustaining the liberation and akedic impulses of his early writing he quotes Isaiah 63:9:

> In their affliction He was afflicted
> Shepherd of the flock . . . He rescued them and lifted them up

The God of history and nature in Moltmann's theology is much like the pervasive spirit of care, justice and goodness lying behind Amartya Sen's economic philosophy and strategy. Moltmann has studied Judaic monotheism carefully with his colleague Lapide and has frequently collaborated with his Tübingen colleague, Hans Küng, on matters of world religions. He has also written on *Islam: The Challenge for Christianity*.

Conversation with Moltmann

In conversation with Moltmann in the summer of 2003 I have probed his interest in *Science and Wisdom* where he works both on *Sophia* as an Hebraic construal and *Phronosis* as an Hellenic rendering of the universal human idea.

He is now engaged at his writing bench, he claims, with the Oneness, unity and householding of God. Reflecting on the great *perichoresis* section of John 17:21ff., he sees the inner connectivity of Godhead in the prayer of Jesus . . . "that they may be One as We (father and son) are One" he conceded to my suggestion that this resonated with the *Shemah* of Israel, with wisdom and with the Abrahamic theology which we are exploring vis-à-vis science.

He further elaborated with what he saw as an affinity of the Abrahamic/akedic model I was exploring with the *Shekinah* model found in thinkers like Franz Rosenzweig who affirm that "God in light" (and gathering) upholds God in us with God above. Like worship, science is an endeavor to "unify, sanctify and glorify the Name"—*Hashem*. In *circuminsession* (circling-enabling movement) and *circumsession* (indwelling-rest) the world is drawn near the divine, becoming His ingratiated dwelling. Trinitarian formulation is Christianity's attempt to name (fathom and work with) the lordship of Christ and the unity of God. Christ the Messiah shows and shines the Father (*Shekinah*). In the Spirit, Son and Father come to themselves and to the beloved world and we on earth "come to our senses" and understand.

In our conversation Moltmann finally invoked the image of the Eastern Church in the great medieval icon of "the Trinity"—in the Cathedral at Kiev—so magnificently studied in Tarkovsky's film, *Andrei Rublev*. Here we find two images: the classic, though disturbing, depiction of the Trinity, as in the era of Velasquez, of God, the lordly yet grieving father, holding, as a pietà, the dead son, with the spirit, as a dove, hovering overhead. Rublev—the great Lucan iconographer—in Eastern transparency and transfiguration—centers on a see-through into eternity—a banquet table and a Ravenna-like Christ as *Cosmocrator*—overarching a display of the resplendent creation. Here all creatures are ingathered, upheld as if forming a home and family bound together by cosmic, sacrificing love. My mind was drawn to the insights of the Oxford Judaist—Geza Vermes—who found in the Akedah of Abraham—who "gave over his only begotten and dearly beloved son" the biblical paradigm for the love of God. The divisibility and unificability, the One for the many, the outgoing for the ingathering, freedom and democracy, aseity and participation—here is the divine mystery that makes science possible. Which brings us back to Amartya Sen.

Excursus: Amartya Sen: A Conversation

He welcomed us into the Master's rooms in Trinity College, Cambridge. As we sat beneath Hans Holbein's full-length portrait of Queen Elizabeth, he commented that he was not sure why of how I would include him in a book on theology for science. Since numerous other theologians had similarly appropriated him he graciously consented to the interview. Referring to a litmus test once made over his faith position at another educational institution he again reiterated that he was non-religious, secular—perhaps even agnostic or atheist . . . Then he began to rehearse the important associations with religion throughout his life. His grandfather, K.M. Sen, a Hindu sage, was the author of the Penguin book on *Hinduism*[23] (London: Penguin, 1976). The English translation was so horrible that young Amartya was asked to translate it while grandpa was dying. This was a formidable chore given his disinterest in religion but filial piety won out. He was also invited, despite his reluctance, by the Vatican and Pope John Paul II to be part of the working group celebrating the centenary of *Rerum Novarum (1891)*, the great encyclical on capital and labor, social justice and care for the poor. *Centesimus Annus* bears the imprint of the 'so called secularist,' Amartya Sen, and a bust of the Pope sits proudly on his desk in the Trinity Gallery.

Throughout our discussion I probed him as to where on the spectrum of the religious and philosophical heritage he positioned himself. He maintains a deep, almost familial esteem for Hinduism and continues to study Sanskrit. He has been deeply influenced by Buddhism (in the first century CE, China called India "the Buddhist Kingdom"), especially with the early traditions of free democratic meetings as early as the fifth century BCE He is intrigued by pre-Christian and Muslim Iran, especially in the town of Sousa, and by Judaism and Christianity. As he heads for a two-year assignment to found and head Harvard's new center for Justice and Economics he will indubitably draw on this rich heritage. As with Leon Kass, we find in Sen a religious heritage that is subliminal and operational rather than cultic and parochial in observance. Yet that heritage is absolutely constitutive of the intellectual and ethical life and faith therefore remains deep and richly pervasive since it is far more than just a set of cognitive assertions. Both are children of the rational enlightenment having jettisoned some of the theological heritage, even of Kant, Hegel, Hume and Adam Smith, as have many contemporary intellectuals.

Sen is publishing this year the second volume of a comprehensive set of his *Oeuvres* with Harvard University Press (Belknap). Volume 1 covers his writings on economics, and Volume 2 the miscellaneous philosophical contributions. After reading his work I am convinced that he has a valuable place in this study. Indeed I have come to feel that he fills out the scientific, ethical and theological conceptualization of my proposal. Though the connection with Hinduism I draw in this study may be strained, Sen does live out that residual and subliminal heritage by his exquisite expression of the Vedic, Upanishadic, Indo-European and ecumenical religiomoral perspective. Dicks' study of the theological import of his work along with numerous articles and dissertations (e.g., Louvain) bear out my hunch as to his essential theological contribution.

As a relatively new science, economics draws on deep theological, philosophical and political springs for its vitality and valuations—convictions and commitments. In the company of contemporary economists Sen stands with R.H. Tawney, Barbara Ward, Kenneth Boulding, Kenneth Galbraith and Herman

---

[23] Kshitmohan (K.M.) Sen, *Hinduism* (Harmondsworth: Penguin, 1961). New edition with foreword by Amartya Sen (Penguin, 2005).

Daly as spokespersons for humanistic, ecologic and, yes, overt and cryptic theological ethics.

As we parted company that glorious July afternoon and stood beneath Newton's clock the words of the Apostle seemed apropos —"I perceive that you are very religious as I see your construction . . . 'to an unknown god'" (Acts 17:23). Sen's offering of thanksgiving to life is the legacy of a brilliant and noble system of ethics and economics—of *theologia* in the Greek sense—an assertion of what is ultimately meaningful and valuable. Theological values finally housed in religious and parochial systems on occasion rise to fill humanistic and universalistic currency—this is cause for celebration and the goal of any theistic value. Freedom, tolerance, justice, peace and respect are values borne out as much in the secular and philosophical heritage as they are in the theological, which is often, especially in the living of these days, captive to narrow confinements of thought and blatant injustice. As such, philosophy of science and moral philosophy must be assumed to be not only a valid *theologos* of modernity, but also a prophetic critique and corrective for theology in any age.

6 Leon Kass
the agapic vector

JÜRGEN MOLTMANN SIGNALED THE crucial assertion in *Science and Wisdom*: "The fear of the Lord is the beginning of wisdom" (Psalm 111:10). Leon Kass titles his study on reading Genesis *The Beginning of Wisdom* (New York: Free Press, 2003). When we were co-founders of the Hastings Center some 35 years ago, we were both young bioethicists: he a scientist, physician and philosopher, and I, a pastor and theologian. We were both social activists, having joined the freedom fighters in Mississippi in the mid-1960s. We both had young children in tow as we attended organizational meetings at Willard Gaylin's home near Hastings-on-Hudson. He was then teaching the great books at St John's College in Maryland, being mentored by my mentor, Paul Ramsey. They both worked with Andre Hellegers, M.D. at the new Kennedy bioethics program at Georgetown. Even as a young man, what always astonished me about Kass was the power and profundity of his theological vision. He would address the issue of cloning by citing C.S. Lewis, *The Abolition of Man*. He would illumine the ethical quandaries of heart transplantation by calling Francis Bacon to witness. Like another of his mentors, Hans Jonas, who had worked on Gnosticism with Rudolf Bultmann and existential philosophy with Heidegger, he was as conversant with Thomas Hobbes as he was with Genesis *Rabah* and Maimonides.

A poet and philosopher surpassed only by his wife, Amy, his career has been known for wise counsel, inspiring teaching and public service. His present post, chairing the President's Council on Bioethics, represents the later contribution. Though our political persuasions were at variance and though we have differed, particularly on bioethical issues across the years[1], I have found him a most thoughtful ethical voice in the field of bioscience. Since the moving on of our elders' generation of "*Die Weisen*"—Paul Ramsey, Theodosious Dobzhansky, René Dubos, Hans Jonas, Ernst Mayer, Harry Beecher, Bob Morrison, and others—Leon has been our stalwart.

---

[1] The Kass-Vaux debate on "Debbie's Dying," published in *Journal of the American Medical Association* (April 18, 1988), framed that provocative issue of assisted dying.

Even our present, now rapidly-graying generation of bioethicists—Eric Cassel, Dan Callahan, Will Gaylin, Tris Engelhardt, Bob Murray, Bill May, Gil Meilander, Art Caplan, Mark Siegler, John Fletcher, and others—look to Leon with his splendid preparation in science, medicine, philosophy and theology and his fearlessness in the lion's den for succor, challenge and camaraderie. One might expect nothing less of the "Whiz-Kid," who started his University of Chicago career at age 15 and was raised on the South Side of Chicago by socialist-learning, Yiddish-culture parents with a strong sense of social justice.

Though labeled a "neo–con," a "closet Christian," a "conservative Jew," the "religious right's favorite intellectual" and other epithets that swirl today in the sandstorm of the bioethics of genetics and stem-cell research debate, these designations are profoundly misleading. He is at heart a serious and observant member of the Jewish faith, a dedicated biblical and rabbinic scholar, a lover of Homer and the Greeks, and one who commonly translates this theological and philosophical heritage into contemporary argumentation. He states points with a radical seriousness, often irony, yet always with earnest respect. A 1997 essay in *The New Republic*, "The Wisdom of Repugnance," demonstrated his unease with a blithe permissiveness that disowns both serious conservative or liberal discourse. He is alarmed at the fact that renegade scientists, thoughtless moralists, opportunistic politicians, or rapacious businessmen, parade themselves as experts on life and death matters. These profound matters viewed in light of the depths of Genesis, the Psalms, and the Prophets—indeed from the broad wisdom of *Tanakh*—are, for him, matters of awe, reverence and holy silence.

He expounds traditional views on sexuality, marriage, life-prolongation, family life, yes, but to call him a puppet for Jerry Falwell or the Pope's (or the Inquisition's) legate on birth control, abortion, homosexuality or cloning, is simply unfair and in error.

As one who apparently coined the term *biomedical ethics* around 1968, I can say that Kass' contributions to this quasi-religious, quasi-political, quasi-philosophical and legal field, have always been most thoughtful, steeped in the deepest wisdom of our heritage. One critic says that in Kass, the Vatican has its foot in the door and Karl Rove is smiling. A recent *New York Times* genealogy chart shows him with the Leo Strauss mafia along with Alan Bloom and Paul Wolfowitz. These dismissals all totally miss the man. He is an irenic person of deep justice and truth. The *Ad Hominems* that he has never practiced science, medicine, or philosophy are the defensive and self-serving jabs of two-bit philosophers. A fair assessor will first scan his impressive bibliography.

Leon Kass: A Selective Bibliography

- 1970 • "Problems in the Meaning of Death" *Science* 170: 1235–36.
- 1971 • "The New Biology: What Price Relieving Man's Estate?" *Science* 174 (19 Nov 1971), 779–788.
  - Review of *Fabricated Man* by Paul Ramsey, in *Theology Today* 28: 105–107.
- 1972 • "Making Babies: The New Biology and the 'Old Morality,'" *The Public Interest* 26: 18–56.
- 1974 • "Averting One's Eyes or Facing the Music? On Dignity and Death" *Hastings Center Studies* 2: 67–80.
- 1975 • "Regarding the End of Medicine and the Pursuit of Health," *The Public Interest* 40: 11–42.
- 1981 • "Patenting Life," *Commentary* (Dec 1981), 45–57.
- 1985 • "The Case for Mortality," *The American Scholar* 52 (2), 173–191.
  - "Thinking About the Body," *Hastings Center Report* 15 (1) 20ff., Feb. 1985.
  - *Toward a More Natural Science*, New York: Free Press.
- 1988 • "Doctors Must Not Kill [debate with Vaux]," *Journal of the American Medical Association* 259 (April 8, 1988).
- 1994 • *Hungry Soul: Eating and Perfecting of our Nature.*
- 1996 • "Courting Death: Assisted Suicide, Doctors, and the 'Law,'" *Commentary* (Dec 1996).
- 1998 • *Ethics and Human Cloning* (with James Q. Wilson).
- 2000 • *Wing to Wing, Oar to Oar: Readings on Courting and Marrying* (with Amy Kass).
- 2002 • *Human Cloning and Human Dignity*
  - *Life, Liberty and the Defense of Dignity*
- 2003 • *The Beginning of Wisdom*
  - "Ageless Bodies, Happy Souls: Biotechnology and the Pursuit of Perfection," *The New Atlantis* (Spring 2003), 9–28.

The Judaic and Biblical Foundation of Kass' Theology for Science

As far as the community of bioethics is concerned, Kass is a *theosoph*—a wise person—of ultimate concern for people amid the distresses of suffering and birth, life and death. The ground structure of his thought appears as you look closely at his work. During the years our children studied at the University of Chicago we urged them all to avail themselves of the award-winning teachings of Leon and Amy—especially Leon's class called Genesis. When Sara and I were more involved in the colleges in Hyde Park, we attended some of his biblical studies, several of which appeared in *Commentary*. Among those we remember

- Regarding Daughters and Sisters: The Rape of Dinah
- Man and Woman: An Old Story
- What's Wrong with Babel
- Seeing the Nakedness of this Father (Noah)
- Father Abraham and the Meaning of Wife
- Farmers, Founders and Fratricide: Cain and Abel
- The Akedah as Final Examination: Abraham *Summa Cum Laude*
- Love of Woman and Love of God: Jacob

These Midrashic meditations took the biblical dramas, carefully mined their theological sense then related them to traditional and contemporary issues all in a truly imaginative and searching presentation. The students in the college found these small homilies intriguing, fresh and highly engaging. They captured for many a long-lost faith, a personal philosophy, which had grown stale or a new vision of life in its challenges and relationships. William Rainey Harper, a graduate of my small college in Ohio (Muskingum), and Robert Maynard Hutchins would have been proud of the instruction of this young master, combining as he did great ideas, great books, great convictions and commitments. It was the genius of Harper's founding of the University that biblical purviews were set against radical historic and contemporary thought all devoted to the end of creating citizens of critical thought and character.

What can one make of this theological philosophy of life in today's deconstructionist culture, which decries any evocation of grand narrative and where deontological ethics are suspect? The whole drama of Leon Kass' career has some of the qualities of a C.S. Lewis, a Catherine Pickstock (here at the Cambridge Divinity faculty where I now work), a

John Milbank, Paul Ramsey, or Jacques Ellul. These all seek to preserve a certain dignity for human persons, a certain coherence and relevance of the religious heritage, a certain disdain for the flippant and faddish. In a critical view they nostalgically seek a cultural synthesis now long gone.

Kass began his career as a surgeon in the public Health Service and a research biochemist at Harvard. One day, in the mid-nineteenth sixties he woke up horrified at the prospect of genetic alteration, cloning and the array of proposed alterations of the human form and substance being offered through the biomedical projections. He had already seen Joshua Lederberg's prognostications about the new genetics.

It was about this time that I was invited to testify before the United States Senate Health Committee, chaired by Senators Kennedy and Mondale. I was asked whether there were ominous trends in biomedical research concomitant with the thrilling and salutary projects—should there be a national commission on bioethics, they asked. Leon Kass' position as head of the President's office is the final affirmation of what was then and repeatedly thereafter voted down. Kennedy's office called me in the Houston Medical Center where I had in the mid-1960s established the first Bioethical Institute. "We're told you are the first and only bioethicist in the country—we need you to testify on the advisability of establishing a bioethics commission." "Who else should we invite?" I suggested Jerry Brauer, Dean at University of Chicago Divinity School, as a statesman of the religious life of our nation. The hearings processed against the backdrop of the assassination of Robert Kennedy and Martin Luther King, Jr. After a parade of medical pioneers testified, saying "no need," "we're good men," "we'll make good decisions" (Debakey, Barnard, Lederberg, Kornberg, Wangenstein, et. al.), Brauer, my associate Albert Moraczewski, a Dominican priest-pharmacologist, and Harry Beecher, Dorr professor of anesthesiology at Harvard, all rose and expressed grave doubts abut such exuberant optimism. Nevertheless, the proposal for a commission was squashed, again and again, until, I believe the 1980s. Leon Kass felt the same premonition we four did about Huxley's *Brave New World*. His life project has nobly sought to prevent that "apocalyptic" scenario from coming to pass and to prepare the way for an "Abrahamic/Akedic prospect"—a far better future.

Though a pious, observant, and thoughtful Jewish thinker, for Kass the answer was not donning the Jewish orthodox prayer shawl and moving to Jerusalem, nor was it to seek with Ken Seeskin, our Northwestern University professor, to establish a new currency for "Jewish philosophy." Like Emmanuel Levinas, Kass has sought to access our liveliest moral heritage (found in the theology and philosophy of Judaism) and retrieve from its treasure its maxims, visions and prohibitions for our secular, pluralistic world. With Paul Ramsey, Kass has sought to search out the fine-grained texture of particular life science issues, biomedical crises and clinical practice agonies, which people face, offering admonition and caution against our Faustian schemes, our harmful economies, our too-early abandonments, our manias to avert pain and achieve immortality and our shrinking from care in its justice and mercy. He is immersed in Aristotle, Homer and the Greeks. The modern philosophers pose a compelling truth and justice for him: Descartes, Locke, Spinoza, Kant and others.

Kass does not explicitly pronounce the dicta and positions of Jewish bioethics as do a splendid circle of faith-oriented scholar-practitioners like David Novak, Peter Ochs, Laurie Zoloth, Fred Rosner and others. Like Maimonides, he is a creative renewer and construer of the tradition. A philosopher at heart, and in his association in the committee for Social Thought at the University of Chicago, he appeals to the precepts of reason and law, shunning any hint of parochialism. Kass, in other words, is a Deuteronomic Jew—one who seeks renewal and refreshment of the divine covenant with Israel, humanity and all creation. He lifts theological wisdom into universal light. He draws humanistic reason into sacred salience. He achieves this reciprocal hermeneutic in the manner of Karl Barth. With the newspaper (or the journal *Science*) in one hand, the Bible in the other, and on the writing desk or lectern before him and the mediating great text of philosophy and literature, he crafts a modern *mitzvah*. All this is done against the backdrop of the anxiety and hope of human beings in their joy and suffering, living and dying. William May, a similarly experiential theologian, responds to this quality in Kass.

William May: An Econmium for Leon Kass

A fellow founder of the Hastings Center and committee colleague on the Bioethics panel, William May has always worked in a style and format similar to Kass. With vivid clinical reference and moving literary illumination, Bill has written excellent books including *The Physician's Covenant* (Philadelphia: Westminster, 1981) and *The Patient's Ordeal* (Bloomington: Indiana University, 1991).

May has offered a tribute to Kass that highlights the theological grounding of Kass' view of science and medicine. He begins with an extraordinary assertion: "In my opinion, *Life, Liberty and the Defense of Dignity: The Challenge for Bioethics* (San Francisco: Encounter Books,

2002) is unquestionably one of the most important books on bioethics ever published."[2] May's essay is so salient that I review it here to further clarify the foundations of Kass' thought.

The first premise of Kass' thought according to May rises from the first commandment "no other gods" (my surmise). Kass writes:

> The most fundamental challenge posed by the brave new biology comes from the underlying scientific thought. In order effectively to serve the needs of human life, modern biology reconstructed the nature of the organic body, representing it not as something animated (a living *Nephesh*, my addition), purposive and striving, but as dead matter-in-motion.[3]

In the Cartesian, Baconian, then the modern Biomathematical and Biomechanical project, implies Kass, an insidious idolatry has displaced the dignity to be accorded to a person as *Nephesh*, living being, *Imago Dei*. It is within the "very triumphs" of medicine and its benevolent impulses that this heretical anthropology is taking form.

From the beginning of my career in biomedicine in the 1960s I have been greatly impressed by what can only be called an "iconoclastic" temper drawn into biomedicine, especially by Jewish and Muslim scientists and physicians, where stipulations like "no other gods," "no false idols" and "no defamation of the Name" seem to subliminally inform their decisions in research, practice and policy. Leon Kass personifies this ethos with its underlying justice, reverence, dignity and care.

May continues his analysis of Kass' work by showing that the modern Cartesian concept, which so deeply shapes science, is "dualistic, setting flesh over against thought, body against mind." The reason I invoke unitary, monistic, monotheistic thought in this proposal for a theology for science, drawing on the likes of Avicenna and Maimonides and ending with Kass is in part to avoid this perennial propensity to dualism and penultimacy by injecting a persistent iconoclasm. Such an approach, I have argued, safeguards theoretical and applied science.

Kass goes on to propose that an emphatic "No!" be offered to the proposal of science in concert with business that "we clone a human being." Recalling Karl Barth's *Nein!* against the *Übermensch* of Hitler's biological dystopia with its eugenic and euthanasiac agenda and even against what he felt was the conducive naturalistic philosophy of Brunner's theology, Kass,

---

[2] Accessed July 31, 2006 at http://www.christendom-awake.org/pages/may/leonk.htm.
[3] Kass, *Life, Liberty and the Defense of Dignity: The Challenge for Bioethics* (San Francisco: Encounter Books, 2002) 20.

in a similarly apocalyptic vein pleas that "we get our hand on the wheel of the runaway train now headed for a post-human world."[4]

I affirm, with Kass, the imperative of such a witness. I also extend his fundamental theistic humanism to see not only the "demonic" mania in utopian genetics but to see also the graceful and salutary helpfulness in the genetics which seeks to ameliorate the anguish of agonizing flaws, diseases and deaths. The perfecting of the human and the building of utopia is, of course, suspect. But healing the sick, alleviating suffering and succoring one another in dying—all in the context of universal justice, is our human vocation and destiny. Here is where Kass must be distinguished from the business, free enterprise, "support the rich, neglect the poor" ethos of the Bush administration (which has sponsored Kass' leadership). That ethos is at profound variance with the biblical ethic of global justice, equality, opportunity and capability (Sen) and can only end in ceaseless occupations, wars and enlarged misery and discontent for "the wretched of the earth." In this troubled world Kass is one of our main advocates of a greater *Shalom*.

At this juncture of his work Kass becomes pointedly biblical, drawing on the book of Genesis' insights of male and female, love and family and children and nurture. This emphasis prompts me to identify his distinctive quality as *agapic* as he adds the color of love to the rainbow spectrum we paint in this study. Human sexuality and relationality is a divine mystery and not a technical and rational manipulation. Cloning, therefore is a "perverse" enterprise, rising in "sin" against this biblical wisdom. I agree completely with what Kass calls the repugnance of this proposal. With our common mentor, Paul Ramsey, we see it as "shaking our fists" in the face of the Creator. I do contend though that many salutary skills do reside potential in the new biology. Here we need to turn to specific instances like fashioning clonal clusters, perhaps from stem cells to bring healing care to Parkinson's patients or victims of the societal epidemic of diabetes (such that we might be able to say, following Isaiah, Jesus and others, "the lame walk, the palsied rest"). Such specific causes are worthy of pursuit on a case-by-case basis. Our science, technology and implemented care for persons should pursue those physical needs.

The *imperativa* and *prohibitiva* are nothing less than of biblical moment. As the biomedical project unfolds, the interhuman commands of the *Decalogue* (which follow the Divine-human commands) are at stake. The akedic construal of this revelatory gift where the earthly crisis of cre-

---

[4] Kass, *Challenge for Bioethics*, 147.

ation, freedom, temptation, fall, rescue, guidance and resurrection manifests a redemptive path for humanity if it will only choose faith and justice rather than arrogance and self-indulgence. Sabbath reverence and rest, honoring parents and children, killing, infidelity, lying, stealing and craving—all bear on this scientific endeavor. These ethical norms hover as a sacred canopy—of grace and judgment—around and over our technical feats. In this akedic purview the lamb—*amnion* of God—the pure and righteous messianic visitor of the world—present in every temptation of freedom—every choice of redemption or damnation—provokes the ire of evil in unjust persons and inspires good works in those who are just and kind. It invites individuals, families and societies to "choose this day who you will serve" (Josh. 24:15).

Commenting on the seventh commandment, Kass holds that we must hold selves in life and love together:

> What is the significance of divorcing human generation from human sexuality, precisely for the meaning of our bodily nature as male and female, as both gendered and engendering? To be male or freedom derives its deepest meaning only in relation to the other, and therewith in the gender-mated prospects for generation through union. Our separated embodiment prevents us as lovers from attaining that complete fusion of souls that we as lovers seek; but the complementarity of gender provides a bodily means for transcending separateness through the children born of sexual union. As the navel is our bodily mark of lineage, pointing back to our ancestors, so our genitalia are the bodily mark of lineage, pointed ultimately forward to our descendants.[5]

Kass is here presenting a Ramseyan, Thomistic, natural law theology of the human corpus, its shape, its solidarity and complementarity and its purpose. One senses that this reflection on origin, design and vocation is derived from *Albertus Magnus* and Aristotle. Yet these convictions are conveyed with Hebraic normativity. Where Kass departs from this Catholic and Hebraic heritage and opts instead for an Orthodox Jewish or more strictly conservative catholic theology of life is on the issue of a "right to die." Here the "vitality" theology insists more on the prolongation of bodily existence than I am prepared to accept. Grounded in a very complex theological heritage running from *L'Chayim* protest against ancient Moloch sacrifice and Roman-Roman euthanasia to the twentieth century Holocaust, it seeks to preserve every last filament of physical vital-

---

[5] Kass, *Challenge for Bioethics*, 101.

ity. This vitalism becomes particularly problematic when we consider the way in which the human organism is modified in its natural life trajectory through medication, surgery and technology especially in its degradation and demise in affluent, business-driven societies. Theocentric Judaism, affirming resolutely that "the Lord gives and takes life," accepts the wisdom of "a time to be born and a time to die." In my view faith and trust in God at this threshold of life often requires deliberation and decision.

Kass' Science

We have introduced Leon Kass and identified his theological and ethical standpoint. We are now ready to see how his theology and philosophy influence his science and his science his theology. His major work in this field is *Toward a More Natural Science* (Macmillan). Here, the maturing philosopher, much in the mold of Weizsäcker, whom we recall prepared as a scientist to be a better philosopher, begins to do that groundwork in philosophy of science which will provide foundation for his subsequent formulations.

The sections of the book which signal the directions in which he will move are Natural Law (Part 3), the Hippocratic tradition (Part 2) and early glimmerings of what I see as his akedic and agapic "God and golem" theology of science where the forebodings of an ominous prospect temper the progressivist manias. In this last emphasis Kass draws out his resonance and dissonance with the traditions of the Jewish Enlightenment as these bear on the modern humanities and sciences (especially the social sciences). Within these Kass interweaves his biblical reflections.

NATURAL LAW

> I only wanted to make the world better
> Not to break the god-boundaries
>
> — Father to Bruce in *Hulk*[6]

Section 3 of *Toward a More Natural Science*, "Deepening the ground: Nature reconsidered," contains Kass' essays on natural philosophy, law and theology. Reacting to Monod's and ultimately to Keith Ward's *Chance and Necessity*, Kass argues for a freedom and spontaneity within the contours of an inherent teleology within a living field and panorama of nature. The

---

[6] *Hulk*, directed by Ang Lee. Written by Michael France, John Turman, James Schamus (Universal Pictures, 2003).

derivation and evolution of bodies, their forms and shapes, their dignities and finitudes, intrigue Kass as he sets out to delve back to the pre-Socratics, Plato, Aristotle, even Albert the Great, to brush away the arid dusts of scholastic philosophy and theology and recover a vital, teleological, Levitical, Hebraic and Hellenic heritage. With Hans Jonas,[7] he decries the violence of the degradation of "man among the animals" in cynical evolutionary thought, all the while celebrating the Hebraic honoring of Spirit and the reality of wholeness in creation.

> In the hue and cry over the indignity done to man's metaphysical status in the doctrine of his animal descent it was overlooked that by the same token some dignity had been restored to the realm of life as a whole.[8]

Kass sets out to establish a contemporary natural law science, grounded in the holism, inspiritedness, courage and gratitude in the face of flaws and finitude, finding dignity and beauty even amid distortion and the grotesque.

In Ang Lee's film the tense antagonism between Bruce (Hulk) and his frankenstinian Father, who is impassioned to improve on corrupted human nature (mediocrity and militarism), sharpens as he decides to subject his own son to profound biological-genetic experiments. Searching for love, respect and inherent dignity within the gargantuan, genetically engineered body which he inhabits, Bruce cuts loose in neurochemical fury when he gets mad —becoming the friendly yet foreboding green giant. Looking all so like the grotesque gargoyles at St. John's and New Colleges, Oxford, the brute seeks to find the gentle human within. Kass' scientific project also seeks to disclose the genuinely human—full of dignity, value and inherent worth—within the "gone haywire" Golem which has become modernity's *Übermensch*. This authentic self and teleological worth he claims is found in ancestry and descendents—"the seed of Abraham." In the complexity of beauty in the organism and its organismic reciprocity with all life; in the transcendence to purposes beyond homeostasis; in meaningful activities and altruism; in freedom and responsibility—immortality and finitude—the divinely defined and destined person is known. This multidimensional goodness or "well-workingness" is the kind of virtue that Kass sees as crucial to true and good science.[9]

---

[7] See Hans Jonas, *The Phenomenon of Life: Toward a Philosophical Biology* (University of Chicago Press, 1982).

[8] Jonas, *Phenomenon of Life*, 58.

[9] See Kenneth Vaux, *Powers That Make Us Human* (Urbana: University of Illinois Press, 1985).

Hippocratic Science and Ethics

Closely related to this naturalism and humanism is the wisdom Kass draws from the Hippocratic tradition. Here the radical, mystical, Pythagorean element is added to the Nature Philosophy of ancient Greece. Kass affirms that the scientist and physician, like the artist, only assists nature, teasing forth her inherent capabilities, virtues, health and excellences from the raw material. Inherent patterns incline toward some purpose (as Michelangelo's marble or Handel's musical imagination are already impregnated with Pietà or Messiah), and Hippocrates sought to harmonize the bodies and souls of persons with those natural, salutary flows of airs, waters, times, seasons and places.

Medicine, and science more generally, serves the "ends" of "healing the sick," "ameliorating suffering," "preventing disease," "preserving life" and generally in achieving homeostasis or seeking ways to harmonize a person's own body and soul with cosmic forces. The physician's actions, decorum, speech and prescribed and proscribed actions seek and serve these "ends" of human respect and service. Picking up on the recognition of the Hippocratic heritage that humans are much more vulnerable and in a precarious state than are the animals. Kass sees this vulnerability and need for interdependence as a clue as to how we are made to serve, depend on and care for one another. For Hippocrates diet, rather than drugs—especially harsh cytotoxic, abortifacient, even mind-expanding substances—should always be used. Exercise, salutary emotions and conviviality ought to be preferred over immobilization, repression and isolation. The science should be disclosive rather than coercive, the therapeutics comfortable and not disabling, the ethics true, honest and faithful and not authoritarian or exploitative—this is the Hippocratic ethos.

God and Golem

Rightfully or wrongfully I sense in Kass an ascetic and near-apocalyptic note, which may account for his foreboding in the face of modern biotechnological power. This final characteristic of Kass' science appears to me Kabbalic, arising out a more urgent, conscientious and sardonic (ironic) Judaic mood. From antiquity the Jew and Jewish community have had to protect life, seek security, enrich and ennoble the ethnic-religious community and serve the poor. This imperative to help and heal is always formed over against the fear that ingenuity and invention will misconceive and create a monster that harms and destroys.[10] This spiritual consciousness of guarded creativity has fashioned the impulse to fund work, seek knowledge and implement care according to the instructions (*mitzvoth*) of the faith.

Kass is taken, even in his scientific views, by this "fear and trembling" in the biblical tradition. In a review of Kass' book on Genesis, Phyllis Trible rightly locates but erroneously critiques what Kass draws from the beginning of the Bible:

> The particular coherence Kass discovers (actually, puts) in Genesis lies in his answer to a question he poses: "Is it possible to find, institute, and preserve a way of life that accord's with man's true standing in the world and that serves to perfect his Godlike possibilities?" Kass asserts that in the beginning Genesis lifts up a double-sided difficulty to this way of life. First the human creature . . . even though created in the image of God, is not perfect. As "merely an image," he is prone to waywardness and disaster. Second, as this creature begins to seek direction for the good life, he learns that it cannot come from the natural world, which is completely indifferent to moral values. Thus the five stories in the beginning of Genesis—the primeval couple in Eden, the fratricide of Cain, the marriages of heaven and earth, the catastrophic flood and the building of the city of Babel—show the dangerous tendencies of humankind toward violence, self-sufficiency and mastery of the other.[11]

Kass is searching for that "Way" which I also seek in this study. While Trible sees this "Way" of Abraham as patriarchal and mistaken, "the beginning of folly," with Kass I find there a liberating word, the annunciation of a way of faith and life which is the beginning of righteousness and the end of destructive patriarchy, chauvinism and feminism, the dawn of a fully human and Godly "way."

The "golem" tradition (an embryo grown amiss) in Judaism searches out this monstrous distortion of humanity and seeks to repudiate it by following the "way" of that Word which is light and life (Psalm 119). When Arno Mayer echoes the Gita when mourning the holocaust "Why did the skies not darken?" or when Tevye laments "If I were a rich man" they reecho the cry of the ages against injustice and affirming that heartfelt

---

[10] Norbert Wiener, *God and Golem, Inc: A Comment on Certain Points Where Cybernetics Impinges on Religion* (Cambridge, Mass.: MIT Press, 1964).

[11] Phyllis Trible, "Of Man's First Disobedience, and So On." Review of *The Beginning of Wisdom: Reading Genesis,* by Leon Kass, *New York Times* (October 19, 2003) 28.

industry be efficacious in human service. Science under the Judaic impetus, from Maimonides on through the Medieval and Renaissance masters, through the decades and centuries of exclusion from society down into the vibrant and flourishing days of modern life—in the academies, in domestic workshops and surgeries—in the early moments of mental and emotional therapeutics—fashions a science toward wellness—a commitment and way of life. Einstein, Oppenheimer and Teller have their clinical counterparts in Kornberg, Lederberg and Heller.

The science is contoured by delight and alarm. Golem the embryonic human can become the wooden robot that turns against its maker. The good cornucopia of substances and secrets in the earth (Wisdom of Sirach) can be conjured up by faithfulness and just-care utilities. In this pistic epistemology (faith-grounded science) knowledge, much in the spirit of Newton, is an afterthought of the divine mind—a mimesis of the divine handiwork. Morally laden it can also turn into unspeakable horror. Hebraic Wisdom—like Greek *phronesis*—is the art of sharing, counsel, admonition and helping. Good work will be efficacious, rewarding and rewarded.

The mood of *agape* and alarm is also clear in the outlook of Leon Kass. This takes several forms. In natural sanctions knowledge and power abused will recoil against us. Apocalyptic horrors will greet us if we overdo, overshoot limits or transgress laws of rights and goods. Wealth abused, knowledge forsaken or retarded, *joie de vivre* and *impulse de vivre* denied, all sadden, cheapen and demean life. Vocation is divinely implanted. We must carefully train and work to realize and universalize this benediction on the earth. Kass exemplifies this science in his descriptive and normative reflections on natality and mortality.

Kass on Natality

A key to understanding Leon Kass' view of reality(his science) and his ethics, with their solid grounding in theology, is to examine the ways in which he addresses issues at the beginning and ending of life—his natality and mortality ethics. I generally follow his lead in my *Birth Ethics* (Crossroads, 1987) and *Death Ethics* (Trinity, 1992).

He begins by discussing cloning, which he sees as a rudimentary and paradigmatic issue. In the American Enterprise Institute volume in which he collaborates with James Q. Wilson, *The Ethics of Human Cloning* (1998, see Kass bibliography), Kass revisits an issue we have been exploring for over 35 years. Our teacher, Paul Ramsey, entitled his essay "Shall we clone a man?" in my book *Who Shall Live* (Fortress, 1970). Kass has explored the issue through the levels of different species—single cells, worms, mice, sheep, and now humans. His points recall Ramsey's objections: untoward and unintended consequences are almost certain in such experimentation; human consent is impossible; divine prerogatives are invaded and all the baser motivations—sensationalism, commercialism and Frankensteinism emerge. The arguments are reminiscent of Ramsey: endless similarity assuring that those will come after us will be exactly like us; diminishing individuality and personality; safeguarding freedom; sustaining family solidarity and responsibility; the right to a unique genetic being and "not playing God."

Because of the theological backdrop Kass provides for his bioethics we find a range of deeper concerns implicit in the exotic new issues such as cloning, stem-cell research, in-vitro fertilization and genomic alteration. Issues such as fatherhood, parenting, divorce, adultery, violence, family life and concern for children are shown to be etiologically and agapically fundamental to the biological issues. They are the meaning of those very issues. While some argue that social meanings do not inhere in the biological endeavors themselves and that such discernments and gate keeping belong only to private consumers or to medical providers, like nuclear issues at the macro level (e.g., the hydrogen bomb) the micronuclear issues are of public concern and consequence. Kass is pleading for holistic and systemic conceptualization—the only way that the religiomoral vector can find relevance in our world where ultimate values are secular and commercial. It is not that the 40 percent of American children (60 percent of African-Americans) who are growing up in homes without fathers are clamoring for cloning. What Kass does assert is that these new procedures emerge within an environment and ethos of high stress on families and profound neglect of children. Animated by the background of thought we have selected, Kass was quoted in the *Guardian*, saying that "it is rare to see a scientist who thinks that nascent human life has any dignity worth respecting whatsoever."[12] This theology of scrutiny and evaluation leads Kass to reject cloning per se and label as mischievous, the distinction now made between "therapeutic" and "reproductive" cloning.

His natality theology, science and ethics reach far deeper. Though a strand of Judaism does not see the *in utero* being as "fully human" and even can consider it an aggressor (*rodef*), Kass claims that as a biologist,

---

[12] Oliver Burkeman and Alok Jha, "Life: The battle for American science." *The Guardian* (April 10, 2003) 18.

"I've come to regard the earliest stages of human life as Something, and if nothing obstructs its unfolding itself [it can] become something like you and me, if all goes well."[13]

More generally Kass affirms both the preciousness of nascent life along with the affirmation of mother and family well-being which is asserted in the Jewish bioethic of the "breath" marking the beginning of the life of a "person." In an interview with Nigel Cameron, Kass confesses that he may "suffer from a late-onset, probably lethal rabbinic gene which has gradually expressed itself, and has taken me over."[14]

Kass gives expression to this genetic impulse by asserting that "we're turning procreation into manufacture, sometimes referred to as "designer babies" in which parents and scientists impose their private eugenic visions on the child-to-be. A child, therefore, ceases to be welcomed as a gift, as a mysterious stranger whose genetic independence from its parents is a kind of emblem of the kind of independence that all our children are raised to acquire."[15]

Kass on Mortality

In 1993 Kass published an essay in the *New Atlantic* entitled "Ageless Bodies: Happy Souls" (see bibliography). It captures his theology and ethics of mortality. He begins with a toast (think of C.S. Lewis, *Screwtape Letters*) to biomedical science and technology:

> May they live and be well. And may our children and grandchildren reap their ever tastier fruit—but without succumbing to their seductive promises of a perfect, better-than-human future, in which we shall all be as gods, ageless and blissful (p. 17).

Genesis—there it is again! The garden—the presumption—the fall—the exile. Kass honors science, technology and especially medicine. These are divine arts since God is a physician (Ex 15:26). The ministry of healing in the world is the commission of science. This mission is to combat the forces that injure, harm, disease and destroy persons, families and communities. He has employed the merciful scalpel; witnessed the bypass machine and respirator; seen those torn-apart in car wrecks miraculously reassembled. He has seen the fruits of Francis Collins' genetic research

---

[13] *Religion and Ethics News Weekly*, WNET, New York (July 18, 2003).

[14] Nigel M. de .S. Cameron, "Defender of Dignity." *Christianity Today* 46:7 (June 10, 2002) 42.

[15] Nigel Cameron, "Defender of Dignity," 42.

on cystic fibrosis, Jérôme Lejeune's on Trisomy 21, William Nyhan on Lesch-Nyhan Syndrome and he thrills and trembles in wonder and fear. Genesis ponders the creation of humanity in freedom and agonizes over its ascent and descent. Kass rightly senses that Genesis is the charter for the assessment of any human endeavor, including the endeavor of science and technology.

Biblical creation narratives theologically construe the ambiguity of human ambitions affirming first the exultant celebration: "Be fruitful, multiply, fill the earth and subdue it" (Genesis 1:28). Trinitarian doctrine is the way that Christian thought comes to terms with God, the creation and fall, and the messianic visitor as the connection of world and God. In the self-constriction of the trinity, the creation and incarnation and the akedic atonement, human knowledge and power are given share in the divine life in order that the world might be fashioned toward its intended possibility.

Between creation and consummation human life resides in a state of acute responsibility as capacities for construction and destruction rapidly intensify. The risks of rebellion and disorder well up when human freedom is not under the sway of faith, justice and love which is the way of Torah and Gospel (*taurut* and *injil* in Islam). The ambiguity of the scientific project is that its knowing and doing reside in this value-fraught matrix. It is therefore an absolute imperative if the world is to go on and develop that transcending parameters bear on the project. "Do it—but carefully" becomes the human call in the creation. Of all of our voyagers on the waters of theology for science, Kass best keeps this tension of creative (and accountable) ambiguity, refusing to collapse the human scientific vocation into either willful agnosticism and technical nihilism on the one hand or delusional utopianism on the other.

In light of this biblical ethic of beginnings and endings the criterion often invoked to evaluate whether or not a biomedical technique is licit is if it is "therapeutic." "Therapeutic" seems to be given a classical Abrahamic, Hippocratic and "Baconian" definition: what "cures diseases, prolongs lives and relieves suffering" is good and obligatory. When these goals are pursued the results are "fruitful" in the biblical language. But when this knowledge and these skills are put to "non-therapeutic" (frivolous, ideological) use they result in "bioterrorism" (e.g., bacteria or drugs to obliterate memory); "social control" (fertility blockers for welfare recipients); or "improvements" (attempts to perfect bodies and minds through genetics or drugs). The implicit evil is not only the consequential harm caused to people but the deontological wrong as persons are thwarted from their more excellent purposes. Again, in Genesis language, the distorted human will seeks to "play God," directing God-given insights and capabilities into "forbidden fruits."

Today—October 22, 2003—the US Congress passed a bill outlawing an abortion procedure medically labeled "dilation and extraction" and called by opponents "partial birth abortions." Though it may not survive a "constitutionality" challenge at the US Supreme Court, it illustrates the ambiguity we address in this issue. In this case we ask if evil can be done to the mother in order that the child's life be spared. On the same day national attention was drawn to the case of Terri Schiavo in Florida, a young woman locked for years in an irreversible coma, whose feeding tube had been withdrawn at the husband's request, supported by the doctors and courts, that decision now overturned and the tube reinserted at the executive order of Governor Jeb Bush. Again the conflict of harms and duties arise amid a plethora of goods and evils.[16]

Kass is also offering another moral parameter on justice, which says that energies diverted into unworthy causes "leaves undone" the other things we should be doing with those resources. Such causes are the treatment of malaria, Aids and malnutrition in which millions of persons die unnecessarily because even though the knowledge and technique are "given" and "ready"—we divert energies to do other things. Here again is the biblical (Deuteronomic) ethic where misdirection provokes a divine sanction and counterproductivity. A part of this moral morass is the haphazard nature of efforts that arise in an atmosphere of free inquiry, free development and free enterprise. We push research into the "biology of senescence" while ignoring the health care needs of poor people and even neglect the care-provision implications of that particular research.

The first dimension of the ambition Kass seeks to evaluate is the quest for "ageless bodies." Organ transplantation and artificial machines and parts; genetic, stem-cell and other biochemical means to slow down the aging process and its deterioration or invigoration of bodily processes (growth hormones to Viagra) fall under his sharp scalpel dividing "bone from marrow."

Regarding "happy souls" Kass enumerates the ways in which we can "eliminate psychic distress or induce euphoria." In all of these endeavors the act of recentering the deviation or bringing disease to an equilibrium or homeostatic state is well and good. Enhancement, manipulation, harm-

---

[16] The conclusion to this matter was the court-ordered removal of the feeding tube as requested by Terri's husband. The moral quandary continues to trouble American health care.

ing or remaking is suspect. This template of evaluation is then brought to bear on the thousands of proposals and possibilities in biomedicine. Antibiotic therapy for meningitis, bypass surgery and Prozac therapy for depression are licit. Cloning embryos and Huxley's Soma raise questions. Kass moves to his normative position by questioning the legitimacy of:

- Using growth hormone to raise big kids who can earn basketball scholarships
- Making it possible for post-menopausal women to bear children
- Having a mastectomy to improve one's golf swing

These admittedly extreme cases presuppose either an Hellenic theological ethic of "natural" contours and entelechies or an Hebraic theological ethic grounded in obedience/ disobedience to God's will, word or way. The tension that arises again centers on freedom. "Why can't I do what I please with the money I earn and own?" "It is my choice if I choose an abortion for convenience sake." "It's my choice if I wish to end my life by refusing life-prolonging therapies."

Kass then takes theology for biomedicine in yet another direction by considering the "giftedness of creation" and evaluating the human responses of gratitude (and acceptance) or ingratitude (want and do something more or different). Here a theology in the train of Boyle, the Puritans, Calvin, Augustine and Paul ultimately flows back to the Deuteronomic equation of blessing/righteousness, curse/sin. Here we are to receive what is given in gratitude, putting the provisions of life to use in generosity. Now the emphasis is not so much in combating evil as in celebrating and distributing the good.

Abraham and Akedah: Theological Parameters in Life's Genesis and Exodus

The salient contribution of Leon Kass to the thesis we unfold in this work is the vital role played by the heritage of Abraham throughout the moral history of humanity down into our modern era of science and biomedicine. The venture of Abraham, by which a new vision of God and human destiny grips humanity and through which a new understanding of nature and history arises, is the intellectual starting point for Kass. The axis point of Abraham's story comes in Genesis 22 when he is called on to love and trust God utterly by offering "the beloved son"—the long awaited, only son—his future. In an act of faith which forever will banish not only the allowance but the command to sacrifice the bodily first-fruits; will forever dignify the intrinsic value of the child and will forever signal the conditions if life and the human project is to be sustained in the earth "take your only child, the one you love"—"do not lay a hand on the child" becomes the metaphor to decipher theodicy and temptation—"What God is doing in the world and why." The saga of Abraham is the tale of humanity down through and forever out into history. The Akedah, as Jon Levenson has shown, in his *Death and Resurrection of the Beloved Son* (New Haven: Yale, 1993), is the central metaphor of God, life and its meaning in Judaism, Christianity and Islam as these Abrahamic faiths struggle with the drama of human freedom and obedience in this world under and before that divine mystery.[17]

Kass calls it the final successful examination for Abraham, in which he attains *summa cum laude*. As we have shown with our pioneer theologian-scientists Avicenna and Maimonides, and as we have reiterated in the depiction of Leon Kass, the venture of Abraham is the dawn of theology and of science. Just as Adam is the proto son of God and Jesus the proto son of Man, Abraham is the proto son of God/Man. Yes there was some continuity, some intimation of what was to come—there had to be with names like Serug, Nahor, Terah—but God always seems to work incrementally—slowly—"When the time was fully come God sent forth His son" (Gal 4:4). And before the patriarchs something was divinely afoot in Noah, Cain, Abel, Eve and Adam. But these are derivative. They appear in all the old-Oriental cosmogonies and anthropoetiologies. But again, God works in those ways—through precursors. Yet Abraham is singular—the first—the first to vaguely perceive, to be addressed, to listen, to believe, to heed. "Go out—I will show you." He is the first to be invited into the "big deal"—the Covenant—"I promise—you trust and obey." God—the originator, perpetuator and consummator of all reality, is now known in nature and history. God is now the God of a person, family, tribe, all nations, and all creation—"from Grover's Corners, New Hampshire . . . to the mind of God[18]"—what an address.

For Kass, in Abraham, viewed in purview of the Akedah, God "institutes His new Way among humankind."[19] Abraham is the founder and father of this primordial pathway of insight and instruction which hereafter

---

[17] See Kenneth Vaux, *Jew, Christian, Muslim* (Eugene, Oregon: Wipf and Stock, 2003).

[18] Thornton Wilder, *Our Town: A Play in Three Acts*. (New York: Coward McCann, 1938).

[19] Leon Kass, *The Beginning of Wisdom: Reading Genesis* (New York: Free Press, 2003) 352.

will teach and guide humanity in its journey in the world. Knowledge and guidance is to be organic and genetic (generational). Because knowledge, science and especially wisdom is transmitted along genealogical and generational pathways, we speak of knowledge being generated as children stand on the shoulders of their parents and innovators stand on the shoulders of their predecessors. Harvey (1653) builds on Vesalius (1543). Galileo (1629) builds on Kepler (1596) who builds on Tycho Brahe (1588).

It is the same with moral history. Wisdom (noble insight chastened by suffering) is conveyed by the witness (martyr) through the display of righteousness (e.g., adherence to the truth, first commandment) in the face of the ridicule and temptation of the world. Science, as I have contended throughout this essay, is an akedic endeavor. In the words of Søren Kierkegaard, a hero is fashioned as one in "fear and trembling" ventures into the unknown in faith and sacrifice. From this crucible of trust in the face of assault, provision and resurrection is claimed, inheritance prevails and the world is given new life. This may sound like a romantic view of science in this post-Cartesian world of facts, data and objects. But Kass belongs to the long sweep of intellectual history where the themes of wresting the known from the unknown, ameliorating the contradictions to well-being, and adventuring in faith and hope, much more explain science than recent and short-lived concepts in philosophy of science like subject-object splits and matter-thought demarcations.

Akedah is the drama of command and promise, interposed (intervened) by human freedom and temptation, consummated by the work of creative wonder.

> Work out your salvation with fear and trembling for it is God who works within you both to will and do His good purpose (Phil. 2:13)

From the faithful human gesture of obedient fear (the beginning of Wisdom) the Lord will see, the Lord will provide, the Lord will remember—and the place is called *Adonai-Yireh*.

While Kass is much to much a scientist in the mood of modernity to use such theological ruminations about science himself, this framework becomes the paradigm for his understanding of human responsibility within the context of knowledge, work (technology) and worship (fashioning a faithful project with the virtuosity we have been given and the modicum of knowledge disclosed), all within the enigma of good and evil as that unfolds within the drama of human knowledge and power on earth—the Genesis saga.

The Agapic Vector of Theology for Science

Geza Vermes, the Oxford Judaist, has identified the Akedah as the annunciation to humanity of "the love of God."[20] It is divine love that is the source of the dispensation of science. The lineaments of human love for God, the world and humanity are the motivation—subliminal or actual—for creative *techne*—work in the world. For theology to be true to its world task—to be conducive to science—it must be full of love. For science to be true to its sustaining and guiding impulse—its theology—it too must be "slow to anger, kind and full of compassion." *Agape* is a distinctive marker of a theology for science.

Excursus: John Polkinghorne's Theology for Science

When one seeks a deeply theological scientist, one whose theology and science thoroughly intertwine, the path may lead from Cambridge, Mass. to Cambridge, England. It likely ends at the office of the one-time professor of mathematical physics, then Vicar of St. Cosmus and St. Damien, Blean, now laureate of the esteemed Templeton Prize—John Polkinghorne. What is the direction of Polkinghorne's thought and what is its affinity to the work of Leon Kass? Like Pannenberg and Moltmann, Torrance and Weizsäcker he moves beyond the deism and dualism so common to this inquiry and like Kass seeks a theology of the living God—the God of Abraham. Though he works on the banks of the Cam like Sylvia Plath he did not ultimately despair as that pastoral setting pronounced the fragile order of nature against the whirlwind of God. Here Newton had observed the falling apple and conjectured the "laws of nature" all the while remaining confident that only divine providence prevented the world from "wobbling apart."

As a young scientist Polkinghorne observed that the pervasive and comprehensive universe of the "divine mechanic" made the hypothesis of divine action dispensable. With Bonhoeffer he came to reject the "god of the gaps"—the explanatory deity that occupied the zones of our remaining ignorance and our projected weakness. He realized the scientific and theological fallacy of this notion, which squeezed God out to the edge of the universe. Through William Temple, C.W. Davies and the great "natural law" philosophers of the recent century, Polkinghorne came to posit a worldview where science and theology were compatible—indeed synergistic.

In recent years (*The Work of Love, The Ends of God and the End of the World*) he has enriched this natural law and process perspective with insights from a more theocentric (Gustafson, Barth) and liberation (Moltmann) perspective.

---

[20] Geza Vermes, *Scripture and Tradition in Judaism* (Leiden: Brill, 1973).

Polkinghorne is now able to weave together even the mystery theology of Monod and Bergson with the indeterminacy theory and relativity of Heisenberg and Einstein all into a universe under the spell and within the presence of the living God of the Bible—the God of Israel. Like Kass he has found a decalogic and kenotic (akedic) deity "One not far-off but near"—One who condescended into this world bringing truth, peace and love. This theology of presence would empower his critique of contemporary scientific theory, which has become excessively expansionist, hegemonic and reductionist. This overweening emphasis of positivist explanations has been especially strong in the biological sciences (Monod and Dawkins), the psychological sciences (Freud and Skinner) and philosophical theory. By contrast, mathematics, physics and chemistry have tendered more modest claims. Polkinghorne's thought resonates with that of Kass in its iconoclastic tenor. Polkinghorne's biblical, theological and pastoral emphasis in contrast to the all-too-prevalent "process" and "deist" tendency of writers in the field of religion and science is colored by etiologic (creation), elpistic (hope) and eschatologic (judgment, end) considerations. The "flux" of human existence—the constant changeover of the constituents of our own bodies and the broader process of transmutation occurring in the world itself—to Polkinghorne accords with the Apostle in Romans 8, where the world is subjected to "futility," not of its own will but by the will of Him who subjected it in hope. The world is not whirling along meaninglessly toward cosmic destruction—"a tale told by an idiot" (Monod after Macbeth)—but as an adventure in hope. In this regard one feels the unmistakable influence of Teilhard on Polkinghorne's thought. He confirms this influence on interview. He knows, as Teilhard knew that ultimately all our theological and scientific theory is just that—speculation and search for more workable explanatory hypotheses. Theology, like science, can be helpful or not. Polkinghorne's bibliography offers the broad scope of his work.

John Polkinghorne: A Selective Bibliography

1985 *Creation and the Structure of the Physical World* (London)

1986 *One World: The Interaction of Science and Theology* (London)

1988 *Science and Creation: The Search for Understanding* (London)

1989 *Science and Providence: Gods interaction in thee world* (London)

1991 *Reason and Reality: The Relation Between Science and Theology* (London)

1994 *Quarks, Chaos and Christianity* (London) *Science and Christian Belief* (Gifford Lectures)

1996 *Beyond Science: The Wider Human Context*

1998 *Science and Theology: An Introduction* (Fortress)

2001 *The Work of Love: Creation as Kenosis* (Eerdmans)

2002   *The God of Hope and the End of the World* (Yale)

2003   *Belief in God in an Age of Science* (Yale)

The Search for a New Natural Theology

Polkinghorne insists on a synthesis of scientific and theological knowledge. Creation, though certainly *creation ex nihilo,* is fully in concord with "big bang theory" and "creatio continuo," therefore it remains under the sustenance and guidance of God who gave it genesis, sustains its bounty, beauty and benevolence—embraces even its evil and suffering in His "good will" for the "gift of love must be the gift of freedom, the gift of 'letting be.'"[21] To protect this emphasis of "letting be" from the deistic "letting-go" is a fine line. Here I side with Torrance in finding the Maxwell, Planck, Einstein, Polanyi universe fully in accord with that of Barth, Calvin and Augustine in their great convictions of providence and contingency. The doctrines of Akedah, incarnation and crucifixion, divine self-limitation and *Kenosis* offer a fruitful conjunction of divine purpose and worldly freedom. Together these form not only a theology conducive to science but an ethic of human justice and amelioration of evil for a suffering world. Seen within this purview the history of science becomes an adventure of theodicy and the natural theology of Polkinghorne becomes successful. In Teilhardian wisdom and thanksgiving he proclaims:

> The cruciform pattern of life through death is the way the world is . . . We are here today because some five billion years ago a star died in the throes of a supernova explosion, scattering into the environment those chemical elements necessary for life[22]

John Polkinghorne's Akedic Theology and Rachmaninoff's Mass of St. John Chrysostom

John Polkinghorne, obviously a parish theologian and pastor, one who struggles with the real life crises people face, takes a theology of science in the directions of this essay toward the actual anguish and hope, death and resurrection of life in the cosmos, under God. He is also a person of cultural breadth indicated in his book *Beyond Science: the Wider Human Context.* In such a purview of reality, truth and meaning one schooled in the wisdom of Pythagoras of Samos will inevitably ponder the interconnection and affinity of mathematics, music and theology—thought in the Pythagorean-Platonic school to be touchstones to the divine. Two quotes set the stage for these reflections:

> All of us will die with business unfinished, hurts unhealed, potentialities unrealized. The vision of a continuing process of purification

---

[21] John Polkinghorne, *Belief in God an Age of Science* (New Haven: Yale, 2003) 13.

[22] Polkinghorne, *Age of Science,* 14.

leading to the inexhaustible experience of the living God, as set out in Dante's *Purgatorio* and *Paradiso* is a necessary part of the fulfillment which alone makes total sense of the assertion of individual value.[23]

The whole range of subjective experience from perceiving a patch of pink, to being enthralled by the performance of the Mass in B Minor . . . cannot be dismissed as epiphenomenal froth on the surface of a universe whose true nature is impersonal and lifeless. . . . metaphysics which fails to acknowledge this is inadequate.[24]

Even intense thunderstorms which darkened for moments the hauntingly beautiful Sanctuary of King's College, Cambridge could not dampen the enthusiasm of listening to one of the world's great choirs singing the Rachmaninoff *Liturgy of St. John Chrysostom* that July evening in King Henry VI's magnificent Chapel founded in 1441. The glorious Mass of the Eastern faith tradition was sung exquisitely, in Russian, by the choir known worldwide for its Christmas Day Service of Lessons and Carols. The "great doctor of the Church," Bishop of Constantinople in the decades following the Emperor Constantine's Christianization of the Roman Empire when corruption and *accidie* had already set in church and society. Like Luther, John was forced to a long walk in inclement weather which caused his death after years of strife with his adversaries. Though the Mass appears widely in the eighth and ninth centuries obviously it springs from Chrysostom's text as well as the older liturgies of St. James (Jerusalem and Antioch) and St. Mark (Alexandria).

Like a Ravenna mosaic from the same period the Mass exudes a theology of Christ, the Good Shepherd, who lays down his life for the sheep. Here also is *Christus Victor* and the great *Cosmopancrator*. Here the human plight is lifted up into the light of the sacrifice of the Lamb of God (Sergius Bulgakov) into the inexpressible glory of the transfigured heaven and earth. The chorus—angels and people—respond to the call of celebrant and deacon in the Great Liturgy:

> *Blagoslovi, dushe moya, Ghospoda*
>
> Bless the Lord—O my soul
>
> And forget not all His benefits
>
> Who forgives all your iniquities
>
> Who redeems your life from destruction
>
> Who satisfies you with good things
>
> So that your youth is renewed like the eagle's
>
> The Lord executes mercy and justice for all who are oppressed

---

[23] Polkinghorne, *Age of Science*, 23.
[24] Polkinghorne, *Age of Science*, 19.

The Little Liturgy continues in the chorus:

> *Slava ottsui Sinu I Svia to mu Duhu*
> Glory to the Father, and to the Son, and to the Holy Spirit
> Only begotten (Genesis 22), Son and Word of God
> Who without change (from God) dids't become man
> And was't crucified, O Christ God, trampling down death by death
> *Votsarstvii tvoyem pomiani nas, Ghospodi*
> Remember us when thou comest into your kingdom
> In Thy Kingdom remember us, O Lord,
> when Thou comest in Thy Kingdom.
> Blessed are the poor in spirit,
> For theirs is the Kingdom of Heaven.
> Blessed are those who mourn, for they shall be comforted.
> Blessed are the meek, for they shall inherit the earth.
> Blessed are those who hunger and thirst after righteousness,
> for they shall be filled.
> Blessed are the merciful, for they shall obtain mercy.
> Blessed are the pure in heart, for they shall see God.
> Blessed are the peacemakers,
> for they shall be called the sons of God.
> Blessed are those who are persecuted for righteousness' sake,
> for theirs is the Kingdom of Heaven.
> Blessed are you when men shall revile you and persecute you,
> and shall say all manner of evil against you falsely for my sake.
> Rejoice and be exceedingly glad,
> for great is your reward in Heaven.

The great hymn of the universe is ultimately the hymn of love. Torrance describes St. John Chrysostom as one of three hierarchs (with Basil of Caesarea and Gregory of Nazianzus) who combine the Hebraic-Christian Spirit into the Greek "beauty of form."[25] The lasting contribution of this combination for our thesis is that we have "a divinely ordained bond between the natural and the moral order . . . [A] covenanted economy of righteousness and grace undergirds and stamps

---

[25] Torrance, *Christian Frame of Mind*, 11.

the whole creation."²⁶ Kass, then Polkinghorne, blend the elements of love and meaning, science and theology, and so culminate our thesis.

---

[26] Torrance, *Christian Frame of Mind*, 12.

Conclusion

WITH THE HELP OF some of the ablest thinkers in theology and science of our time and ages past I have formulated my convictions and commitments for consideration by the international community who find these issues intellectually vital and ethically crucial to our times. I have listed a set of criteria of theology and science that seem indispensable and have chosen an exponent to delineate each dimension. I have accounted alethic, aesthetic, etiologic, eschatologic, ethical and agapic dimensions as worthy and essential attributes of science making it intellectually truthful and ethically valuable to our society. A search for truth and beauty, regard for the inception and culmination of reality, all built on the impulses of justice and love conveys the radical normativity of God into the endeavors of science and technology.

These parameters all devolve out of what I have called an Abrahamic/Akedic matrix. Abraham—the first religio-historic (post-mythic) person, ventured a new vision of God and the world and can thus be called the father of faith and of science. Both Jesus and Paul connect messianic and cosmic meaning to this reality. Judaism, Christianity and Islam—the religions of science—trace their origin and sustenance to this epicenter of religioethical reality. For me this becomes a rich and thick metaphor embracing not only faith (the known), order, hope, venture, right and freedom but also doubt (the unknown and uncertain), chaos, loss, opacity, evil and contingency. Science is such an ambivalent adventure. It resembles Plato's *Mimesis*, Newton's afterthought of God's thoughts, Girard's sacrifice or Dali's crucifixion arched over, out and into the cosmos. It seizes the known from the unknown, the now from the not-yet—all in the joyous anguish of new birth (Romans 8).

The "I Am" of the Exodus, the promulgator of the Decalogue, is the One who has established cosmic natural law. The incarnation of wisdom (*Logos*)—the Word—is the creative order of the world. The quest of science and theology is how that light, law, love is implicit in the spatio-temporal structures of the cosmos. Why is the way of wisdom the way of humiliation? Why has sacrifice, even the anguish and yearning of the cosmos, reflected this Way? As Torrance has affirmed, I have seen my deepest purpose in this study to be what he calls "evangelical"—to "evangelize the foundations of all human thought and life."[1] What shall occur in the world as the disorder, introduced by man, is reordered by "The Man"— this is the quest of a theology for science.

> Then first humanity triumphant passed the chrystal ports of light and seized eternal youth. Man, all immortal—hail, hail . . . heaven all lavish of strange gifts to man. *Thine is the Glory—Man's the bounded bliss.*[2]

Paris, 2004

---

[1] Torrance, *Transformation and Convergence*, x.
[2] William Billings, Lyrics excerpted from "Easter Anthem." *Sacred Harp,* 3rd ed. (1860).

www.ingramcontent.com/pod-product-compliance
Lightning Source LLC
Chambersburg PA
CBHW071449150426
43191CB00008B/1290